The Validation of Risk Models

Applied Quantitative Finance series

Applied Quantitative Finance is a new series developed to bring readers the very latest market tested tools, techniques and developments in quantitative finance. Written for practitioners who need to understand how things work 'on the floor', the series will deliver the most cutting-edge applications in areas such as asset pricing, risk management and financial derivatives. Although written with practitioners in mind, this series will also appeal to researchers and students who want to see how quantitative finance is applied in practice.

Also available

Oliver Brockhaus
EQUITY DERIVATIVES AND HYBRIDS
Markets, Models and Methods

Enrico Edoli, Stefano Fiorenzani and Tiziano Vargiolu
OPTIMIZATION METHODS FOR GAS AND POWER MARKETS
Theory and Cases

Roland Lichters, Roland Stamm and Donal Gallagher
MODERN DERIVATIVES PRICING AND CREDIT EXPOSURE ANALYSIS
Theory and Practice of CSA and XVA Pricing, Exposure Simulation and Backtesting

Daniel Mahoney
MODELING AND VALUATION OF ENERGY STRUCTURES
Analytics, Econometrics, and Numerics

Zareer Dadachanji
FX BARRIER OPTIONS
A Comprehensive Guide for Industry Quants

Ignacio Ruiz
XVA DESKS: A NEW ERA FOR RISK MANAGEMENT
Understanding, Building and Managing Counterparty and Funding Risk

Christian Crispoldi, Peter Larkin & Gérald Wigger
SABR AND SABR LIBOR MARKET MODEL IN PRACTICE
With Examples Implemented in Python

Adil Reghai
QUANTITATIVE FINANCE
Back to Basic Principles

Chris Kenyon, Roland Stamm
DISCOUNTING, LIBOR, CVA AND FUNDING
Interest Rate and Credit Pricing

Marc Henrard
INTEREST RATE MODELLING IN THE MULTI-CURVE FRAMEWORK
Foundations, Evolution and Implementation

The Validation of Risk Models

A Handbook for Practitioners

Sergio Scandizzo
Head of Model Validation, European Investment Bank, Luxembourg

palgrave
macmillan

First published 2016 by
PALGRAVE MACMILLAN

Palgrave Macmillan in the UK is an imprint of Macmillan Publishers Limited, registered in England, company number 785998, of Houndmills, Basingstoke, Hampshire RG21 6XS.

Palgrave Macmillan in the US is a division of St Martin's Press LLC, 175 Fifth Avenue, New York, NY 10010.

Palgrave Macmillan is the global academic imprint of the above companies and has companies and representatives throughout the world.

ISBN: 978–1–137–43695–5

This book is printed on paper suitable for recycling and made from fully managed and sustained forest sources. Logging, pulping and manufacturing processes are expected to conform to the environmental regulations of the country of origin.

A catalogue record for this book is available from the British Library.

A catalog record for this book is available from the Library of Congress.

Contents

List of Figures

List of Tables

Acknowledgements

I am grateful to Carlos Freixa, Juraj Hlinický, Stefania Kourti and Aykut Özsoy in the EIB Model Validation team for many useful discussions on many of the topics covered in this book. Thanks also to Peter Baker and Josephine Taylor and to the editorial staff at Palgrave Macmillan for many improvements to the manuscript and for an efficient and effective editing process.

The views expressed in this book are those of the author and do not necessarily represent those of the European Investment Bank. Any remaining mistakes or inaccuracies are entirely my own.

Introduction: A Model Risk Primer

On March 29, 1900, at the Sorbonne University in Paris, Luis Jean-Baptiste Alphonse Bachelier, at the time a 30-year-old postgraduate student, successfully defended a dissertation titled *Théorie de la Spéculation*. In this work Bachelier singlehandedly introduced the idea that in an efficient market, the absence of unexploited profit opportunities means that the mathematical expectation of the speculator's gain is zero, and hence, the current price of an asset is the best predictor of its future price. He showed how stock prices followed a stochastic process, developed the mathematics of Brownian motion to model such a process and came up with a formula for pricing options that is not that far from the Nobel Prize-winning solution to the same problem proposed by Fischer Black, Myron Scholes, and Robert Merton in 1973. This was all well before Einstein used essentially the same diffusion equation to model the Brownian motion in 1905, before Andrey Markov began working on continuous-time processes in 1906, and before Andrey Kolmogorov published his 1931 paper laying the foundations of the general theory of Markov processes.

Bachelier's work is widely considered the seminal, albeit long unrecognized, scientific work on the modelling of financial markets. Many of the mathematical models used today and virtually all of their basic underlying assumptions can find their roots in this dissertation, whose true value took more than fifty years to be fully recognized. Yet, in the very first paragraphs of this work, Bachelier felt the need to introduce the following caveat:

> The influences which determine the movements of the Stock Exchange are innumerable. Events past, present or even anticipated, often showing no apparent connection with its fluctuations, yet have repercussions on its course. Beside fluctuations from, as it were, natural causes, artificial causes are also involved. The Stock Exchange acts upon itself and its current movement is a function not only of earlier fluctuations, but also of the present market position. The determination of these fluctuations is subject to an infinite number of factors: it is therefore impossible to expect a mathematically exact forecast.

Although Bachelier's remark meant undoubtedly to emphasize the impossibility of a deterministic forecast as opposed to a probabilistic one, I like to think that the tone of his words also suggests a certain fundamental prudence in the interpretation and use of such forecasts.

1 Uncertainty and irreversibility

Ursula LeGuin wrote in *The Left Hand of Darkness* (1987): "*The only thing that makes life possible is permanent, intolerable uncertainty: not knowing what comes next.*" A world without uncertainty would be, well, unexpected indeed. For a start, it would be a reversible one. Any outcome could be obtained, not just once, but as many times as needed through processes that would never fail to perform in their "expected" way, and thus, any outcome could be perfectly anticipated.

Most people are familiar with the second law of thermodynamics and not just because it is taught in school. People are familiar, sometimes painfully so, with the concept of irreversibility, with the idea that, as time goes by, changes cannot be fully reversed and the shape of things and the guise of people can never be fully recovered. This idea is an ancient one. "*All things give way; nothing remains,*" writes Plato in one of his dialogues (*Cratylus*, 402.a.8), explaining the philosophy of Heraclitus of Ephesus. And everybody knows the nursery rhyme that recounts the sad fate of Humpty Dumpty.

> Humpty Dumpty sat on a wall,
> Humpty Dumpty had a great fall.
> All the king's horses,
> And all the king's men,
> Couldn't put Humpty together again.

It was only, however, at the beginning of the nineteenth century that French mathematician Lazare Carnot suggested that movement represents a loss of what he called "moment of activity," a sort of tendency to the dissipation of energy. Twenty years later, his son Sadi Carnot proposed that, like the fall of a stream that makes a mill wheel turn, the "fall" of heat from higher to lower temperature can make a steam engine work. Sadi went further by postulating that, although in an ideal model the heat converted into work could be reinstated by inverting the motion (cycle) of the engine, in practice some heat is always lost so that no real engine could be perfectly efficient. The second law of thermodynamics was about to be born.

A few decades later German physicist Rudolf Clausius formulated the law by at the same time coining the word "entropy," a word he chose because of the meaning of the Greek words *en* and *tropein*, "content" and "transformation" (in German, *Verwandlungsinhalt* -- luckily the Greek terminology stuck). Entropy is the concept Clausius used to explain the loss of usable heat, the one produced through friction, postulated by Carnot and which appear in the most famous formulation of the second law of thermodynamics.

> *The entropy of an isolated system which is not in equilibrium will tend to increase over time, approaching a maximum value at equilibrium.*

What has all this to do with uncertainty? As a matter of fact, a great deal. Towards the end of the nineteenth century, another German physicist, Ludwig Boltzmann described entropy in terms of the number of microscopic configurations (i.e., the number of different positions of its individual particles) that a gas can occupy by contrasting those microstates corresponding to lower levels of energy to those corresponding to higher levels. He argued that providing heat to a gas, thus increasing its entropy (in the thermodynamic sense) also increases the kinetic energy of its particles, thereby increasing the information needed to determine the exact state of the system. Entropy is therefore a measure of the amount of uncertainty in a system for a given set of macroscopic variables. It tells us, for given values of temperature and volume, how much information we need (and thus how uncertain we are) about which exact microscopic configuration a gas will take. The more states available to the system with appreciable probability, the greater the entropy or, otherwise said, the greater the *variety*, the greater the entropy.

The statistical formulation of the second law establishes therefore a relationship between irreversibility (heat always goes from the body at higher temperature to the one at lower temperature) and uncertainty (providing heat and increasing thermodynamic entropy increases the uncertainty about the configuration of a gas' particles) and ultimately variety.

Imagine now having to write a computer program that produced a particular string of symbols. If the string is, say:

> xyzxyzxyzxyzxyzxyzxyzxyzxyzxyzxyzxyzxyzxyzxyzxyzxyzxyzxyzxyzxyzxyzxy
> zxyzxyzxyzxyz

then you can write a short program that says something like

> Print (24 times): "xyz."

which is much shorter than the string to be printed.

If, however, the string to be printed is:

> Dkd78wrteilrkvj0-a984ne;tgsro9r2]3"., nm od490jwmeljm io;v9sdo0e,.
> scvj0povm]]-

the program most likely will have to look like:

Print (once):

'Dkd78wrteilrkvj0-a984ne;tgsro9r2]3"., nm od490jwmeljm io;v9sdo0e,. scvj0povm]]-'

which is longer than the string to be printed.

The difference between the two cases is that in the former, uncertainty about the outcome can be resolved by providing a short sentence that completely identifies the string (*xyz* 24 times) without any need for spelling it out in full. In the latter case, lacking a short description of the string, the only way to identify it is to write it down. We may say that in the latter case the need to spell out the string in full within the computer program somehow defeats the purpose (what is the point of having a computer printing out something we have to write down ourselves anyway?) and that is precisely where the link between uncertainty and irreversibility lies.

Andrey Kolmogorov, the Russian mathematician who first formulated the concept of algorithmic randomness, defines a string as random if it is shorter than any computer program producing that string. Random is something that, like the second of the strings considered above, cannot be identified other than by writing it down in full. In other words, in order to know such a string, we need to *wait* until all its characters have been written or printed. By contrast a string is not random if it can be identified through a program which is shorter than the string itself, thereby allowing us to identify the string *before* it is fully written down or printed out. Randomness therefore has to do with the impossibility to anticipate, or predict a certain outcome. We cannot get to know that outcome (by computing it by hand, through a computer or otherwise) more rapidly than waiting for that outcome to happen.

2 Uncertainty and models

Foreseeing an outcome without having to wait for it to happen or, in other words, telling the future, is of course a very basic, perhaps the most basic human endeavour, and mankind started devising means of doing it well before computers were invented. In one way or another, all those means had in common the idea that a relationship can be established between our reason and the outside world and that therefore our reason can internally represent whatever part of the world it wants to study.

A model in this sense is an internal representation sharing at least certain properties of the outside world and from which outcomes can be derived without, or before, having to witness their happening. Models are of course Newton's or Maxwell's equations, but models are also planetariums or cartographic maps. Even human beings can be models, as in the case of twins who grow up in different families and whose study may allow scientists to pinpoint the role of genes, or of the environment in the development of personality.

In this work, however, we are concerned with models used in finance, and to this end, let us now review some basic definitions.

The U.S. Office of the Comptroller of the Currency, the U.S. banking supervisor, defines a models as "... a quantitative method, system, or approach that applies statistical, economic, financial, or mathematical theories, techniques, and assumptions to process input data into quantitative estimates" (OCC, 2011–12).

In one of the very first papers on the subject of model risk, Derman (1996) classifies models as follows:

1. A fundamental model: a system of postulates and data, together with a means of drawing dynamical inferences from them;
2. A phenomenological model: a description or analogy to help visualize something that cannot be directly observed;
3. A statistical model: a regression or best-fit between different data sets[1].

Crouhy et al. (2000) essentially ignore phenomenological models and focus on the first and the third, renaming them structural models ("They employ assumptions about the underlying asset price process and market equilibrium conditions to ... draw inferences about the equilibrium prices") and statistical models (that "... rely on empirical observations that are formulated in terms of correlation rather than causation"), respectively.

This is broadly in line with Cont's (2006) distinction between econometric model (which specify a probability measure in order to capture the historical evolution of market prices) and pricing models (where a risk-neutral probability measure is used to specify a pricing rule).

This distinction hints at another way to classify financial models, which is particularly relevant to the scope of this book: the one between pricing and risk measurement. Sibbertsen et al. (2008) distinguish between derivatives pricing and the measurement of credit and market risk. Kato and Yoshida (2000) use the same two categories to analyse two related risks. One is the risk that the model does not accurately evaluate the price of a security or is not consistent with mainstream models in the market. The other is the risk of not accurately estimating the probability distribution of future losses.

This in turn leads us to the need for defining and classifying model risk. Indeed Kato and Yoshida's definition of the risks in a pricing model reflects the two main contributions to the topic: those of Dermann (ibid. 1996) and Rebonato (2003). For Derman the risk of using a model to value a security comes from the potential failure in devising a realistic and plausible representation of the factors that affect the value. For Rebonato, the issue with every valuation model is rather how close its results are to the market consensus. Using a more realistic and plausible model than the rest of the market may actually lead to potentially large differences between the *mark-to-model* value of a security and the price at which it is eventually traded, and hence to correspondingly large losses. Morini (2011) notes that during and following market crises, market consensus tends to move towards models that are simpler to implement while at the same time appearing more realistic in light of the events. Following Rebonato, he also summarizes the potential for model risk by means of the following four cases.

1. Model used is different from market consensus.
2. Model used is in line with market consensus, but there are operational errors.
3. Model used is in line with market consensus, but suddenly market consensus changes.
4. There is no market consensus.

The following quote from Keynes (1937) comes to mind: "*Knowing that our individual judgment is worthless, we endeavour to fall back on the judgment of the rest of the world which is perhaps better informed. That is, we endeavour to conform with the behaviour of the majority or the average.*"

When trying to estimate the risk from the changes in value of a security or of a portfolio of securities, what is commonly indicated as trading market risk, the definition and identification of model risk is slightly less straightforward. In this case the risk is the under-estimation of the market exposure and the subsequent potentially incorrect decisions that this may entail. Notice the two-pronged nature of the problem. While with pricing models the "revealed inaccuracy" in the model-based valuation is also, by and large, a measure of the loss, with risk models the inaccuracy in the estimation of the relevant probability distribution translates into smaller or larger losses depending on the way such distribution is used in the risk management process. For example, a market or a credit risk measure may be used for computing economic and regulatory capital, for pricing, for provisioning, for assessing the eligibility of a transaction or a counterpart, for establishing a portfolio, counterparty, country or other limit, for negotiating guarantees or other security. Consequent inaccuracies in each of these quantities, in turn, may have financial consequences, and estimates of model risk should aim at capturing the potential for such losses. Figure I.1 – incompletely – summarizes uses and risks related to risk models.

Furthermore, even the simple ex-post identification and measurement of a discrepancy between the model-based estimate and the actual probability distribution may be problematic. While losses due to a discrepancy between model-derived prices and the prices at which a security eventually is traded can be observed and measured, the same is not generally the case for probability distributions.

The vast literature available on model risk describes in depth all the key assumptions on which the majority of risk models are built and which turn out not to correspond to empirical evidence. Such assumptions (normality, independence of returns, absence of fat tails, constant volatility and so on) are very well understood to be false. They

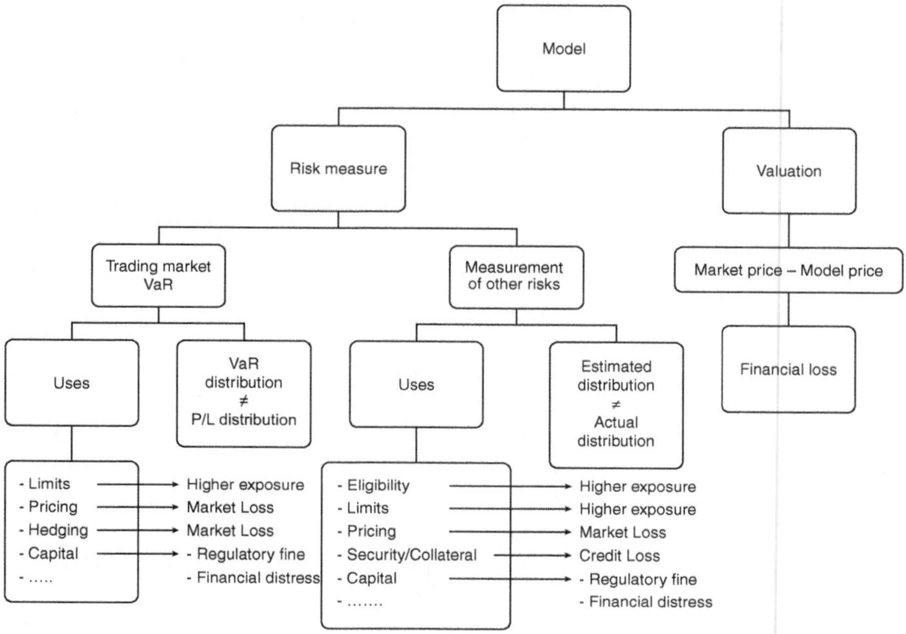

Figure I.1 Risk models: uses and risks

are, however, used either because they allow substantial simplifications to be made to the models (with obvious advantages on costs and transparency of the model itself) or because, more rarely, they are thought not to cause substantial differences in the results, at the level of precision required by the specific application. Abandoning such assumptions does not eliminate model risk, albeit presumably leading to more accurate models, as new ones need to be added in order to estimate the additional parameters and variables required by their very abandonment. For instance, instead of assuming constant volatility, this can be forecasted through regression models. But this choice implies the adoption of an additional, fairly complex model which in turn requires its own additional assumptions. As statistician George Box (1987) once put it, "all models are wrong, but some are useful."

Model risk is therefore only marginally a problem of inappropriate choice and incorrect implementation. Aside from pure and simple mistakes in developing, specifying and implementing the model – which do happen, but can be, at least in theory, minimized through due diligence and controls – model risk is fundamentally a manifestation of the so-called problem of induction, as formulated by philosopher David Hume, "who argued that from the strict logical point of view we have no justification in generalizing from instances we have experience of to those of which we have no experience" (as quoted in O'Hear, 1989). Taleb (2004) used a suggestive version of Hume's problem to highlight the pitfalls of allowing induction to guide risk assessment and predictions in finance, namely John Stuart Mill's reformulation of the problem of induction. "No amount of observations of white swans can allow the inference that all swans are white, but the observation of a single black swan is sufficient to refute that conclusion."

Inductions are generalizations. Some sequence of events is observed a certain number of times and then a law is derived which purports to apply to all other instances of the same phenomenon. We see thousands and thousands of white swans and we not only find it wholly unsurprising, but conclude that the whiteness of swans is a law of nature. Sextus Empiricus once wrote: '*Based on constancy or rarity of occurrence, the sun is more amazing than a comet, but because we see the sun daily and the comet rarely, the latter commands our attention*' (Trans. R.G. Bury, Harvard University Press, Cambridge, 1933).

Our efforts in risk measurement, however, could be unsuccessful for a more subtle and devastating reason, because we fail altogether to take into account one or more key elements of the risk profile: In other words, we could ignore the very existence of one or more risks. Our models may be working just fine under the assumptions made except that those assumptions fail to consider what former U.S. defence secretary Donald Rumsfeld[2] inspiringly called "unknown unknowns."

Model risk can be a special case of risk ignorance. Our misunderstanding of the uncertainty inherent in financial transactions can lead us to a failure in identifying the risks we are exposed to and this can eventually translate into estimating our exposure incorrectly, but just as easily can lead us into products, markets and deals that we should better stay out of.

This is of course most likely to happen when dealing with new and complex products, operations or environments and can have potentially devastating consequences as proven in such high profile cases like Long Term Capital Management, the 1998 Russian financial crisis, and, more recently, in the sub-prime crisis or in the JP Morgan "London Whale" losses.

3 Model validation as risk measurement

Although both academic literature and regulatory guidance provide theoretical references and practical methodologies for model validation, precious little is available when it comes to the measurement of model risk. This may sound surprising as one would imagine that the latter is an inevitable by-product of the former and that the results of the model validation process should somehow be translated into an adjustment to model-based risk measures. Still, current literature falls short of giving a risk manager or a validator practical tools to develop a measure of model risk that can be computed, and reported, by model and by transaction thereby becoming an integral part of the overall risk measure for the bank's portfolio.

One exception may be the work of Karoui et al. (1998) in the context of plain vanilla options pricing and hedging using the Black-Scholes formula, where a profit/loss can be computed when the pricing and hedging volatility is different from the realized one. Avellaneda et al. (1995) and Lyons (1995) derived a somewhat similar, but definitely less practical solution in the case of exotic or non-convex payouts.

Sibbertsen et al. (2008), building on the work of Kerkhof et al. (2002) and of Artzener et al. (1998) suggest two approaches for the measurement of model risk: Bayesian and worst-case. In the Bayesian approach the average of the risk measures computed by all candidate models is taken, by using appropriate prior distributions on both the parameters and the probability that a specific model is the best one. Needless to say, the need to specify such priors constitutes the main practical hurdle in applying this method. The worst-case approach, on the other hand, equates model risk to the difference between the risk measure of an individual model and the risk measure under the worst-case model. Here the challenge lies in the determination of the worst-case and in distinguishing between the risk of estimation error and that of mis-specification on the individual model.

A possible alternative consists in treating model risk as a type of operational risk, thereby modelling it as a set of possible events (model failures) occurring according to a (discrete) probability distribution, each potentially causing a financial loss according to a (continuous) conditional probability distribution.

In the aggregate loss model, originally developed in actuarial science in order to treat insurance-related problems, the aggregate loss is seen as a sum of N individual losses $X_1, \ldots, X_N$.

$$S = X_1, \ldots, X_N \quad N = 0,1,2,\ldots$$

One needs to determine, the probability distributions of the events (frequency) and the conditional probability distribution of the loss (severity) given an event. The aggregation of these two into an overall probability distribution will allow the estimation of model risk with a desired level of confidence. The distribution of the *aggregate losses* may be derived either analytically (in simpler cases) or numerically by means of convolution integrals or Monte Carlo simulations. A closed-form approximation of the model, particularly well-suited for heavy-tailed loss data, was derived by Böker and Klüpperberg (2005) to treat operational risk data. A comprehensive analysis can be found in Klugman, Panjer and Willmott (1998).

In conclusion, if we define measurement, following Hubbard (2007), as "*A set of observations that reduce uncertainty where the result is expressed as a quantity,*" the measurement of model risk is still far from being a straightforward task, especially when it comes to the part of the definition about reducing uncertainty. Model validation is therefore both about assessing model risk and about overcoming our shortcomings in trying to assess it.

According to the Merriam-Webster dictionary the word "validation" means:

- To make legally valid
- To support or corroborate on a sound or authoritative basis.

Whether we choose to emphasize the correspondence to formal requirements or the rigour and soundness of the underlying analysis, validation refers to the process of ascertaining that something satisfies a certain, predefined set of criteria. Validating a model consists therefore in comparing it with something else, in benchmarking it against a scale, which in turn can be a set of rules, a description of practices, a set of empirical observations, the outputs from another model and so on. In other words the essence of validation is the measurement of a model (including the output, the quality of the data, the process around it and the way it used) against one or more recognized yardsticks. It follows, of course, that, as in all measurements efforts, a validator needs to be aware of the principle known as "Wittgenstein's ruler," which, simply stated, says that if you want to use a ruler to measure a table and you do not trust the ruler, you might as well use the table to measure the ruler (Taleb, 2010).

A typical application of Wittgenstein's ruler is the so-called case interviews that management consultancies use in their recruitment activity. The interviewer typically asks the candidate to solve a particular problem, say, to determine the size of a market or the profitability of a company, and the candidate is expected to work out an answer in a limited time and with little or no data. The objective of the interviewer is not to find out the correct answer (she may even ignore it altogether), but to judge the candidate's ability to make reasonable assumptions, develop a methodology and reason towards a solution. In true Wittgenstein's fashion, the recruiter uses the table to measure the ruler. The candidate is the (untested) ruler and the problem is the table. It is actually interesting to notice that most case interviews are indeed measurement problems, wherein the measurement process is inverted, and what gets measured in reality is the candidate and not the quantity mentioned in the case.

"Measuring the ruler" is what validation is ultimately about. Suppose we need to validate a derivative pricing model. Normally the model is used to measure (i.e., to produce an estimate of) the value of certain derivative products. In order to validate it, we would use observations about the values of those products and compare them with the estimates yielded by the model with the objective of assessing how accurate the model estimates are. In other words when we validate a pricing model, we look at it as a ruler we are not sure we can trust for measuring a table (for example the value of a financial product), and hence we use a table (for example a set of market observations) to assess how good the ruler is.

What happens when market observations are not readily available? What happens when we have a ruler that we do not fully trust and no table readily available to test the ruler? In that case of course we need to find another table, that is, another benchmark against which we can test our model. This may be the results obtained from another, trusted, model, for instance one provided by a reputable vendor, or one built by another expert in the same organization. It may also be one obtained from an independent, trusted, third party, as in the case of consultancies specialized in model validation or of the credit ratings and default data obtained from an international rating agency.

Note that even when validating the underlying theoretical structure, the set of equations used, the implementation in an IT system or even the deployment of the model within a specific organizational process, we are still measuring the object of our validation against a benchmark. This may be a set of theoretical results accepted by the relevant scientific community, an industry standard in programming and testing, or an established practice for developing procedures and controls.

Martini and Henaff (2010) argue that model validation encompasses a smaller or larger scope depending on the interpretation taken by each financial institution. It could be a purely technical and qualitative exercise focussing on whether a certain methodological choice is fit for the intended purpose. It could, in addition, encompass the implementation of a certain methodology and hence cover the IT choices made, internally developed code and/or vendor solutions. Validation could also include, beside the model and its implementation, the whole process through which the model is deployed within the organization, thereby encompassing data, calibration, use test, and the related internal controls.

4 Conclusions

As validation in general does not mean to produce a single monetary measure of model risk, but involves comparing various aspects of a model against different yardsticks, it is essential to be able to interpret its results and act, or recommend action, accordingly. For instance, if validation encompasses the comparison between the price provided by a model and the market price, what is an acceptable result? When comparing a model-derived default probability with an observed default rate by means of a statistical test, when is it that the null hypothesis can be rejected? What constitutes an appropriate implementation of a given mathematical model? When is it that a model is adequately documented? And so on.

A similar problem arises when philosophers look at how a scientific theory could be accepted or rejected depending on how good it proves to be at predicting things. Whereby logical positivists stated that a theory can be proven true ("verified") by cumulative observations consistent with the theory's predictions, others, the most eminent of which being Karl Popper (1959), argued that, whereas a theory can be conclusively rejected on the basis of even a single experimental result contrary to its predictions, it can never be conclusively established as true (i.e., verified) and as such will only be provisionally retained, until the first counterinstance will force us to discard it.

This approach solves the problem of induction by rejecting it outright as a means to establish the truth of a theory, but it also implies that every theory should be simply thrown away as soon as a counterinstance is found. In fact, the main criticism to the Popperian approach has precisely been the observation that it is very difficult, if not impossible, to put into practice, and that, in the real world, a theory is not immediately rejected at the first counterinstance. Rather, the theory is revised, and changes are made in one or more of the hypotheses in order to accommodate the new results. While Popper maintained that this approach salvages a theory at the cost of lowering, or destroying, its scientific status, other thinkers, the most authoritative of which was Willard Quine (1970), countered that, as experiments are fallible both ways, they can neither conclusively falsify nor verify a theory, and therefore scientists should better be sceptical revisers (rather than sceptical falsifiers) and try to save theories rather than to refute them. He went on to suggest that for any body of evidence confirming a theory, there might well be other theories that are also well confirmed by that same body of evidence.

Validation is therefore rarely a pass or fail process, and rarely one can conclusively accept or reject a given model. Validators should never forget that the limits of model-making apply to their work as well and that they should consider their results with the same healthy scepticism with which they consider the results of any model they examine.

In a sense, all risk is model risk. If the map were the territory, we could run our models and predict the future. And there would be no surprises.

Notes

1. In a more recent work (Derman, 2011) he gives a definition that is more general and akin to the one considered earlier in this chapter: "*Models* stand on someone else's feet. They are metaphors that compare the object of their attention to something else that it resembles."
2. "Reports that say that something hasn't happened are always interesting to me, because as we know, there are known knowns; there are things we know we know. We also know there are known unknowns; that is to say we know there are some things we do not know. But there are also unknown unknowns - the ones we don't know we don't know," D. Rumsfeld, 2003.

References

Avellaneda, M., Levy, A. and Paras, A., "Pricing and Hedging Derivative Securities in Markets with Uncertain Volatilities," *Applied Mathematical Finance*, Vol. 2, 73–88, 1995.

Bachelier, L., J.-B., A., Théorie de la spéculation, Annales Scientifiques de l'École Normale Supérieure, 21–86, 1900.

Board of Governors of the Federal Reserve System, Office of the Comptroller of the Currency, OCC 2011-12, Supervisory Guidance on Model Risk Management. Sec. III, p. 3.

Box, G. E. P. and Draper, N. R., Empirical Model-Building and Response Surfaces, Wiley, 1987.

Böcker, K. and Klüpperberg, C., *Operational VAR: a Closed-Form Approximation, Risk,* December 2005.

Cont, R., "Model Uncertainty and its Impact on the Pricing of Derivative Instruments," *Mathematical Finance,* Vol. 16, No. 3, 519–547.

Crouhy, M., Galai, D. and Mark, R., *Risk Management,* McGraw Hill, 2000.

Derman, E., *Model Risk.* Technical Report, Goldman Sachs, New York, 1996.

Hubbard, D. W., *How to Measure Anything: Finding the Value of Intangibles in Business,* Wiley, 2010.

Karoui, N., Jeanblanc-Picquè, M. and Shreve, S., :Robustness of the Black and Scholes Formula," *Mathematical Finance,* Vol. 8, No. 2, 93–126, 1998.

Kato T. and Yoshida T, "Model Risk and its Control," *Monetary and Economic Studies,* December 2000.

Kerkhof, J., Melenberg, B. and Schumacher, H. "Model Risk and Capital Reserves," *Journal of Banking and Finance,* Vol. 34, No. 1, 267–279, 2010.

Keynes, J. M., "The General Theory of Employment," *Quarterly Journal of Economics,* February 1937.

Klugman S. A., Panjer H. H. and Willmot G. E., *Loss Models, From Data to Decisions,* J. Wiley & Sons, New York, 1998.

Le Guin, U., *The Left Hand of Darkness,* Ace Books, 1987.

Lyons, T., "Uncertain Volatility and the Risk-Free Synthesis of Derivatives." *Applied Mathematical Finance,* Vol. 2, No. 2, 117–133, 1995.

Martini, C. and Henaff, P., "Model Validation: Theory, Practice and Perspectives," *The Journal of Risk Model Validation,* Vol. 5, No. 4, 3–15, Winter 2011/12.

Morini, M., *Understanding and Managing Model Risk,* Wiley, 2011.

O'Hear, A., *Introduction to the Philosophy of Science,* Clarendon Press, Oxford, 1989.

Popper, K. R., *The Logic of Scientific Discovery,* Basic Books, New York, 1959.

Rebonato, R., "Theory and Practice of Model Risk Management," in Field, P. (editor), *Modern Risk Management,* Risk Books, London, 223–248, 2003.

Quine, W. *The Web of Belief,* Random House, New York, 1970.

Sibbertsen, P., Stahl, G. and Luedtke, C., 2008. *Measuring Model Risk,* Hannover Economic Papers (HEP) dp-409, Leibniz Universität Hannover, Wirtschaftswissenschaftliche Fakultät.

Taleb, N. N., *Fooled by Randomness,* Thomson Texere, London, 2004.

Part I

A Framework for Risk Model Validation

1 Validation, Governance and Supervision

In recent years the difficulties and the failures of corporate governance in banks have been a constant point of focus of both scientific literature and public debate. This should not surprise us in light of both the opaqueness of their business activities and of their role and relationship with the wider economy, features that set banks apart from other kinds of companies.

Banks are much more highly leveraged than other companies and, since they charge higher interest rates than those they pay on their debt, their profitability goes up with the size of their loan portfolio. This growth should be checked by the progressive premium creditors will demand as the bank's leverage (and hence its probability of default) increases as well as by the regulatory capital requirements, but such constraint critically depends on the ability to assess the risk inherent in the bank's balance sheet and to estimate the probability of default. This is not a straightforward task, and is complicated by the fact that banks' balance sheets are more opaque than those of other firms. Of course, all firms are, to an extent, opaque. Banks, however, take this feature one (big) step forward as the assets they take on their balance sheet are precisely those they are better able to assess and monitor. Those assets are therefore by definition better understood by insiders than by outsiders. In other words, banks' opaqueness is fundamentally linked to its key activity: risk-taking. The profile resulting from this risk-taking may change, sometimes sharply, even if the bank does not take new positions or alter the composition of its portfolio. Furthermore, the presence of derivatives, asset-backed securities, or securities with embedded options may render the bank extremely sensitive to changes in market conditions with dramatic consequences on its balance sheet.

These are some of the reasons why governance in banks is at the same time so critical and so difficult, and nowhere more so than when it comes to governing the complexity that surrounds the quantitative treatment of risk measurement and management.

1 The relationship between governance and model risk

Corporate governance in financial institutions has come under intense scrutiny since the 2008–2009 financial crisis. Such scrutiny has primarily focussed on the processes and responsibilities underpinning the making of decisions – in particular risk-taking decisions – and the system of incentives provided to managers and directors. However, another aspect of governance that has been singled out as both surprising and disturbing is provided by the many examples of board members and top executives who, in the aftermath of the financial crisis, have admitted to having misunderstood or even ignored the extent and complexity of risk-taking in the institutions they were supposed to oversee and manage. Indeed many widely esteemed top managers and directors alike have claimed limited understanding and even outright ignorance of some of the most risky deals their institutions had entered into on the basis that they were too many, too complex and too difficult to comprehend. And this worrying phenomenon has proven to be remarkably resilient to legal and supervisory provisions.

Years after the worst of the financial crisis, in 2012, JP Morgan, at the time the largest American investment bank and the only one to go through the 2008–2009 financial crisis relatively unscathed, announced a loss in excess of $6 billion (although the final amount might have been larger) related to the hedging (!) activities of their London based Chief Investment Office (CIO), whose head was promptly fired. JP Morgan's CEO, possibly the most respected top banker in the country, admitted he had not properly understood the nature of the deals transacted in the CIO and that those activities should have gotten more scrutiny from the bank's executives. The scrutiny, it turns out, should have focussed on model building and model validation alike. As extensively explained in JP Morgan's task force report on the CIO losses (JP Morgan, 2013), CIO traders were convinced that the model used to compute portfolio Value at Risk (VaR) was too conservative in the way it accounted for correlation and thus did not recognize the whole impact of diversification in the CIO portfolio. The bank therefore developed a new model that went live in January 2013, shortly after a series of VaR limit breaches had been recorded using the old model. The use of the new model immediately produced substantially lower VaR values that were accepted without further enquiry until May 2012 when, following large losses, a review of the model showed a number of operational errors, including wrong Excel formulas, affecting the way correlation was computed.

The JPMorgan "whale" scandal highlighted once more the importance of effectively linking corporate governance and risk management. Risk management as a mere exercise in quantitative analysis is of no use in absence of a solid management process. Such a process should ensure that roles and responsibilities are clearly established, that quantitative models are developed and validated according to certain minimum quality standards and that the recognition of their limitations is matched by consequential management decisions. It is worth quoting the Federal Reserve (2011) on the subject.

> *Model risk management begins with robust model development, implementation, and use. Another essential element is a sound model validation process. A third element is governance, which sets an effective framework with defined roles and responsibilities for clear communication of model limitations and assumptions, as well as the authority to restrict model usage.*

McConnell (2014) goes even further to argue that market risk management should be split between risk modelling and process management, with a separate team of operational risk experts in charge of the latter.

The above discussion suggests that the use of ever more sophisticated quantitative models for risk analysis allows a financial institution to better understand and control certain risks while at the same time exposing it to another kind of risk linked to the potential inadequacy of the model employed. The idea that risk is pushed out of the door only to come back in through the window is not a new one. Hedging market risk through a derivative contract, for instance, reduces exposure to market factors while introducing a new exposure to the credit risk of the derivative counterpart. The use of collateral reduces credit risk while creating an exposure to potential operational failures in the related management process, and so on. More generally, technical progress, while freeing us from a number of needs and risks, has a tendency to create new ones. Writing in a context far removed from today's global finance, Beck (1986) argued that technological advances generate ecological risks that are global and radical, and that defy our ability to control and insure them. His analysis focussed on the sociological consequences of this globalization of risk and in particular on how the mechanics of the distribution of risks differ from the traditional ones that govern the distribution of wealth.

Over the past few decades, the practice of finance has reached an unprecedented level of sophistication, thereby expanding enormously the access to equity and debt finance for companies, countries and societies, but, as a by-product of that very sophistication, risks have emerged that are unpredictable, global, potentially catastrophic and difficult to hedge or insure. Model risk is a prominent example of such risks: It arises as the result of technological progress and of the attempt at managing other risks (market, credit and operational) in a more effective way; it is difficult to measure and to account for; it is hard to manage and is obscure to all but the most specialized experts. In other words, it is precisely the kind of risk that those tasked with overseeing the soundness and the stability of the financial system should worry about.

2 Model validation as assurance

Validation is about confirming an understanding of something complex. It is needed whenever there is an information gap about an object that by its nature is to be used primarily, if not exclusively, by experts. In risk management the role of experts is critical not just because of the heavy reliance on complex mathematics and statistics, but because of the global and radicalized nature of risks mentioned in the previous section. And when the full extent of certain risks is not realized by the experts, we start to question "not only the limits of, or the gaps in, expert knowledge, but ... the very idea of expertise" (Giddens, 1990). Validation is therefore aimed simultaneously at those that have to rely on the work of experts to make decisions as well as at the experts themselves.

In finance, knowledge of quantitative models, as a fundamental tool in managing innovative and complex financial products, plays a role not dissimilar to that of technological innovation in other industries, but with one fundamental difference: time. In the pharmaceutical industry, for instance, the process of bringing a new drug to the market, from the initial idea to the actual commercialization of it, is normally a matter of years, in some cases decades, both due to the research effort required and the internal and external tests a new product has to undergo (including the subsequent clinical trials and regulatory reviews that are required before a new drug can be licensed for medical use). In recognition of the costs the company has to sustain, regulation also allows for a period during which the profits afforded by the new product can be enjoyed exclusively. This allows for the full exploitation, for a limited number of years, of the competitive advantage generated by the innovation.

In banking, the relationship between product development and competitive advantage exists as well, but in a manner that is very different from the one in other technology-based industries. The development effort is shorter, and the approval process is much less formal and rigorous. No specific test is performed before selling the new product to the public, although one might argue that "trials" along the line of the ones performed for drugs would be advisable in order to ascertain the potential toxicity and side effects of certain financial products. Furthermore, once the product has been launched, there is no such thing as a patent for the product that would grant the bank the exclusive right to use it. To the extent that other firms can master the same know-how, nothing prevents them from selling the same product, thereby starting to erode the profit margins of the original innovator.

The speed and pattern for developing and launching a new financial product creates, however, two critical knowledge gaps, the most visible of which is the one between the innovating firm and its competitors. The more complex and innovative the product is, the longer it will take for competitors to bridge that gap. But there is another knowledge gap created by financial innovation: one between the front office (the people developing and selling the product) and the rest of the firm. In a pharmaceutical company, before a product reaches the customer, the analysis and the scrutiny it undergoes within the company are so comprehensive that knowledge about the product and its potential effects is by and large documented and widely shared. Although surprises can still happen, the product only gets out the door when a number of control functions within and outside the company, and not just the scientific team who developed it, are comfortable that the product and its effects are well understood. By contrast, in banks it can take a long time before the risk management or the compliance functions, let alone the auditors and the accountants, develop an understanding of a new product comparable to that of the front office. And by then the product has already been launched and transacted many times over. This, in itself, is a source of risk; it is difficult to control somebody's activities when our understanding of those activities is inferior to the one that we are supposed to control.

The practice of systematic model validation is an attempt at bridging this internal information gap and at ensuring that at least the technical capacity for valuation and risk measurement of the financial products, usually the key component in a bank's understanding and ability to manage them, are independently and transparently tested.

Like other assurance-type functions, however, model validation can fail in its mission as much because of inadequacies in the people performing the task as because of the approach, process and methodologies followed.

Achim, Achim and Streza (2008) identify the following four types of causes for audit errors:

- Failure to sufficiently understand the client's business;
- Failure to verify management's observations and explanations;
- Lack of exercising professional scepticism on unusual or last-minute transactions;
- Inadequate appreciation and evaluation of risks.

It is easy to see how these causes relate to a trade-off between competence and independence that also applies to model validation. A failure to understand the business and the related model's purpose, as well as an inadequate appreciation of risks, may come from an excessive distance from the reality of the business because the analysis relies too much on documentation and too little on extensive interaction with staff or simply from not spending enough time and resources on the job. On the other hand, a lack of diligent verification and professional scepticism may come from a false sense of security and understanding as a consequence of spending too much time interacting with the model developers and from having a long-lasting relationship, precisely the kind of behaviour that would otherwise facilitate a better comprehension of what goes on within the modelling team.

On top of this trade-off, anyway, there is always a potential conflict of interest arising from the fact that model validators are rarely completely independent from a hierarchical point of view and do not, as a rule, have the authority and status of auditors. Although the latter feature may help them develop a more productive and less conflictual relationship with model developers and owners, it can also generate problems when, for instance, their input is sought during the development of a new model, something an auditor would normally refuse to do. While it may be useful, and it may save time and resources in the long run to have the opinion of an independent validator during the development effort, such an opinion should always be carefully qualified. In fact, a validator's understanding of the chosen solution will necessarily be high-level, in view of the lack of a full-functioning model prototype, and the opportunities for testing any hypothesis or assumption will be limited by the limited time available and by the lack of a complete dataset.

A good model governance structure should provide for the appropriate level of oversight by board and senior managers who should approve and regularly review the overall framework (scope, objectives, policy, methodologies and infrastructure), supported by the assurance provided by the internal audit team. Ownership and control of the models should reside with the relevant business unit charged with developing and using them, as supported by the appropriate quantitative and IT expertise, while validation should be the responsibility of a team with the required resources and expertise which is independent both from the staff responsible for developing the model and from those using the model on a regular basis. Figure 1.1 summarizes this governance concept. In the next chapter we will expand on the appropriate allocation of responsibilities in model management.

3 Model validation from a supervisory perspective

The evolution of prudential supervision, as outlined in the various versions of the Basel Accord, has progressively put the issue of risk measurement, and therefore of risk modelling, at the centre of the supervisors' attention. While during the 1990s supervisory requirements were confined to trading market risk models (1996

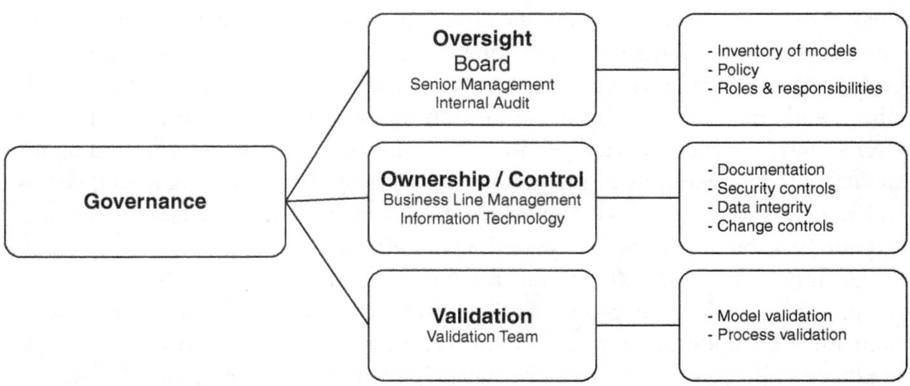

Figure 1.1 The governance of risk models

amendment to the first Basel Accord), the twenty-first century has seen the codification of quantitative models for credit risk and operational risk (the second Basel Accord), and, during the post-crisis scramble for reform, a substantial toughening of the modelling requirements for market and counterparty credit risk (the so-called Basel 2.5).

Banks' use of quantitative models is therefore driven by the regulatory framework that prevails in their jurisdiction, starting with the choice, still relevant in several countries, between Basel I and II. Within Basel II, a substantial difference is determined by the choice of the Internal Rating Based (IRB) approach, foundation or advanced, for credit risk and by that of the Advanced Measurement Approach (AMA) for operational risk. A further component in the supervisory framework driving the use of models is the choice of the internal model method for the derivative book and the related requirement for computing counterparty credit risk. These choices have in turn an effect on the incentives banks face in their choice of assets (Le Leslé, and Avramova, 2012), as can be seen, for instance, in the difference between American and European banks, the former favouring assets carrying a low risk weight (fostering a stronger capital ratio), while the latter favour assets with higher returns (allowing them to respect a generally more stringent leverage ratio).

For instance, the BCBS (2013) published an analysis of the variation in risk-weighted assets for credit risk in the banking book, where several drivers of such variations were identified from discretionary choices allowed under the Basel framework to deviation in the national implementation from Basel standards. Amongst these: varying credit risk approaches taken by banks (partial use of Standardised approach, Foundation vs. Advanced), treatment of securitization, conservative adjustments to IRB parameter estimates and differences in banks' modelling choices, like choice of reference data, or methodological differences, such as Probabilities of Default (PD) master scales, definition of default, adjustment for cyclical effects, like long-run PD, downturn effects in Loss Given Default (LGD) and Credit Conversion Factors (CCF), the treatment of low default portfolios through expert judgements and the calculations of defaulted exposures. All these elements are likely to have a relevant impact on RWAs.

For example, in modelling PDs, some regulators require that clients be weighted in the denominator by number of active months, others ask that all be equally weighted, and still others require that all good clients who have left the bank be removed. Some allow for continuous rating scales while others do not. In extrapolating central tendency for PDs, some regulators allow the use of external default data, while others allow it with a conservative add-on, and others forbid it altogether. Some require adjustments for cyclicality while others do not. In LGD modelling, there are considerable variations across jurisdictions on conservative buffers, on the inclusion of unresolved cases in development samples, on the exclusive use of recession years in development, on collateral haircuts, on discount rates used to compute recoveries and so on.

These differences are not confined to credit risk. Some regulators, for instance, require Value at Risk (VaR) to be computed as the maximum of a simple average and an exponentially weighted average, while others require a simple average only. All regulators apply multipliers to the computed VaR that can vary from 3 (the minimum established in the Basel Accord) up to 5.5. In both market and operational risk calculations, not all regulators allow the recognition of diversification benefits across countries, and analogous differences arise in the recognition of insurance mitigation benefits for operational risk. Being able to distinguish which differences in the various risk measures are due to the different practices from those that are due to the actual risk of the assets is fundamental for effectively managing model risk.

The most problematic effects of modelling choices, however, come from the fact that the very act of measuring an exposure is not irrelevant to the exposure itself. Perhaps the most famous example of this phenomenon is given by the so-called volatility skew or "smile," as it is often called.

According to the Black-Scholes (1973) option pricing model, the implied volatility as a function of the exercise price looks like a horizontal straight line. This means that all options on the same underlying asset and with the same expiration date should have the same implied volatility, even with different exercise prices. As every trader knows, however, this is not what happens in practice. The plot of the implied volatility is U-shaped for a call option, as it goes from deep in-the-money to at-the-money and then to deep out-of-the-money (Derman and Kani, 1994), or vice versa for a put option. MacKenzie and Millo (2003) argue that the assumptions behind the Black-Scholes model were quite unrealistic and that empirical prices differed systematically from the model. It was the financial market that gradually changed in a way that fit the model. This was in part the effect of option pricing theory itself. Pricing models came to shape the very way participants thought and talked about options, in particular via the key, entirely model-dependent, notion of "implied volatility." The use of the Black-Scholes model in arbitrage had the effect of reducing discrepancies between empirical prices and the model, especially in the econometrically crucial matter of the flat-line relationship between implied volatility and strike price.

Similarly, by means of a computational model using agent-based simulation techniques, Vagnani (2008) shows that the "smile" in the implied volatility curve is likely to emerge in an environment in which traders rely on their subjective beliefs to resolve their uncertainty about the underlying stock volatility and use the widely accepted Black-Scholes formula to price options.

This property of complex systems, also named *reflexivity* in some studies (Giddens, 1990, ibid.), played a destructive role in the latest global crises. As pointed out by Daníelsson (2002), both in the 1987 and in the 1998 crashes, the widespread use of risk measurement models substantially contributed to extreme price movements and losses. In 1987 the use of portfolio insurance, with its complex, futures-based, option-replicating hedges, was a major factor in the collapse of future markets when all the major players reacted to the increase in volatility by putting in place the same hedges. In 1998 a similar increase in volatility and correlations caused a generalized breach of limits with subsequent flight to stable assets. This in turn increased volatility even more and dramatically drained liquidity.

Adrian and Shin (2008) explain how before and during the 2008-2009 financial crisis, banks' risk and leverage went up as asset prices rose, and they went down as asset prices fell. The phenomenon is a consequence of banks targeting a certain level of risk and adjusting their balance sheet accordingly in order to remain close to that chosen target when asset prices, and the related risk measure, move. Figure 1.2 shows the mechanism in case the risk measure chosen is leverage. However, the same argument applies in the case of Value at Risk or other risk measures.

The effect is amplified, however, if banks, as it happens, all use the same kind of model to measure risk. This in turn points to a different regulatory problem: On one hand, the supervisors do not want to see too much variation in risk measures amongst similarly capitalized banks. It may suggest that some banks are "gaming the system" or that some models used are not conservative enough. On the other hand, if all banks were 100% consistent in their reported risk measures, that would not be reassuring either. It could suggest that most banks are using the same kind of model which, ceteris paribus, is producing the same results. In case the widely chosen modelling approach proved unable to effectively anticipate large movements and losses, as arguably was the case in late 2007 and early 2008, it could contribute to a systemic build-up in risk across the industry. In other words, looking at the financial system as a whole, a supervisor wants to see neither too much variety nor too little in the individual risk assessments. In the former case it is impossible to decide which ones are right; in the latter they might as well be all wrong. As Michel de Montaigne (1533–1592) once wrote, "If our faces were not alike, we could not distinguish man from beast; if they were not unlike, we could not distinguish one man from another."

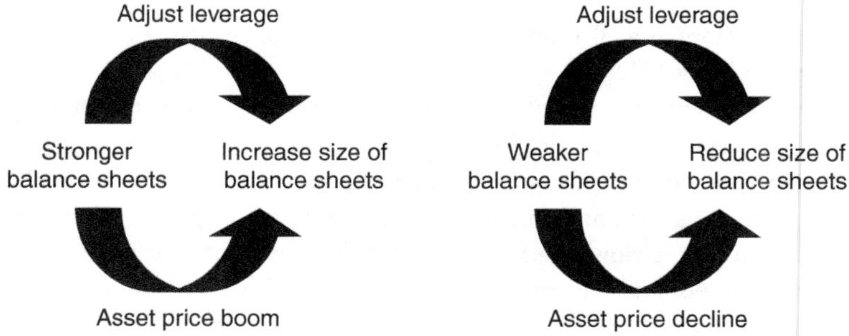

Figure 1.2 Reflexivity and pro-cyclicality

Accordingly, Le Leslé, and Avramova (ibid. 2012) argue that, although reported Risk Weighted Assets (RWAs) show substantial differences within and across countries, a full harmonization and convergence may be neither achievable nor desirable. However, improvements in supervisory policy and banking practice should focus on enhancing the transparency and understanding of outputs and on providing common methodological guidance. Given the central role of models in computing RWAs across ever larger parts of the financial sector, such objectives shall at least in part be served by a systematic and effective application of model validation standards.

4 Conclusions

It is interesting to note how, historically, regulation and supervision also have followed the economic cycle. Stricter provisions and stronger supervisory powers are enacted during and immediately following financial crises, while a lighter touch, both in rule making and in enforcement, is adopted in times of economic expansion. This approach is reflected in financial institutions' perception and assessment of risk, which in turn pushes them to lobby for easing of regulations when times look good. Such a market-driven approach to risk assessment may look reasonable from the perspective of banks and their shareholders, who after all see their capacity to absorb losses go up with asset prices and the likelihood of negative scenarios go down with every passing day of positive market data (which go on to boost the database on which their risk measures are founded), but it is not conceptually sound for regulators and legislators to follow, no matter how well one can understand the social and political dynamics at play.

Since the aftermath of the 2008–2009 crisis, regulators and governments around the world started to question the way financial institutions were managed and how people at their helms were held accountable for their decisions. The result was a major overhaul of laws and regulations that only a few months earlier had looked very much state of the art. One non-irrelevant component of these regulatory changes hinges on the quantitative estimates of values and risks produced by financial institutions as well as on how to ensure that such estimates are both reliable and understood.

The issues encountered in both corporate governance and in risk management stem from the asymmetrical distribution of information and on the constraints we encounter in interpreting and comprehending it. The complexity of the mechanisms we devise to manage risk and to control a corporate entity present therefore costs and limits, and this is nowhere more evident than in the widespread reliance on quantitative models and the resulting model risk. The opaqueness to outsiders of implementations and results, as well as the difficulty in piercing this veil in a manner that is both reliable and unbiased by management interests create one more potentially dangerous gap in the governance of a financial institution. How to possibly bridge these gaps is the subject of the next chapters.

References

Adrian, T. and Shin, H. S., "Liquidity, Monetary Policy and Financial Cycles," *Current Issues in Economics and Finance*, Vol. 14, No. 1, January/February 2008.

Basel Committee on Banking Supervision, "Strengthening the Resilience of the Banking Sector," Bank for International Settlements, December 2009.

Basel Committee on Banking Supervision, "Analysis of Risk-Weighted Assets for Credit Risk in the Banking Book," Regulatory Consistency Assessment Programme (RCAP), July 2013.

Beck, U., *Risikogesellschaft. Auf dem Weg in eine andere Moderne*. Suhrkamp, Frankfurt a.M. 1986.

Blochwitz, S. and Hohl, S., "Validation of Banks' Internal Rating Systems: A Supervisory Perspective," in Engelmann, B. and Rauhmeier, R., *The Basel II Risk Parameters*, Second Edition, Springer, 2011.

Board of Governors of the Federal Reserve System, *Supervisory Guidance on Model Risk Management*, SR Letter 11-7, Washington, April 2011.

Daníelsson, J., "The Emperor has No Clothes: Limits To Risk Modelling," *Journal of Banking & Finance*, Elsevier, Vol. 26, No. 7, 1273–1296, July 2002.

Derman, E. and Kani, I., "Riding on a Smile," *Risk*, Vol. 7, 32–39, 1994.

Giddens, A., *The Consequences of Modernity*, Stanford University Press, Stanford, CA, 1990.

JP Morgan, Report of JP Morgan Chase and Co. Management Task Force Regarding 2012 CIO Losses. Report, January 16, 2013, JP Morgan Chase, New York. URL: http://files.shareholder.com/downloads/ONE/2272984969x0x628656/4cb574a0-0bf5-4728-9582-625e4519b5ab/Task_Force_Report.pdf.

Le Leslé, V. and Avramova, S., *Revisiting Risk-Weighted Assets*, IMF Working Paper No. 12/90, March 2012.

MacKenzie, D. and Millo, Y., "Constructing a Market, Performing Theory: The Historical Sociology of a Financial Derivatives Exchange," *American Journal of Sociology*, Vol. 109, No. 1, 107–145, July 2003.

McConnell, P., "Dissecting the JPMorgan Whale: A Post-Mortem," *Journal of Operational Risk*, Vol. 9, No. 2, 59–100, 2014.

Montaigne, M., III, 13, p. 1070, éd. Villey, PUF, Quadrige, Paris, 1992.

Organisation for Economic Co-operation and Development, *OECD Principles of Corporate Governance*, Paris, 2004.

Scandizzo, S., *Risk and Governance: A Framework for Banking Organisations*, Risk Books, London, 2013.

Vagnani, G., "the Black-Scholes Model as a Determinant of the Implied Volatility Smile: A Simulation Study," *Journal of Economic Behavior & Organization*, 2008, Doi: 10.1016/J.Jebo.2009.05.025.

2 A Validation Framework for Risk Models

It follows from the previous chapter's discussion that model validation has one main goal: to manage and, if possible, minimize, model risk. It does so, within the broader context of a model risk management framework, by fulfilling what auditors call the "second line of defence" role. The three lines of defence model (BCBS, 2012) foresees the following structure of controls: a set of controls performed within a given business process by the business unit primarily responsible for the process (the "business owner"); a set of meta-controls, performed by an independent entity within the organization (the second line of defence), aimed at ensuring that the controls in the first line have been properly performed and that exceptions have been properly identified, followed up and resolved; a regular review of the business process and of the related controls performed in the first and second lines of defence, whose objective is to ensure that the business process is effected according to documented procedures, that both sets of controls are performed properly and that all exceptions are promptly followed up and resolved. This last activity, the third line of defence, is usually performed by Internal Audit at periodic intervals and involves, amongst other things, both a review of activities against documented procedures and a set of tests on the available records.

In order to develop a framework for model validation, we need first to define the key concepts, establish the objectives and the guiding principle of the model validation activity, and establish the fundamental elements of a governance framework, including roles and responsibilities. We should also give an outline of the model risk management framework to be implemented under these provisions.

1 Definitions and objectives

The BCBS, in the second Basel Accord and in other papers, as well as a variety of national regulators, have regularly written about the need for "appropriate policies and procedures" in the management of risk. Although they refer potentially to a large number of documents governing the complexity of risk management activities, in this chapter and throughout this book the term "model validation policy" refers to a single document, approved and regularly updated by the board that outlines the bank's approach to model risk and spells out definitions, appetite and responsibilities at a sufficiently high level to be understood unequivocally by everyone inside and outside the bank, but also with sufficient detail so as not to leave any doubt as to what the objectives of model validation are and who is responsible for what.

Although the responsibility of the board of directors for risk management has repeatedly been established in regulatory documents, you cannot reasonably expect the board to rule on every single issue arising from the implementation of a model risk management framework. To the greatest extent possible, you want to go to the board with thought-out solutions for approval rather than with a problem to solve. Consequently, it has to be at the same time comprehensive in scope and specific enough to provide the necessary leverage when dealing with the misunderstandings, and inevitably the outright resistance, that you will encounter in the implementation of your model risk management framework. The first step in achieving this goal is to define the key concepts at hand.

Establishing definitions may seem a straightforward task in such a technical field, but one may be surprised to see how fuzzy things can get when applied within the context of a banking organization. Let us start with the definition of a model. It may be straightforward to identify a scoring sheet and related PD mapping as a model, but what about the computation of asset-liability gap? The set of equations and related implementation used for the computation of the Value at Risk of a trading portfolio is certainly a model to be validated; but is it the same for the projection of funding and liquidity requirements? And is every calculation performed for any ad-hoc reporting purpose and implemented in a spreadsheet to be considered a model and a candidate for validation? There is also a ton of calculation routinely performed by accounting departments in their day-to-day activity. Are those models to be validated too?

Amongst the several definitions provided by the Merriam-Webster dictionary, the following is probably the more relevant in our context: "a system of postulates, data, and inferences presented as a mathematical description of an entity or state of affairs." However, this is definitely too broad and would be of little use when it comes to answering some of the questions above.

More specific guidance on what should be the object of regular validation is given in the Basel Accord and related guidance (BCBS, 2006 and EBA, 2007). This guidance, however, refers specifically to models used for credit, market and operational risk, and, although certainly covering a lot of ground in terms of supervisory relevance, it does not provide a general definition.

The U.S. banking regulator (OCC) is to date the only one that provides overall definitions. In one of its papers (OCC, 2011) it defines a model as "a quantitative method, system, or approach that applies statistical, economic, financial, or mathematical theories, techniques, and assumptions to process input data into quantitative estimates[1]", model risk as "the potential for adverse consequences from decisions based on incorrect or misused model outputs and reports[2]", and model validation as "the set of processes and activities intended to minimize model risk, i.e., to verify that the models are performing as expected, in line with their design objectives and business uses[3]".

The objective of a model validation policy is also to establish the relevant responsibilities, the process and the guiding principles to be followed as well as the documentation to be produced in order to minimize the *model risk* associated with the models and the related risk estimates.

2 Key principles

An example of key validation principles is provided by the Basel Committee on Banking Supervision, who established the following principles of validation (BCBS, 2005). Although developed for the validation of internal rating models, they provide nonetheless a useful frame of reference.

Principle 1 – Validation is fundamentally about assessing the predictive ability of a bank's risk estimates and the use of ratings in credit processes

The risk assessments made by the bank should not only be (theoretically) predictive of the underlying risk, but the rationale underpinning the methodology and process employed should be supported by historical experience.

Principle 2 – The Bank has primary responsibility for validation

The primary responsibility for validating the risk models lies within bank itself. This certainly should reflect the bank's self-interest and the need for the bank to have a system in place reflecting its business.

Principle 3 – Validation is an iterative process

A state-of-the-art validation framework necessitates the presence of monitoring and review processes facilitating the timely identification of any material divergences from expectation, the analysis of such divergences and (if appropriate) the consequent evolution of the various models. This criterion recognizes that a risk assessment methodology and/or its application should be dynamic in nature. Therefore, the monitoring of performance and identification of difficulties in application or process should be an ongoing exercise rather than an occasional review exercise.

Principle 4 – There is no single validation method

Many well-known validation tools like back-testing, benchmarking, replication, etc., are useful supplements to the overall goal of achieving sound and reliable risk modelling. However, there is unanimous agreement that there is no universal tool available that can be used across portfolios and across markets.

Principle 5 – Validation should encompass both quantitative and qualitative elements

Validation is not a technical or solely mathematical exercise. Validation must be considered and applied in a broad sense, its individual components like data, documentation, internal use and all processes the risk model uses are equally important.

Principle 6 – Validation processes and outcomes should be subject to independent review

For all risk models, there must be an independent review within the bank. This specifies neither the organigram in the bank nor its relationship across departments, but the review team must be independent of both the designers of the risk models and of those who implement the validation process.

3 Roles and responsibilities

The Board and senior management should be responsible for approving and periodically reviewing the bank's model validation policy.

Following the three-lines-of-defence approach discussed above, the *first line of defence* responsibility should be assigned to the *model owner*. *Model owner* is defined as the team(s) responsible for development, operation and maintenance of the model/estimate under consideration. Ownership of a model may be assumed by one or several units within the bank. The owner(s) of each model is (are) to be clearly identified.

The owner(s) of a model is (are) the primary people responsible for taking the necessary measures to contain the model risk arising from the models under their responsibility (e.g., by ensuring that complete and clear documentation on the model and the related processes are accessible to relevant parties, by conducting the necessary tests to check and monitor the model outputs' performance by demonstrating the validity of model assumptions, and by ensuring the quality of the data used for development purposes or during model operation and so on).

A dedicated team should be responsible for setting up the processes and controls, and for performing the activities in order to minimize the model risk associated with the models and the risk estimates, following the appropriate validation methodologies and the validation process, as well as for producing the documentation discussed further below in accordance with the timeline specified. The validation team acts primarily as a control and advisory function, and fulfils this responsibility via independent assessment of the models, the estimates and the related processes developed by other units within the bank. Following an independent review exercise, they may issue recommendations that aim at improving the models and the estimates as well as the related processes throughout the bank.

An in-depth assessment of a model as performed during a validation exercise is very rarely carried out more often than once a year. However, this does not mean that no assessment of any kind is performed in between validation exercises. Depending on the nature of the model and the related exposures, this may be done on a monthly, weekly, or even on a daily basis. This regular monitoring activity is an essential component of model risk management. It tends to be more automated and quantitative-based and is usually performed under the responsibility of the model owner, but it naturally presents a number of synergies with regular validation work. In fact, individual validation analyses that are deemed more suitable for ongoing monitoring purposes are usually transferred to the model owner.

Finally, Internal Audit intervenes as the third line of defence in model risk management, and bears the responsibility for assessing whether the first and second lines of defence can fulfil their roles adequately.

There is, however, a further governance dimension to consider. Because most models will involve different departments/functions within the bank as developers, owners, users, validators, respectively, differences in views and in interpretations of results, when not outright conflicts, are inevitable. Furthermore, the three-lines-of-defence model itself relies on the conflict, or at least on the lack of alignment, amongst the interests of different functions to ensure independence and effectiveness of controls. This implies that a kind of overall governance body needs to be in place to provide a forum to analyse and make decisions on validation results as well as to resolve any conflict that validation work may engender. In some institutions, this is provided by an escalation mechanism involving the appropriate levels of senior management, while in others, one or more interdepartmental committees are in place to ensure all views are represented, validation findings are clearly understood and timely decisions are taken.

All the teams within the bank should provide access to all documentation, databases, computer applications and other information needed for the model validation activities. They should provide advice and explanations on the functioning of the models. The teams are also responsible for implementing the changes and updates needed in a timely fashion to address any inconsistencies, errors or weaknesses highlighted by the validation process.

4 Scope and frequency of validation activities

A comprehensive Inventory of Models should be the first step in establishing the scope of validation activities. It should comprise a detailed list of all the models used in the bank and should be developed and maintained by the validation team, in cooperation with all the other relevant teams (users, owners, developers). Managers should be responsible for ensuring that details of all new models or changes to existing models are promptly communicated to the validation team so that they can be considered in the planning of validation activities.

Like all human activities, a validation function needs to deliver results by using as few resources as possible. While it would be ideal to take all the time and expert staff needed to thoroughly analyse every single model on a regular and frequent basis, all manner of constraints will render this goal unattainable. The most obvious of these constraints is human resources. It is rare that enough skills and manpower are available, both because of budget limitations and because the required combination of knowledge and expertise required for model validation in modern finance is overall in short supply. A less obvious problem comes from the nature of model development and maintenance. Models are not normally developed one after the other so that validation work be neatly and sequentially organized nor are they kept stable until the next validation exercise is scheduled. More often than not, a validation team has to deal with models that have been in place and used for quite a while, others that are brand new and others still that are more or less drastically updated. On top of that, regulatory pressure may also quite unevenly bear at times more on certain models than on others, overhauling whatever priorities the bank had tried to set up. As a result, validation teams need to manage a trade-off between prioritization of the model's portfolio and the breadth and depth of the validation work. Usually this is done on one side by classifying models according to some measure of their risk and on the other side by establishing different levels of validation. The following is an example of such an approach, but every institution will have to develop the structure that best fit the size and the complexity of its portfolios.

An independent validation may be performed according to the following three levels:

- extended validation: includes complete qualitative and quantitative assessment of the whole model structure
- standard validation: includes qualitative assessment pertinent to any changes introduced in the validated model, and complete quantitative assessment of all the model components
- light validation: includes qualitative assessment pertinent to any changes introduced in the validated model, and high-level quantitative assessment of the model

The required depth and the extent of the analysis performed in validating each model may be determined by the validation team taking into account peculiar characteristics of the model under consideration. Examples of criteria for prioritizing models are:

a. Size (nominal) of related portfolio;
b. Size (Risk Weighted Assets) of related portfolio;
c. Whether the model is subject to supervisory approval;
d. Whether the model is linked to production of the bank's financial statements;
e. Whether the model's output is sent to third parties outside the bank (clients or other institutions).

These two dimensions can be combined in order to establish a frequency of the validation exercise that is compatible with the resources available. For instance, given that most regulators will require that key models be validated at least on an annual basis, the following approach can be adopted.

- Extended validation
  - For models subject to supervisory approval, over a 1-year cycle;
  - For all other models over a 2–year cycle.
- Standard validation
  - For models subject to supervisory approval, over a 1-year cycle;
  - For all other models, over a 2–year cycle.
- Simpler models may be regularly subject to a light validation exercise.

Model changes

Any validation plan however may be upset by the need to validate changes in the existing models. A model may need changing for a number of potential reasons, such as:

a. A change in institution-specific business conditions, due to, for example, the introduction of/expansion into new business areas, mergers and acquisitions, changes in the organisational structure, etc.;
b. Relevant external events in the markets where institutions operate, and/or in technology, and/or in macro-economic systems;
c. Developments in risk management and measurement systems; evolution of relevant best practices;
d. Changes to own funds and/or other regulatory requirements;
e. Outcome of a previous validation exercise.

The decision to change a model should rest with the responsible teams within the bank. However, any material changes in a model should be accompanied by the following actions:

Table 2.1 Traffic light scheme for validation

Red	Material changes or extensions (e.g. those which, in a supervised institution, would require prior supervisory approval)	Extended validation
Amber	Moderately material changes or extensions (e.g. those which, in a supervised institution, would require prior notification to the supervisory authority)	Standard validation
Green	Minor changes or extensions (e.g. those which, in a supervised institution, would require notification to the supervisory authority on a yearly basis)	Light validation

a. Reason for the changes should be described in detail and added to the model documentation;
b. Changes should be tested, and detailed documentation should be put on file for audit purposes;
c. The relevant head of business should formally sign-off on the new model;
d. Business specifications for the relevant software applications should be amended accordingly;
e. The relevant procedures should be amended accordingly;
f. An independent validation should be performed before the new model is used for the first time.

The scope and depth of the validation to be performed will depend on the materiality of the model change. It should be the responsibility of the relevant teams to assess the materiality of any model extension or change. The following "traffic light" scheme is an example of how the validation levels described above may apply.

Specific guidance on how to assess the materiality of extensions and changes can be found in the European Banking Authority "Regulatory Technical Standards" (EBA, 2013).

5 The validation process

The validation process constitutes an integral part of the model life cycle.

The model life cycle broadly consists of the following stages:

- **Initiation stage:** The activities that need to be performed *before* the effective design of the model starts. Activities at this stage include definition of the (target) risk measure that is going to be modelled and estimated, identification of the risk measure's intended uses, identification of the business requirements, and the technical (infrastructure) requirements as well as the regulatory requirements – if any.
- **Design stage:** The design of the methodology (including definition of assumptions) and development of a prototype (coding or implementation in a software environment) that will serve to produce estimates of the risk measure.

- **Roll-out stage:** The roll-out of the prototype in a production environment. Both the roll-out in the technical infrastructure (i.e., input data processes, output/reporting processes) and the roll-out in the organization (i.e., production and distribution of user manuals, training of users, etc.) are considered here.
- **Operations (Use):** The regular use of the model (e.g., on a daily/monthly/yearly basis) by the users (be it users from the business units or the risk management units).
- **Review stage:** All the review activities that need to be conducted on the model on a regular basis (daily, monthly or yearly) in order to assess and ensure adequacy of the models and the risk estimates with respect to the requirements outlined in the Initiation stage. This stage provides a feedback loop to the Initiation and the Design stages.

The validation activities occur at two stages throughout this model life cycle in two designated types of validations, respectively (as shown in Figure 2.1):

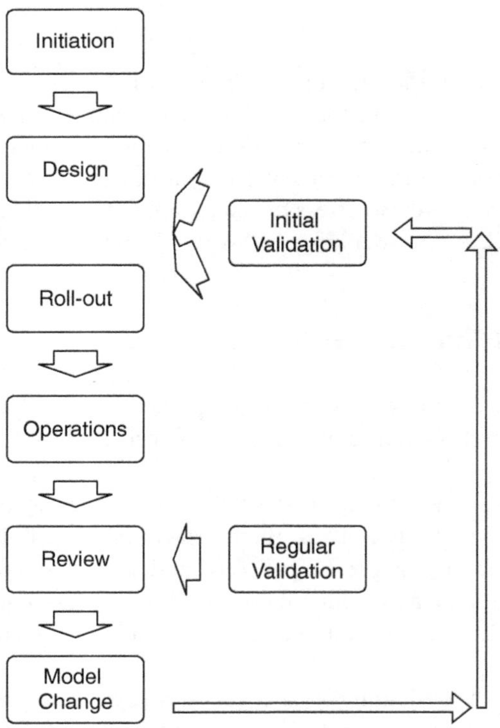

Figure 2.1 Model and validation cycle

- **Initial validation:** Independent end-to-end assessment of the Initiation and/or Design and/or Roll-Out stages following an initial development or a material change in the model design.
- **Regular validation:** In contrast, this type of validation concerns the models that are already being employed actively in operations. It aims at independently assessing and complementing, where necessary, the regular review activities conducted by the model owner[4].

5.1 Structure of validation activities

The structure of validation can be described as encompassing the validation of the model itself as well as the process in place around it. For both Initial and Regular Validations, this is comprised of validation of the model itself and of the process around it.

Validation of the model will cover the conceptual and theoretical design of the model as well as the model's output and performance.

The validation of the model design is the first step in assessing whether the model is "fit for purpose," or adequate for fulfilling both the intended objective and the specified requirements. This means verifying both whether the approach followed is adequate and whether the model is actually applied to the right cases, in particular to the kind of counterparts or client segments for which it is intended. To validate the model design means to look closely at the first two stages of the model life cycle depicted in Figure 2.1, namely the initiation and design stage. This task should be fulfilled through an accurate review of the model documentation followed by discussion with the model owner to ensure no part of it remains obscure or ambiguous. The objective of the review of documentation is to assess whether it ensures full transparency around the business requirements, the model design and its roll-out in the organization. In particular, it should give confidence about the alignment between the design of the model and its intended use.

The review should cover conceptual design, assumptions, data and analytics, including:

a. Appropriateness and adequacy of the methodologies; verification that the model is used for the intended purpose;
b. Explicit identification of assumptions made during development and assessment of their validity under the prevailing conditions;
c. Availability of the relevant risk factors, assessment of their adequacy, how they are treated in the model and of any missing one;
d. Adequacy of prototype development in a software environment;
e. Suitability of model implementation (e.g., model may be conceptually correct, but is it applied to the right set of products?).

The validation exercise should also focus specifically on the output of the model and in particular should ensure that a thorough testing of the model's components and its outputs' performance has taken place (possibly by complementing the tests already performed by the model owner), including:

a. Sensitivity analysis/stress testing/model replication (where necessary);
b. Model performance and stability;
c. Back-testing, benchmarking, and other relevant testing.

Validation of the process shall cover the data, both those used during the development of the model and those related to the model's period of operation under analysis, the model implementation and the use test. In particular, the availability and quality of data, historical as well as current, should be reviewed, covering:

a. Data used for development and calibration
b. Data used for regular output production
c. Data quality, appropriateness and availability

Model implementation should accurately represent the developer's conceptual description of the model and the solution to the model. The review should include:

a. Code review
b. Comparison with alternative implementation
c. Deployment in IT system
d. Deployment in organization

The use test, as introduced in the Second Basel Accord for credit and operational risk models, reflects the supervisors' concern that when regulatory capital is computed using internal risk estimates, such estimates are not produced for the sole purpose of regulatory compliance, but are truly employed for internal risk management purposes. The idea is that this would minimize the incentive to favour capital minimization over accuracy of measurement, and thus give additional confidence to supervisors on the reliability of the estimates produced. The Basel Committee on Banking Supervision (BCBS, 2006) identifies three main areas where the use of components of an Internal Rating Based Approach (PDs, LGDs, EADs) should be observable: strategy and planning, credit exposure and risk management, reporting.

Strategy and planning refers to how the bank identifies its objectives, establishes policies, develops plans and allocates resources. Evidence of the use test in these areas may include how economic capital is allocated to the various projects; how credit risk assessment influences the decision to enter a new market or to launch a new product; or how IRB components are used in determining the bank's levels of activity. Credit exposure covers all the activities that a bank enacts in controlling and managing credit risk: credit approval, portfolio management, loan pricing, limit setting, provisioning, performance assessment and remuneration thereof. Finally, reporting refers to the flow of risk-related information from risk management to the other parts of the organization and to senior management and board of directors. Figure 2.2 summarizes the structure of validation activities.

Finally, the validation process should be properly documented in order to provide a complete track record for audit and regulatory purposes, but also to ensure that its findings are fully explained and agreed upon and that proper follow-up can be ensured.

The documentation should be structured as follows:

a. An executive summary should contain a synopsis of the activities performed and their results. It should state that the validation of the model has been performed in accordance with the provisions of the policy and should describe the results of the validation process. In particular, it should explicitly state whether or not the risk estimates obtained through the model can be used for capital and other management purposes. In case of a negative result (e.g., significant model limitations), it should also list what actions are needed in order to obtain more reliable estimates and the timeframe for performing such actions.
b. An assessment of the model specifications, model performance and model design, including input/output datasets and/or data feeds should be described in detail. The process should be documented alongside samples of the data analysed, the tests performed and all the relevant results.

6 A note on model documentation

The model owner should develop and maintain the model documentation, describing and recording the responsibilities discussed in section 2. The Basel Committee is explicit, if a bit generic, in requiring exhaustive model documentation as a key tool for model risk management. The following is a relevant quote from the Second Basel Accord (BCBS, 2006).

> *The burden is on the bank to satisfy its supervisor that a model has good predictive power and that regulatory capital requirements will not be distorted as a result of its use. Accordingly, all critical elements of an internal model and the modelling process should be fully and adequately documented. Banks must document in writing their internal model's design and operational details. The documentation should demonstrate banks' compliance with the minimum quantitative and qualitative standards, and should address topics such as the application of the model to different segments of the portfolio, estimation methodologies, responsibilities of parties*

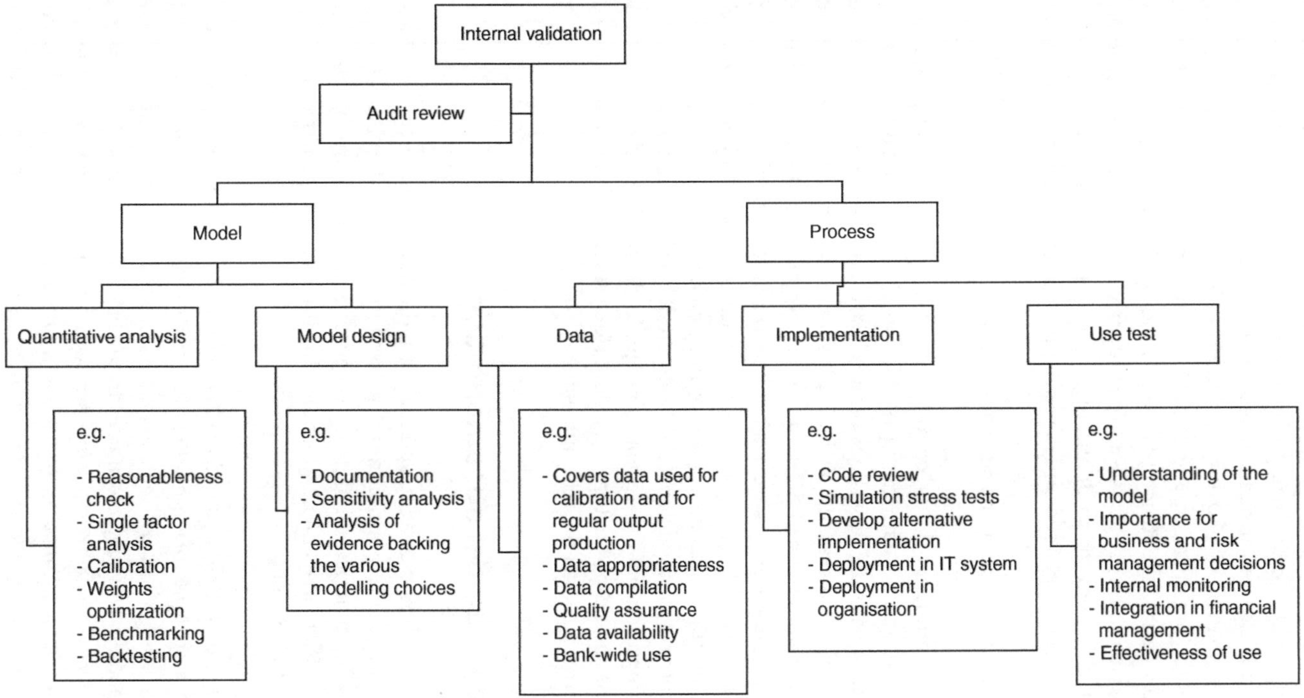

Figure 2.2 Structure of validation activities

involved in the modelling, and the model approval and model review processes. In particular, the documentation should address the following points:

(a) A bank must document the rationale for its choice of internal modelling methodology and must be able to provide analyses demonstrating that the model and modelling procedures are likely to result in estimates that meaningfully identify the risk of the bank's equity holdings. Internal models and procedures must be periodically reviewed to determine whether they remain fully applicable to the current portfolio and to external conditions. In addition, a bank must document a history of major changes in the model over time and changes made to the modelling process subsequent to the last supervisory review. If changes have been made in response to the bank's internal review standards, the bank must document that these changes are consistent with its internal model review standards.

(b) In documenting their internal models banks should:

- *provide a detailed outline of the theory, assumptions and/or mathematical and empirical basis of the parameters, variables, and data source(s) used to estimate the model;*
- *establish a rigorous statistical process (including out-of-time and out-of-sample performance tests) for validating the selection of explanatory variables; and*
- *indicate circumstances under which the model does not work effectively.*

(c) Where proxies and mapping are employed, institutions must have performed and documented rigorous analysis demonstrating that all chosen proxies and mappings are sufficiently representative of the risk of the equity holdings to which they correspond. The documentation should show, for instance, the relevant and material factors (e.g. business lines, balance sheet characteristics, geographic location, company age, industry sector and subsector, operating characteristics) used in mapping individual investments into proxies.

In summary, institutions must demonstrate that the proxies and mappings employed:

- *are adequately comparable to the underlying holding or portfolio*
- *are derived using historical economic and market conditions that are relevant and material to the underlying holdings or, where not, that an appropriate adjustment has been made; and*
- *are robust estimates of the potential risk of the underlying holding.*

Documentation should cover exhaustively all the relevant requirements: the business purpose of the model as well as all the technical, functional and regulatory requirements. Such information is not merely descriptive or background: It is an essential input to assess whether or not the model works as intended and is fit for purpose. This in turn is a prerequisite to submit the model to the use test, which means to verify that it is actually used for the intended business purpose and not just to satisfy a regulatory requirement.

Documentation of model development serves a number of other purposes besides facilitating the validation process. One such purpose is to capture the relevant organizational knowledge, thereby managing the risk that model knowledge is confined to a too limited number of people (and sometimes even to just one person). Another is to provide information to model users so that they can better understand the implications of employing each particular model. It also provides confidence to senior management and external parties (auditors and supervisors) that appropriate best practices are followed and that key controls (in the first line of defence) are in place. What follows is a list of key features that effective model documentation should have and that should be checked during a model validation exercise.

a. Versioning and security around documentation (incl. access rights). Quality of model documentation should be properly controlled and evidence of such controls, like senior level sign-offs, should form an integral part. Versioning information highlights how current the information contained in the documentation is.
b. Structure and clarity of the documentation (technical documentation, user manuals, guidelines, etc.)
c. Traceability of assumptions and choices made during model design and model roll-out. All key assumptions should be clearly described and justified, but also the implications of each assumption should be investigated and analysed. To the extent possible, documentation should contain evidence of this analysis rather than just a conceptual explanation of the bank's choices.
d. Transparency around model testing. Model developers should be required to thoroughly test newly developed models before they are subjected to independent validation and eventually implemented. Documentation around testing should cover the nature and results of the tests performed as well as how the test results have been interpreted and why. Standard components of this section will be: sensitivity analysis and stress testing (aimed at gauging the level of uncertainty associated with the models estimates) as well as back testing and benchmarking (aimed at assessing the predictive power of the model).
e. Ease of review, validation, as well as a potential take-over by a knowledgeable third person/party. Finally, model documentation should be accessible. This means that it should be properly organized and self-contained, but also that its style, structure and complexity should be adapted to the intended purpose and readership. This could be done by having different levels of documentation for executives, validators and users, as well as by appropriately segmenting, structuring, cross-referencing and signposting a single, all-purpose document. In particular, technical language should be used to clarify how the model was developed and implemented, and should be employed to clarify rather than obscure the key aspects of the model.

Finally, we present a sample structure for model documentation.

1 Version summary, document review & sign-off process (author, reviewer, committee, etc.)
2 Model history (a history of relevant major changes in the model, reference to earlier version documentation)
3 Model purpose (rationale)
   3.1. Description of the risk measure or estimate (e.g., probability of default event, loss in case of default event, portfolio loss under a severe stress scenario)
   3.2. Uses of the model (i.e., related reporting & decision processes both in risk management and business activities)
   3.3. Model scope (geographical coverage, business lines, counterpart types, product types)
   3.4. External requirements (e.g., regulatory framework and requirements) and internal requirements (e.g., requirements implied by the uses of the model, such as, through-the-cycle calibration, distribution percentile)
4 Model design (should be given in sufficient details so as to allow independent reproduction of the model development process and the final model specification by a knowledgeable person)
   4.1. Methodological choices (detailed outline of the theory, assumptions, proxies and/or mathematical and empirical basis of the parameters, variables)
   4.2. All prototypes, datasets and code used in development, calibration and testing (descriptions of data sources, data sourcing operations, descriptions of data tables, data fields, etc.)
   4.3. Expert judgments with justifications
   4.4. Circumstances under which the model does not work effectively (e.g., due to assumptions becoming invalid)
5 Model implementation and operations
   5.1. Input processes (i.e., input data sources and their owners, processes to follow to source and prepare data, including involved controls)
   5.2. Operation process (i.e., process to follow to run the model in order to produce the model outputs, IT systems, owners of the process steps including involved controls)
   5.3. Output processes (i.e., storage in systems, preparation of reports, involved controls)
   5.4. Use procedures (e.g., user guidance, manuals)
   5.5. Monitoring (e.g., description of monitoring tests, process to follow for regular monitoring, reports, datasets and codes used in monitoring)
   5.6. Calibration (e.g., description of calibration methodologies, process to follow to calibrate the model, owner of the process steps, including involved controls)
6 Reference documents

To facilitate the search and retrieval of the documentation produced, a centralized storage location should be maintained. As well as containing the formal model documentation, this location should also contain model development and other relevant data & information. Below is a list of what documentation, information and data should be stored and maintained.

- Formal Model Documentation. Both current and historical model documentation should be stored, providing a trail of the changes to the model. Appropriate naming conventions shall be used to identify last change author, time period, and version.
- Model development. The relevant information and data needed to understand and validate the development process should include: prototype (only final prototypes, not early versions), code, data used for development and test results.
- Production system and tools. This should encompass the current code, the code history and the test results.
- Decisions concerning the model. This should include relevant accompanying information to back up any decisions relative to the model, such as internal memorandums, minutes of meetings, and relevant email messages.
- Results of validation exercises. The outcome of validation exercises should also be stored with a history of those exercises, which should include validation reports, recommendations and agreed actions as well as the related audit trail.

7 The model validation team

The following is a typical list of qualifications as found in an ad for a model validation position at a major investment bank.

- Advanced degree (Ph.D. or M.Sc.) in a mathematically based subject;
- High level of proficiency in programming (VBA, Matlab, C++);
- Previous experience in a relevant quantitative role such as Front Office Quant or Derivatives Model Validation;
- Understanding of stochastic calculus and its practical applications in finance;
- Understanding of quantitative risk management techniques is desirable;
- Thorough theoretical understanding of financial derivatives and associated pricing issues including collateral discounting and XVA.

From the above description, one could be forgiven for thinking that all it takes to do the job properly is a good academic degree and a familiarity with mathematics. However, things are more complicated than that. To start with, validation is inherently about other people's work and hence about interaction with other, usually equally if not more qualified, experts. In such interactions, the human element, especially insofar as the validator is expected to challenge assumptions in design and look for flaws in implementation, is bound to have a relevance one might not normally suspect in such a highly quantitative line of business. Quants are usually proud of their expertise and their work and strongly opinionated, at least in those areas – and there are surprisingly many in financial modelling – where opinions matter, and so the scope for lengthy and unproductive disputes on the methodology and results of a validation exercise is potentially quite large. Successful model validation therefore requires a fair amount of flexibility in managing professional sensitivities and outright egos as well as negotiation skills.

Also, given that validation is nowadays both best practice in model management and a key compliance requirement, auditors, supervisors and senior managers are key stakeholders in the process and some of the main users, if not of all the findings of a model validation exercise, of its results. As they are rarely in a position to fully appreciate the technical content, it is a further responsibility of the model validation team to make at least the conclusions, the resulting recommendations and their impact on the business, intelligible and therefore defendable in broader contexts, that is, to an audience other than one made of math PhDs. The ability to translate complex technical issues into understandable and manageable business concepts is thus another very valuable skill a model validation team should have – a skill, by the way, that is rarely taught in university programmes and that needs to be developed and fostered on the job.

Finally, validation is a risk management activity and as such needs to balance the company's appetite and tolerance levels for model risk with the limited resources available. This means that an ability to manage trade-offs, to eschew theoretical perfection in favour of practical results, to prioritize and be able to deliver high quality work within deadlines is a trait of paramount importance that should rank fairly high within the necessary set of technical and scientific requirements.

It may be tempting to structure a validation team simply around the type and size of the various portfolios, and hire a number of experts by model category on the basis of how many models of each kind need to be validated in a given period. However, this approach may prove very inefficient and even be counterproductive. As validation is performed on a yearly basis at most, yet needs to be done quickly when new models are produced or changes to existing models are made, experts dedicated to a narrow set of models may find themselves with nothing to do in some periods and almost overwhelmed in others. The resulting need to ensure efficiency may conflict with the need for backups – for instance, when people are absent or when an unexpected concentration of validation jobs occur. Also, as quantitative modelling covers more and more of the whole spectrum of financial activities, the nature and number of models may grow so diverse – ranging from the more traditional credit, market and operational risk to funding and liquidity, asset-liability management, all kinds of fair valuations, results projections and so on – as to make it almost impossible to hire a specific expert for each. A financial institution should strive to hire people with a broad combination of both competence and experience, who are willing to learn and develop new skills as well as to share their expertise with others. In the end, a group of employees that does not share tasks or expertise is not really a team but a collection of experts, who may be individually very good at their jobs, but who will ever achieve the synergies, the effectiveness and the organizational value added that is the ultimate goal of any corporate function.

One last issue worth mentioning is how to recruit, motivate and retain people in a validation function. Validation is a challenging and interesting job that keeps changing in line with the evolution of the business, the regulatory environment and the theoretical and applied knowledge of models and their uses. However, from the perspective of a highly educated and strongly quantitative expert, it has one major drawback: It focusses almost exclusively on the work done by other people in the organization, whereby developing, or contributing to the development of original models is one of the most challenging and ultimately satisfying tasks a quant can undertake. In other words, especially if compared to model development, validation is not perceived as really creative work.

In addition, the ultimate test for a model developer is whether the model works or not, as proven by peer review, market test, business use and, of course, validation results. For model validation, however, the quality of the work performed may be of impeccable technical quality and still be criticized on grounds of feasibility and business opportunity, misunderstood by senior managers or auditors, and also simply opposed and undermined just for reasons of turf protection or professional pride. This is one of the reasons why, as explained above, quantitative skills are necessary, but not sufficient conditions for the successful performance of validation work.

One may consider a parallel with the well-known distinction between accuracy and precision in the scientific method. Accuracy refers to how close a measurement result is to the true value, while precision refers to the reproducibility of the measurement. Similarly, in model validation, one needs accuracy – that is, results must be technically correct – but at the same time those should not be questionable on the grounds that they hold only under certain circumstances (timeframes or datasets) or depend on subjective judgment. This quality of precision in the assessment may require refraining from making observations or recommendations that, although very reasonable in principle, cannot be undisputedly backed by empirical evidence, and may also require distinguishing between conclusions that any well-informed third party would draw and those that reflect more the expert opinion of the validator.

However, the need to negotiate consensus, to communicate, to find compromises when necessary, could be demotivating to anybody if not properly managed. It is the task of the manager of the model validation team to ensure that the political dimension of is taken care of without damaging either the technical standards or the compliance requirements of the job.

8 Conclusions

The responsibilities of a validation unit are not limited to a quality review of a model after development or every time it undergoes changes, but they encompass all model development decisions and assumptions as well as the way a model is implemented and rolled out in the organization. The independent opinions and recommendations expressed by a validation unit should be considered at the same level as those of internal audit, and it should be the responsibility of the model owner to either implement them or to demonstrate that they do not affect the model's performance.

Model development work in modern financial institutions may happen in a front office, for example trading or lending departments, as well as in risk management, typically within market, credit and operational risk teams. The organizational position of the validation team can vary depending on size, structure and culture of the financial institution. Typically, a smaller organization will find it difficult to devote more than a few resources to the task and may even struggle to have a fully dedicated team. In such cases the need for independence in the review of models may be achieved by assigning validation tasks to staff within the same model development team in such a way that each expert will never have to validate models that they have developed or contributed to develop. This may be acceptable in certain cases, but will remain less than ideal both because it may be impossible to ensure a complete segregation during development work and because there may be a tendency to resolve any disagreements over validation results in favour of model development.

Larger organizations will typically have a dedicated team, which would report higher in the hierarchy with respect to the model development teams. The ideal solution from a control and compliance perspective would of course be to have a complete organizational and reporting line separation. This solution, however, is by far the most expensive, as it implies a complete duplication of the modelling skills present throughout the organisation.

Notes

1. Board of Governors of the Federal Reserve System, Office of the Comptroller of the Currency, OCC 2011–2012, *Supervisory Guidance on Model Risk Management*. Sec. III, p. 3.
2. Ibid., Sec. III, p. 3.
3. Ibid., Sec. V, p. 9.
4. The model owner is defined as the business unit responsible for development and maintenance of the model and the estimates under consideration.

References

BCBS, Basel Committee on Banking Supervision, "The Internal Audit Function in Banks," *Basel*, June 2012.

BCBS, Basel Committee on Banking Supervision, "International Convergence of Capital Measurement and Capital Standards," *Basel*, June 2006.

BCBS, Basel Committee on Banking Supervision, "Studies on Validation of Internal Rating Systems," WP 14, *Basel*, May 2005.

Board of Governors of the Federal Reserve System, Office of the Comptroller of the Currency, OCC, "*Supervisory Guidance on Model Risk Management,*" 2011–2012.

Crouhy, M., Galai, D. and Mark, R., "*The Essentials of Risk Management,*" McGraw-Hill, 2006.

European Banking Authority, "*Final Draft Regulatory Technical Standards on the conditions for assessing the materiality of extensions and changes of internal approaches when calculating own funds requirements for credit and operational risk in accordance with Articles 143(5) and 312(4)(b) and (c) of Regulation (EU) No 575/2013 (Capital Requirements Regulation – CRR),*" Brussels, December 2013.

European Banking Authority, "*Final Draft Regulatory Technical Standards on the conditions for assessing the materiality of extensions and changes of internal approaches when calculating own funds requirements for market risk under Article 363(4) of Regulation (EU) No 575/2013 (the Capital Requirements Regulation — CRR),*" Brussels, December 2013.

Part II

Credit Risk

3 | Credit Risk Models

The development of models for the assessment of credit risk has evolved in response to a number of macroeconomic factors as well as to radical shocks of both financial and regulatory nature (Altman and Saunders, 1998; Hao, Alam and Carling, 2010). In the years following the end of the Bretton-Woods agreement, the main determinants of this evolution were the increase in volatility and consequent number of bankruptcies as well as the technological advancements behind progressive disintermediation and the rise of off-balance-sheet derivative instruments. More recently, impulse for ever more refined credit risk analysis has come from competition in margins and yields, driven by low interest rates and globalization, and, unsurprisingly, from the fallout and industry-wide soul-searching that has followed the 2008–2009 financial crisis. The refinement of credit scoring systems, the incorporation of more accurate measures of credit risk in derivative valuation, and the increasing focus on measuring risk at the portfolio level are only some of the directions lately taken by credit risk model research in academia as well as in the financial industry.

As we have discussed, in order to compute regulatory capital for credit risk, the Second Basel Accord foresees an Internal Rating Based approach (in the two "Foundation" and "Advanced" versions) where average PDs estimated by banks are mapped through a given supervisory formula in order to obtain the conditional PDs required within the ASRF framework. As the name of the approach suggests, banks' estimation of average PDs is in turn derived from ratings, i.e., the assigning of debtors to classes according to their creditworthiness. This type of approach has been long applied in the financial industry by the main rating agencies (Standard & Poors, Moody's and, more recently, Fitch) aimed at supporting investment decisions in corporate bonds. At the same time banks have developed similar classification systems, aimed at assessing the creditworthiness of their clients (corporate, SMEs or retail) and usually called "scoring" systems, to reflect the more quantitative nature of the approach. Although these two approaches have evolved separately, the first as an expert-based methodology focussed on large corporates' traded bonds and the second as a statistically based methodology focussed on banks' clients, the vast majority of banks supervised under the Second Basel Accord follows some kind of combination of the two, whereby a mix of quantitative and qualitative elements are combined within a statistical framework that also incorporates expert inputs or adjustments. These ratings identify classes to which the various debtors belong, in such a way that debtors belonging to the same class shall have, in principle, the same credit risk.

1 Credit risk models

There are broadly two main types of credit risk models: structural models and reduced-form models. The former, also known as asset value models or option-theoretic models, view default risk as a European put option on the value of the firm's asset (Black and Scholes, 1973; Merton, 1974). When these fall below the level of the firm's debt obligations at maturity, a default occurs. A structural model is therefore one where credit risk, as well as its key components like PD and LGD, is a function of the structural characteristics of a firm, like leverage or asset volatility. A reduced-form model, on the other hand, does not try to establish a causal explanation of default, but rather considers it as part of a random process, while the loss given default is specified exogenously. Not unlike aggregate loss models (Klugman, Panjer and Willmot, 2008) used in the insurance industry, reduced-form models are data-driven and model the probability of an event (the default) separately from the corresponding loss and then produce an aggregate measure of risk through numerical methods. Default events are assumed to occur unexpectedly due to one or more exogenous events, independent of the borrower's asset value. Observable risk factors include changes in macroeconomic factors such as GDP, interest rates, exchange rates, and inflation, while unobservable risk factors can be specific to a firm, industry or country. Correlations among PDs for different borrowers are considered to arise from the dependence of different borrowers on the behavior of underlying economic factors.

Key instances of structural models are the Merton model and the KMV model. The Merton model assumes that the firm has made one single issue of zero coupon debt and equity. If V is the value of the firm's assets and D the value of its debt, when debt matures, debt holders will receive the full value of their debt, D provided $V > D$. If, on the other hand, $V < D$, debt holders will receive only a part of the sums due and equity holders will receive nothing. Hence the value received by the debt holders at time T will be: $D - max\{D\text{-}V_T, 0\}$. But D can be seen as the pay-off from investing in a default risk-free instrument and $- max\{D\text{-}V_T, 0\}$ is the pay-off from a short position in a put option on the firm's assets with a strike price of D and a maturity date of T. Therefore, the holding of risky debt can be considered equivalent to holding a risk-free bond plus having sold a put option with strike price D, and the value of this put determines the price differential between risky and riskless debt. As the volatility of the firm value increases, so does the value of the put, and so does the spread on the risky debt (the price difference between a risky and a riskless obligation).

The *KMV Credit Monitor Model* turns the problem on its head and considers it from the perspective of the borrower. It assumes that there are only two types of debt, the first maturing before the chosen horizon and the other after, and that default tends to occur when the market value of the firm's assets drops below a critical point that typically lies below the book value of all liabilities, but above the book value of short term liabilities. The model computes a proxy measure for the probability of default: the distance to default. As the distance to default decreases, the company becomes more likely to default and as it increases, becomes less likely to default. It can be computed as:

$$\frac{lnV_0 - lnD + (r - \sigma_v^2 / 2)T}{\sigma_v \sqrt{T}}$$

Once the default point D the firm value V and the volatility σ have been identified, the *distance to default* provides the number of standard deviation moves that would result in a firm value falling below D (this step may prove difficult without assuming normality of the distribution). On this basis, one can use the KMV proprietary database to identify the proportion of firms with the same distance-to-default who actually defaulted in a year. This is the expected default frequency.

As an example of a reduced-form model, the CreditRisk+ model (CSFB, 1997) applies an insurance approach where default is an event similar to other insurable events (casualty losses, death, injury, etc.) These are generally referred to as *mortality models* which involve an actuarial estimate of the events occurring. Default is modelled as a continuous variable with an underlying probability distribution, while loss severities are distributed into bands. The frequency of losses and the severity of losses produce a distribution of losses for each band. Summing across these bands yields a loss distribution for a portfolio of loans.

The predictive power of the model may depend heavily on the size of the sample of loans, as the observed distribution of losses may have a larger variance than the model shows. Thus the model could underestimate the corresponding exposure. This may also be due to the assumption that the mean default rate is constant within each band and to the fact that default rates across bands may be correlated due to underlying state variables that have broader impact on borrowers.

Alternatively, one could classify credit risk according to how the model's parameters are determined either empirically, by applying mathematical methods to known data, or on the basis of expert judgment. In particular, when a bank does not have sufficient data to build a model statistically, a set of risk factors are chosen by experts. A borrower is scored against each of these factors, and creditworthiness is expressed through an overall score that is a weighted average of the ones attributed to the individual factors. There is a virtually infinite number of combinations of risk factors and scoring methodologies that can be used, but by and large, most models rely at least on the same kinds of factors, namely: financial factors (like typically balance sheet ratios and other financial indicators) and non-financial ones (like management capability, financial flexibility, supporting parties) as well as behavioural factors (like delinquency status, credit utilization and limit breaches). Lastly the rating can be adjusted upward or downward for additional reasons like parental support, as a warning signal, as well as for any other factor not being considered by the model (with the appropriate justification provided).

Today's financial institutions' approaches to a credit risk model are principally focussed on the estimation of the key parameters required under the Second Basel Accord: the probability of default (the probability that a given company will go into default within one year) the loss given default (the losses incurred on a defaulted loan as a percentage of the outstanding balance at time of default) and the exposure at default (the expected outstanding balance if the facility defaults, which is equal to the expected utilization plus a percentage of the unused commitments). Banks can calculate their regulatory capital charge for credit risk on the basis of these estimates. The risk measure to be used in credit risk models is therefore both accepted and standardized. However, related definitions are neither clear cut nor entirely homogeneous.

A default event is defined by the BCBS as occurring when the obligor is either more than 90 days late in its payments or is unlikely to pay its obligation. While the first part of this definition may or may not imply losses (an obligor may well repay all its obligations in full even after a delay longer than 90 days), the second part implies a somewhat subjective judgment which may or may not turn out to be correct (Lehman Brothers was certainly likely to default, and indeed it did, but so was Merrill Lynch, who in the end did not). In structural option-theoretic models, a firm is in default if the value of its assets falls below that of its liabilities, while several scholars use actual bankruptcy, in the sense of Chapter 11 reorganization under U.S. law, as the default criterion. Both definitions, of course, must allow for the fact that obligors may in the end pay in full even while technically being bankrupt.

Loss given default is the loss on a credit exposure when the counterpart defaults. Such loss, however, can be computed in different ways. One way consists in considering the recovered part over the debt workout period discounted to the default date. This "workout" approach requires the estimation of a cash flow which is not, in principle, known in advance (post-bankruptcy settlements may occur at different times and be made in cash as well as in non-liquid assets) as well as the selection of an appropriate discount rate (in itself not always a straightforward task). If the counterpart is a large organization whose bonds are traded on the market even after a bankruptcy, one can estimate the LGD from the market price of bonds (or other tradable debt) after the default has occurred. Needless to say, the application of this "market" approach is quite limited. Finally, in the "implied market" approach one can look at the market value of risky, but not defaulted bonds using theoretical asset pricing models.

EAD is the actual exposure at the time of default and its computational challenge required an approach that is facility-specific (e.g. distinguishing amongst fully drawn lines, secured loans, undrawn lines, derivatives, guarantees and other off balance sheet items). Modelling of the simultaneous variation between default probability (PD) and exposure at default (EAD) is particularly important in the context of derivative instruments, where credit exposures are particularly market-driven. A worsening of exposure may occur due to market events that tend to increase EAD while simultaneously reducing a borrower's ability to repay debt (that is, increasing a borrower's probability of default). This phenomenon is called wrong-way exposure.

There may also be correlation between exposure at default (EAD) and loss given default (LGD). For example, LGDs for borrowers within the same industry may tend to increase during periods when conditions in that industry are deteriorating or vice-versa. LGD is often modeled as a fixed percentage of EAD, with actual percentage depending on the seniority of the claim, but in practice, LGD is not constant and should be modelled as a random variable or as dependent on other variables.

2 The Basel II formula

As our principal aim is to provide guidance for practitioners working on the validation of risk models in financial institutions, the content of this second part of the book will be structured around the estimate of the key parameters for an Asymptotic Single Risk Factor (ASRF) model as discussed in BCBS (2005).

The Merton model can be generalized to a credit portfolio model. As in Merton's model, default happens when the value of the assets falls below that of the company's obligations and such value is linked to a standard normal random variable, but the portfolio losses will depend on a combination of n specific risk factors ξ_i and a systematic risk factor Y, representing the state of the economy. The number of defaults over a given period will be given by:

$$d_n = \sum_{i=1}^{n} 1_{\left\{\sqrt{\rho}Y + \sqrt{1-\rho}\xi_i \le t\right\}}$$

where 1_e takes the value *1* if event *e* happens and value *0* if it does not.

Provided the portfolio is large enough and no individual loans dominate the others, the cumulative distribution function of loan losses, for a given state of the economy Y, converges to a limiting type taking the following form (Vasicek, 1987 and 1991):

$$P(L \leq x) = P(p(Y) \leq x) = N(-p^{-1}(x)) = N\left(\frac{\sqrt{1-\rho}N^{-1}(x) - N^{-1}(p)}{\sqrt{\rho}}\right)$$

where L is the portfolio percentage gross loss, $p(Y)$ is the conditional probability of loss on a single loan under the given scenario. The average of these conditional probabilities over the scenarios provides the unconditional probability of default.

By turning the model around with the average probabilities of default as an input, one might derive an expression for the threshold x through the inverse normal distribution function and a conservative value of the systematic risk factor by applying the same inverse normal function to a pre-determined confidence level. By weighting the threshold and the systematic factor through correlation, a conditional default threshold is obtained that can be, in turn, fed into the (direct) Merton model to obtain a conditional PD. This way, the first part (in square brackets) of the well-known supervisory formula is obtained (BCBS, 2005).

$$K(Capital) = \left[LGD \cdot N\left[\frac{1}{\sqrt{1-R}} \cdot INV(PD) + \sqrt{\left(\frac{R}{1-R}\right)} \cdot INV(0.999)\right] - PD \cdot LGD\right]$$
$$\cdot \frac{1}{(1 - 1.5 \cdot b(PD))} \cdot (1 + (M - 2.5) \cdot b(PD))$$

In the above formula, N is the standard normal distribution which computes the conditional PD, with the threshold plus the conservative systematic factor as argument, while INV is the inverse of the standard normal distribution.

The default threshold is given by INV(PD), the systematic factor by INV(0.999), and their sum is weighted using the asset class-specific correlation coefficient R.

The asset correlation parameter R reflects the borrower's exposure to the systematic risk factor Y in the ASRF model, and hence it is interpreted as a measure of the correlation of a borrower's assets to those of the other borrowers.

The loss given default parameter is, in Basel parlance, a "downturn" LGD, as it is supposed to reflect losses on defaulted loans occurring during a period of economic downturn, hence presumably higher than those occurring in normal business conditions. The LGD is multiplied by the conditional PD in order to estimate the conditional expected loss:

$$LGD \cdot N\left[\frac{1}{\sqrt{1-R}} \cdot INV(PD) + \sqrt{\left(\frac{R}{1-R}\right)} \cdot INV(0.999)\right]$$

and by the average PD to estimate the expected loss[1]: $PD \cdot LGD$.

The 0.999 in the argument of the inverse standard normal is the confidence level for the estimate of capital, while M represents the maturity in the expression computing the maturity adjustment, $\left(\frac{1}{(1-1.5 \cdot b(PD))} \cdot (1+(M-2.5) \cdot b(PD))\right)$, which is intended to reflect the higher riskiness of longer-term credits with respect to shorter-term ones.

3 Model philosophy

Rating models may be built in line with different "philosophies," namely, they may be aimed at measuring the creditworthiness of a borrower either in its current state in its current economic environment or over a complete economic cycle. The former approach is called Point-in-Time (PIT), while the latter is called Through-the-Cycle (TTC). If we imagine a rating approach where obligors are first placed in a rating class to which, subsequently, a probability of default is assigned, we can describe the consequences of the two philosophies as follows.

A fully TTC model should display close to a fixed distribution of PDs per rating grade (conditional probabilities of default) over time, and borrowers would migrate from grade to grade only for idiosyncratic reasons. Grade migrations would therefore be uncorrelated to the changes due to the economic cycle. One would see the effect of such changes ex post in how the realized default rates of each rating vary over time. A fully PIT model, on the other hand, explains changes in default rates as arising from changes in the ratings and conditional PDs of many obligors or, alternatively, that the same rating grade corresponds to different levels of creditworthiness, depending on the state of the economy. In other words, cyclical changes will manifest themselves as large-scale ratings migrations while PDs per rating grade will be more stable over time. Needless to say, the different philosophies also reflect different business purposes. A widespread adoption of fully PIT models for the purpose of establishing capital requirements is likely to magnify the effects of the economic cycle both in upturn and downturn periods with undesirable impact on overall financial stability (Adrian and Shin, 2008). On the other hand, a fully TTC model is unlikely to meet a bank's business needs when it comes to pricing the risk of a transaction or monitoring the creditworthiness of a borrower as the economic cycle is one, very key component of the set of relevant risk factors. In practice, rating models will always exhibit a hybrid combination of TTC and PIT characteristics because of the presence of both cyclical and idiosyncratic risk factors. In practice, to completely eliminate all cyclic effects would be as challenging as to get rid of all idiosyncratic ones.

Following the 2008–2009 financial crisis, there has been increasing regulatory emphasis on reducing cyclicality in prudential regulation. Although this may be interpreted as, and may explicitly lead in the future to, a regulatory preference for TTC models, the current requirements, e.g., the prescription for computing PDs as long-term averages of default rates, should not necessarily be interpreted in this way. The Basel Accord prescription that PDs be based on a "long-run average of one-year default rates" (BCBS, 2005), should in fact be a feature of both point-in-time and through-the-cycle rating models. Both PD estimations should be done by averaging over many years of data, and a model will be PIT to the extent that it includes explanatory variables that track the credit cycle. In other words, it is the combination of risk factors that determines where on the PIT/TTC scale the model sits, and the difference between the two is very much a matter of model design rather than of mere PD calibration.

Note

1. Note that the latter is subtracted from the former in order to obtain a capital charge that only reflects the "unexpected" portion of the risk capital estimate.

References

Adrian, T. and Shin, H. S., "Liquidity, Monetary Policy and Financial Cycles," *Current Issues in Economics and Finance*, Vol. 14, No. 1, January/February 2008.

Altman, E. I. and Saunders, A., "Credit Risk Measurement: Developments Over the Last 20 Years," *Journal of Banking & Finance*, Vol. 21, 1721–1742, 1998.

Basel Committee on Banking Supervision, "The IRB Use Test: Background and Implementation," Basel Committee Newsletter No. 9, September 2006.

Basel Committee on Banking Supervision, "An Explanatory Note on the Basel II IRB Weight Functions," Bank for International Settlements, July 2005.

Black, F. and Scholes, M., *"The Pricing of Options and Corporate Liabilities," The Journal of Political Economy*, Vol. 81, No. 3, 637–654, May–June, 1973.

Credit Suisse First Boston, *"CREDITRISK+ A Credit Risk Management Framework,"* 1997. Available at: http://www.csfb.com/institutional/research/assets/creditrisk.pdf.

Hao, C., Alam, M. M. and Carling, K., *"Review of the Literature on Credit Risk Modelling: Development of the Past 10 Years,"* Banks and Bank Systems, Vol. 5, No. 3, 2010.

Merton, R. C., "On the Pricing of Corporate Debt: The Risk Structure of Interest Rates," *The Journal of Finance*, Vol. 29, No. 2, 449–470, 1974.

Vasicek, O. A., *"Probability of Loss on Loan Portfolio,"* KMV Corporation, available at www.kvm.com, 1987.

Vasicek, O. A., *"Limiting Loan Loss Probability Distribution,"* KMV Corporation, available at www.kvm.com, 1991.

4 Probability of Default Models

Validators should ensure that all model components and the related outputs have been thoroughly tested. Let us recall that the first of the BCBS (2005) validation principles is that "Validation is fundamentally about assessing the predictive ability of a bank's risk estimates and the use of ratings in the credit process." We will follow Tasche (2008) in interpreting this somewhat vague requirement as meaning that validators should examine PD models' performance in terms of their discriminatory power and calibration.

The discriminatory power of a PD model can be examined from the perspective of each individual factor as well as in terms of the combined performance of all the model's factors, that is, through a univariate and a multivariate analysis, respectively. The review of a model's calibration, on the other hand, is based on analysing through statistical tests how close the predicted probabilities of default are to the actual default rates, as observed within a financial institution's own history or by means of an external benchmark.

1 Univariate Analysis

The objective of univariate analysis is to appraise the relative power of each individual factor in reflecting the creditworthiness of an obligor. Each factor is examined on a stand-alone basis to develop a better understanding of its potential for measuring an obligor's level of credit risk. The validation team should test each individual model factor to identify biases, concentrations, or skewing; pinpoint components that contribute little to no information to the model; test effectiveness in ranking against benchmark; identify redundancies and unacceptable factor correlations; highlight counterintuitive and flat relationships with default probability; and measure the ability to discriminate between good and bad obligors.

If a factor does not satisfy the above criteria, it should be subjected to additional scrutiny. Such scrutiny may result in the need to change a factor, for example to rescore or re-aggregate answers or, in extreme cases, to exclude a factor from the model. Factors should be intuitive, in the sense that an experienced risk manager should be familiar with the factor and its relationship with credit risk given the credit culture in which they operate. Their behaviour should be consistent with expectations and any deviations should be easily explained. Factors should also ideally exhibit a high degree of discriminatory power on the basis of credit risk. However, a single risk factor should never be discarded on the sole basis of its standalone predictive power, as the same factor may, in combination with others, exhibit an overall much higher predictive power.

1.1 Factors distribution

The analysis of factors distribution should cover both qualitative and quantitative factors. For qualitative risk factors, validators should look in particular for missing values in large quantities, bias or undesired skewness with respect to expected results (some of which may be inherent in certain questions) as well as concentrations. Significant differences between the observed distribution of responses and the expected or intuitive distribution may help identify factors in need of augmentation, e.g., changed to a modifier or have re-scoring of answers. In some instances, differences may simply point to an aspect of the model that needs to be better understood before it can be included in the final model or signal the need to have training issues flagged. For example, an answer distribution with a high concentration in the best or worst input could indicate that the wording of a question or the relative answer list is inappropriate. It may therefore be necessary, in order to prevent a potential bias, to modify the structure of a question in order to foster a more intuitive distribution, not overly concentrated or skewed. The analysis of answer distributions can also help identify:

- Factors with a high frequency of "not known" or missing answers could indicate that a question is poorly understood by users or that the relevant information is not readily available for the model. If missing or "not known" answers account for more than 10% of total responses, additional investigation of the factor is required. The proportion of missing data is directly related to the quality of statistical inferences. Yet, there is no established cut-off from the literature regarding an acceptable percentage of missing data in a data set for valid statistical inferences. For example, Schafer (1999) asserted that a missing rate of 5% or less is inconsequential. Bennett (2001) maintained that statistical analysis is likely to be biased when more than 10% of data are missing. Furthermore, the amount of missing data is not the sole criterion by which a researcher assesses the missing data problem. Tabachnick and Fidell (2012) posited that the missing data mechanisms and the missing data patterns have greater impact on research results than does the proportion of missing data.
- Factors with a clustering of responses in only one of the possible answers.
- The level of granularity in the answers may need to be increased in order to reduce the concentration of responses in a single answer.

The answer distribution for each and every factor can be analysed in several ways. A histogram can be used by creating an appropriate binning scheme as shown in Figure 4.1 below.

For quantitative factors, a scatter plot can be used to display values for two variables within a set of data, like for instance the value of a given factor/ratio and the corresponding probability of default. This is a useful tool to observe data concentrations, correlations, trends and relationships. Alternatively, a table showing the different quantiles (particularly the very low and high ones) may provide more information than histograms, especially in the presence of heavy outliers.

When categorical risk factors (for instance assessed on a scale like: "good," "quite good," "average," "bad") are used, one may want to analyse whether the default rates depend on the outcomes in a certain (expected) way. One way to perform such analysis is to construct a table ordering the categorical risk factor outcomes with respect to the default rate expectation within the single outcomes study to determine whether the default rates actually increase over this ordering scheme. For such qualitative factors, a histogram provides a graphical display of frequencies to help identify unintuitive concentrations, potential bias, clustering and/or skewness of answers in different answer categories. The observed distribution should be compared with an expected one based on expert judgment or intuition, like a bell-shaped curve in the case of answers concentrated around a mean and with decreasing frequency towards the tails, or a decreasing/increasing one across the range of answers, e.g., from best-to-worst or vice-versa.

1.2. Information entropy

Information entropy is a measure of the information contained within a given variable, which corresponds to the diversity of possible responses to a subjective question. This metric is used to identify questions that may be contributing little or no information to the model due to a high concentration of responses within a limited set of answers.

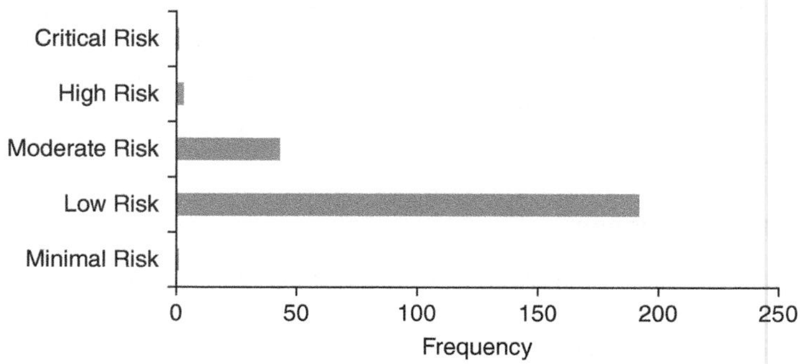

Figure 4.1 Sample histogram

Information entropy is defined as the minimum number of bits (the smaller quantity of information measurable) required for retaining the information contained within a given question. For example, a question with 4 answers – all equally likely – would require 2 bits to store the information since $2^2=4$ possible combinations. If the answers are not equally likely, fewer bits are required for the same amount of information.

Given a question with n possible answers and the probability P_i for the answer being i, the information entropy (H) is defined as minus the mean of the logarithms of the probabilities of the answers. In formulas:

$$H = -\sum_{i=1}^{n} p_i \cdot \log_2 (p_i)$$

The information entropy is maximum when the answers are equally likely, i.e., $P_i = \frac{1}{n}$. A relative measure of information entropy can be computed as the ratio of the observed entropy to its maximum value (relative entropy ratio). This measure can be interpreted as the percentage of possible information conveyed by the question. When the amount of information is low, the usefulness of a question becomes doubtful, and it may indicate a source of over-fitting.

This should not suggest that a factor with high relative entropy is automatically a powerful one within a mode. A factor with a strong measure of information entropy may actually perform poorly in its ability to discriminate between "good" and "bad" obligors.

Although one can use thresholds to identify factors that perform better than the rest, it is very difficult to establish absolute thresholds for relative entropy ratios. Commonly adopted thresholds, like 0.7 or 0.5, can be justified intuitively. In the classical example of a coin toss, the entropy is maximum (i.e., equal to 1) if the coin is fair (i.e., probability of each side equal to 0.5). An entropy value of 0.7 corresponds to probabilities of around 0.2 and 0.8, while an entropy value of 0.5 to probabilities of around 0.1 and 0.9. In the case of a question with 10 possible answers, a relative entropy value of 0.7 can correspond, for example, to half of the answers being equally likely (that is, having probability of 0.2) and the rest having zero probability, while an entropy value close to 0.5 (0.48) can correspond to only 3 of the answers being equally likely (probability equal to 0.33) and the other 7 having zero probability.

1.3 Predictive power

One of the most common ways to measure a risk factor's predictive power is through the so-called Cumulative Accuracy Profile (CAP, Sobehart et al., 2000) which allows for a clear comparison amongst factors. The CAP is a plot of the cumulative empirical distribution of the defaulting debtors against the cumulative empirical distribution of all debtors. It is a direct and visual means to assess the performance of a predictive model.

The CAP can be created through the following steps.

1. "Score" each data point according to its factor level and rank the scores from the highest to the lowest (n observations in total, $i = 1, \ldots, n$, with the nth observation having the lowest score);
2. Loop through the ranked dataset counting the cumulative number of "bad" clients captured for each ranked data point;
3. Plot the percentage of all observations on the x-axis against the percentage of "bad" clients on the y-axis.

The result of this procedure is a curve that joins the origin to the point (100%, 100%) as in Figure 4.2 below.

The y-axis shows the percentage of bad clients captured for each percentage of the full sample on the x-axis. Consequently, if a factor discriminates between "goods" and "bads" well, the initial slope of the curve will be steep as many "bads" are captured by the lowest values of the factor. To quantify discriminatory power, the Accuracy Ratio is computed as the area 1 divided by the combined areas 1+2. Thus the perfect model would have an accuracy ratio of 100% and a random model would have an accuracy ratio of 0%.

The straight dotted line joining the origin to the point (100%, 100%) is often drawn to represent the performance of a model that assigns scores at random, a model therefore with no discriminatory power. This random model represents a factor that has no ability to order clients from bad to good (for example, when the first 50% of the population has been looked at, only 50% of the "bads" should be among them). Intuitively, the greater the area between the curve itself and the dotted line, the greater the predictive power of the model.

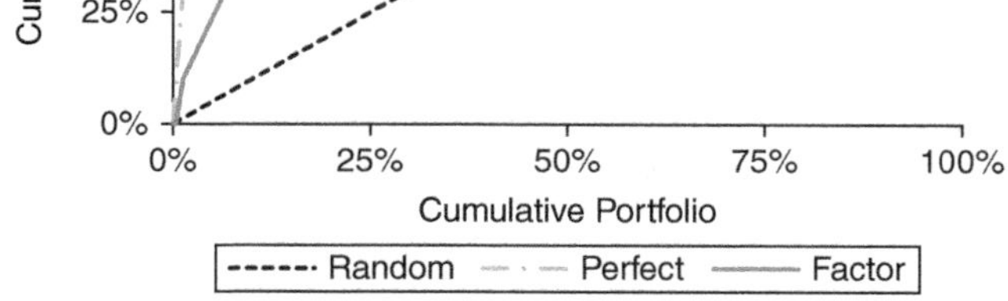

Figure 4.2 CAP curve

The Gini coefficient (or Gini "index") is probably best known as a measure of the inequality of income and is used by economists to measure the distribution of a society's wealth. However, it can also be used to measure the performance of a predictive model. The simplest definition of the Gini coefficient is in terms of the area under the CAP curve – it is twice the area between the curve and the diagonal line joining the origin to the point (100%, 100%).

Typically, no hard thresholds for predictive powers on single risk factor level are given, since even risk factors with very low individual predictive power might provide a high predictive power gain on the multivariate level. Nevertheless, deteriorations of predictive power over time since development indicate disadvantageous changes of the rating model over time and should be analysed.

1.4 Using bootstrapping to estimate confidence intervals

Error estimates are of course especially important in dealing with predictive power measures, and the Gini coefficient just described is calculated from a sample and so is a sample statistic. Ideally, we should try to estimate the uncertainty surrounding our estimates of the Gini coefficient and the *AUC*, so that we can assess whether deterioration over time in the value of either statistic is statistically significant. Hence we should try to estimate its sampling distribution and confidence intervals. Since this is not analytically simple, bootstrapping techniques (Davison and Hinkley, 1997) are usually employed to estimate the error around the point estimate of this statistic.

The idea behind bootstrapping is that the distribution is that the distribution of our statistical measure (in this case the GINI coefficient) over the range of all possible portfolios, which is unknown, can be approximated by its distribution over (many) subsets of the actual portfolio at hand (the historical sample we have used to compute the statistics).

The bootstrap procedure consists of the following steps:

1. Prepare the historical sample;
2. Resample the original dataset used to construct the model, *with replacement*, to construct a new dataset with exactly the same number of observations;
3. Re-compute the Gini coefficient over the new dataset. Note that the structure of the model is unchanged – it is only the parameter values that are re-estimated;
4. Repeat steps 2 and 3 many times (ideally at least 1,000 times), and save the values of the statistics for each repetition;
5. Calculate the mean, standard deviation and percentiles of the resulting bootstrapped distribution to provide an estimate of the statistics' predictive power and error.

The confidence intervals calculated by this method should be used as a guide in the context of several alternative assessments of model performance over time rather than as a rigid decision criterion upon which to trigger a model refitting exercise.

1.5 Relationship to probability of default

One would expect that the relationship between each model factor and the creditworthiness of the borrower, as measured by the probability of default, to be intuitive and easy to explain. For example, in most cases, a monotonic relationship (as the factor value increases, credit quality goes consistently up – or consistently down) is expected in such a way that a "better" factor value implies, everything else being equal, a better score. This is not always the case, however, and the factors that have more complex relationships with risk must be transformed in order to maximize their usefulness in rank-ordering obligors. In this case, other univariate analyses (discriminatory power, for example) may be sensitive to non-monotonic transformations.

In order to analyse the relationship to the probability of default, one needs to rank-order all results for a given factor according to their factor value. Observations are then grouped into a defined number of bins and plotted against the corresponding default probability. Figure 4.3 below shows statistics of the distribution of PDs associated with different (qualitative) values of a given factor. One can analyse this kind of chart to check for heteroscedasticity (that is, if variability is not constant within the sample considered) as well as indication of counterintuitive and flat relationships.

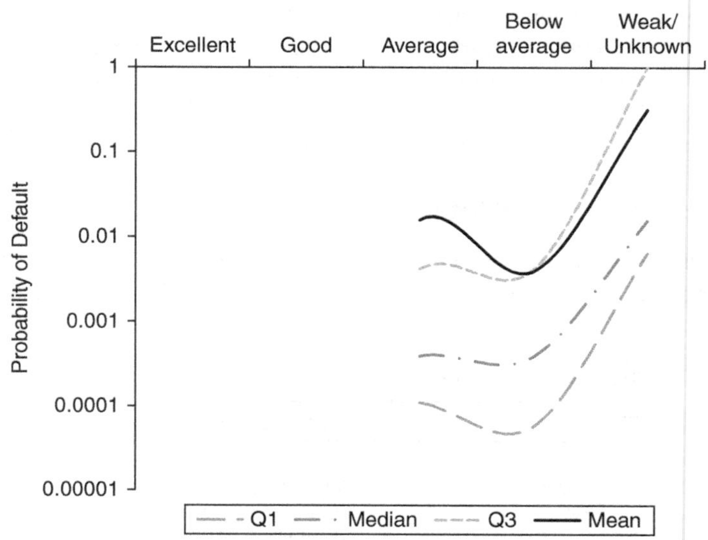

Figure 4.3 Probability of default relationship

2 Multivariate Analysis

2.1 Correlation/Multicollinearity analysis

A high correlation between two factors may suggest that the factors are capturing similar information and that the inclusion of both may add unnecessary complexity and even potentially over-weight a given dimension in the model. For instance, the inclusion of two highly correlated measures of indebtedness may lead to the over-weighting of that dimension as a factor in the model's rating. By analysing the correlations between factors, we may identify independent factors and, as a result, minimize the likelihood of over-weighting any specific dimension. Correlations are typically measured by rank order correlations, Spearman's Rho correlation and Kendall's Tau correlation, since these are robust against outliers (in contrast to, e.g., Pearson linear correlations).

In most cases, Spearman's Rho and Kendall's Tau deliver similar values; nevertheless, the two should not be considered identical. Spearman's Rho measures the proportion of the variability in a given rank ordering that is explained by the variability in another rank ordering. Kendall's Tau measures the difference between the probability that two sets of observed data are in the same rank-order versus the probability that they are not in the same rank-order.

For many distributions exhibiting weak dependence, the sample value of Spearman's Rho is larger than the sample value of Kendall's Tau (see for example Fredriks and Nelsen, 2006 and Capéraà, P., Genest, 1993). What constitutes a satisfactory coefficient is dependent on the purpose for which it is to be used, and on the nature of raw data. The following Table 4.1 provides a rule-of-thumb scale for evaluating the correlation (see Asuero et al., 2006).

The analysis of multicollinearity is a generalization of correlation analysis to more than two dimensions. Whereas correlation is always a pair-wise property, the aim of multicollinearity analysis is the detection of linear dependence of three or more risk factors, which are not visible on correlation level.

2.2 Predictive power of the score

The analysis of predictive power can be extended to the overall score produced by the model. It is advantageous to use the same functionality as used in 1.3

Table 4.1 Scale for interpreting correlation

Size	Interpretation
0.90 to 1:00	Very high correlation
0.70 to 0.89	High correlation
0.50 to 0.69	Moderate correlation
0.30 to 0.49	Low correlation
0.00 to 0.29	Little if any correlation

for the analysis of predictive power of the individual risk factors. However, it is advisable to define a threshold for the predictive power of the full score, on the basis of the properties of the portfolio at hand and the available risk factors. Although there is no analytical method to determine what a threshold should be to judge the model discriminatory power, it is common knowledge amongst practitioners that most commonly used rating models show values of the Gini coefficient in the 0.40-0.60 range. For evidence, one may refer to Blochwitz et al. (2000), who report on the benchmarking of Deutsche Bundesbank's Default Risk Model and KMV Private Firm Model. They compute the Gini coefficient using the Deutsche Bundesbank database (containing more than 125,000 balance sheets and 950 defaults). While the values for the entire sample fall between 0.54 and 0.68, values for individual financial ratios fall between 0.25 and 0.6. Hence the thresholds chosen reflect the understanding that values above 0.5 are presumably in line with the performance of models widely used in market practice, while values below 0.2 are to be considered not up to market standards. It should be noted that the high threshold is merely used to qualitatively identify factors that perform "better" while the low one is used to identify factors that may be potentially discarded or replaced.

2.3 Explanatory power of the score

The relationship to the probability of default can be studied for the overall score by analysing to what extent the PD for a given score (the conditional PD) explains the actual (observed) default rate.

The Brier Score (Brier, 1950) is defined as: $\frac{1}{N}\sum_{i=1}^{N}(p_i - d_i)^2$, where p_i is the PD forecast at the beginning of a period for obligor *i*, and d_i is the actual default indicator (d_i=1 or d_i=0) observed at the end of the same period. The Brier Score, also called the Mean Square Error (MSE), expresses how far the forecast is from the actual observation and is a measure of the accuracy of the forecast. The latter will be better the smaller the squared difference with the observed default indicator and hence the lower the MSE/Brier Score result.

2.4 Stability

Stability of the ratings can be investigated using migrations matrices year over year between validation samples. In order to build a migration matrix (see an example in Figure 4.4 further below), the following steps should be followed:

- Preliminary analysis of data and identification of a common portfolio (a set of borrowers who have all been rated for two consecutive years) for year-on-year analysis;

Rating Migration 2014\2013	1	2+	2	2–	3+	3	3–	4+	4	4–	5+	5	5–	6+	6	6–	7	8
1	0	0	0	0	0	0	0	0	0	0	0	0	0	0	0	0	0	0
2+	0	1	0	0	0	0	0	0	0	0	0	0	0	0	0	0	0	0
2	0	0	2	0	0	0	0	0	0	0	0	0	0	0	0	0	0	0
2–	0	0	0	0	0	0	0	0	0	0	0	0	0	0	0	0	0	0
3+	0	0	0	0	11	1	0	0	0	0	0	0	0	0	0	0	0	0
3	0	0	0	0	1	19	1	0	0	0	0	0	0	0	0	0	0	0
3–	0	0	0	0	0	1	45	0	0	0	0	0	0	0	0	0	0	0
4+	0	0	0	0	0	0	0	61	3	0	0	0	0	0	0	0	0	0
4	0	0	0	0	0	0	0	5	52	5	0	0	0	0	0	0	0	0
4–	0	0	0	0	0	0	0	0	6	61	2	0	0	0	0	0	0	0
5+	0	0	0	0	0	0	0	0	1	5	71	4	0	0	0	0	0	0
5	0	0	0	0	0	0	0	0	0	0	2	47	0	0	0	0	0	0
5–	0	0	0	0	0	0	0	0	0	0	1	1	39	2	0	0	0	0
6+	0	0	0	0	0	0	0	0	0	0	0	0	0	18	0	0	0	0
6	0	0	0	0	0	0	0	0	0	0	0	0	0	1	11	1	0	0
6–	0	0	0	0	0	0	0	0	0	0	0	0	0	0	1	17	1	0
7	0	0	0	0	0	0	0	0	0	0	0	0	0	0	0	3	15	0
8	0	0	0	0	0	0	0	0	0	0	0	0	0	0	0	0	0	3

Shift band	Percentage
+/– 1 notch	99.62%
+/– 2 notch	100.00%
+/– 3 notch	100.00%

Shift type	Percentage/Notch
downgrades	41.67%
upgrades	58.33%
overall shift	0.02

Figure 4.4 Stability analysis

- Portfolio analysis and rating distribution analysis for each pair of consecutive years in the sample;
- Computation of the yearly transition matrix over the common portfolio for each pair of consecutive years in the analysis;
- Convergence analysis or graphical representation of the matrix to investigate the stability of the risk estimates from one year to next.

As for other measures, absolute thresholds are not straightforward to develop. Cantor and Mann (2003), discussing the stability of Moody's rating system, observe that, in any typical year, fewer than a quarter of the issuers experience a rating change of any type, less than 5% experience large rating changes, and only about 1% experience a reversal of a previous rating change. Some years may be atypically volatile, but the absolute percentages are still relatively low (28%, 8%, and 0.8%, respectively). So one might consider 25% or fewer one-notch ratings change as an upper threshold for a (presumably) very stable rating system and twice that (50%) as a threshold below which stability is considered poor.

2.5 Treatment of missing values

Any rating model has to have some mechanism to cope with missing risk factor values, which have to be conservatively considered. An analysis of missing values should provide both the percentage of missing values per risk factor and an indication of whether missing values are treated conservatively. One simple measure would be to calculate the percentage of risk factor outcomes that are worse than the missing value replacement. If this number is higher than 50%, this would be an indication that missing values are not treated conservatively as one would usually expect. These results could simply be provided in tabular format.

3 Calibration

The term "calibration" refers to the estimation of a model's parameters. For example, if our PD model is developed on the basis of a logistic regression, calibration means estimating the coefficients in the equation of the logistic regression. In the practice of risk model validation, however, testing the calibration of a PD model means to verify the accuracy of the estimate of the conditional default probability given the score, usually by comparing historically observed default rates with predicted ones (PDs). Observed default rates and predicted PDs will never perfectly agree, even for a well-calibrated rating model. However, their alignment can be tested on the base of certain distributional assumptions to the extent that the tests employed can distinguish between deviations that come from statistical fluctuations and deviations that come from a model's shortcomings.

Calibration tests can be classified in more than one way. For instance, some tests are conditional on the state of the economy, and some are not. As already discussed, PD estimates may be conditioned on the current state of the economy (PIT) or based on a full economic cycle (TTC). As observed by Tasche (2008), assuming statistical independence of defaults for PIT estimates may be acceptable, because dependences should have been captured by the incorporation of the economic state into the model. The same cannot be said for TTC estimates, however, because such estimates will be, presumably, independent of the state of the economy, and therefore dependencies will not be explained by macroeconomic variables.

Also, tests can be aimed at testing a single rating grade at a time rather than several rating grades simultaneously, or at being applied to a single time period rather than to multiple time periods (Blochwitz et al., 2011; Rauhmeier, 2011).

Binomial Test

The Binomial Test assesses the hypothesis:

> H0: The observed default rate is not higher than the forecasted PD, against the alternative:
>
> H1: The estimated PD is lower than the observed default rate.

The binomial test is conducted for each rating category, over a single time period, under the assumption that default events are independent amongst borrowers within each grade. The null hypothesis H0 is rejected at a confidence level equal to α if the observed default rate r within a given grade is not lower than the critical value r_α, defined as:

$$r_a = \min\left\{r : \sum_{i=r}^{N} \binom{N}{i} p^i (1-p^i)^{N-i} \leq 1-\alpha\right\},$$

where p is the forecast probability of default for a given rating grade, and N is the number of obligors in that grade.

A simpler expression for the critical value can be obtained by applying the central limit theorem and assuming that the binomial distribution approximates the normal distribution as the number of obligors grows larger. In that case the critical value r_α will be given by:

$$\hat{r}_\alpha = N \cdot p + \Phi^{-1}(\alpha) \cdot \sqrt{N \cdot p \cdot (1-p)}$$

where Φ^{-1} is the inverse of the cumulative standard normal distribution.

This will be generally true whenever $N \cdot p \cdot (1-p) > 9$, which, although verified in most cases, will not normally hold for portfolios with low default probabilities and few credits in each rating grade.

Hosmer-Lemeshow test

When we want to test PD forecasts for several rating grades, doing so separately might result in some of them being erroneously rejected (Tasche, 2008). The Hosmer-Lemeshow test (Hosmer, Lemeshow, Klar, 1988) computes squared differences of forecasts from realized default grades at a group level, and then weights them by the inverses of the variance of the forecast defaults:

$$H = \sum_{i=1}^{m} \frac{(n_i p_i - d_i)^2}{n_i p_i (1 - d_i)}.$$

where p_i is the forecast probability of default for rating grade i, d_i is the corresponding observed default rate, n_i is the number of borrowers with grade i, and m is the number of rating grades.

If observations are independent and the sample size is large enough, the statistic H is χ^2 distributed with m degrees of freedom, when $p_i{=}d_i$ for each i.(as it is, in fact, the sum of m independent squared normally distributed random variables). On this basis, one can determine the critical values of testing the hypothesis that the estimated PDs perfectly forecast the default rates, i.e., that $p_i{=}d_i$ for each i.

Spiegelhalter test

The MSE indicator described in 2.2.4 as : $\frac{1}{N}\sum_{i=1}^{N}(p_i - d_i)^2$ can also be used to test the accuracy of the forecast PD over several rating grades. As the MSE measures the distance between forecast PDs and observed defaults, it can be shown that, if the forecast is perfect ($p_i{=}d_i$), then the expected value of MSE is:

$$E(MSE_{p_i - d_i}) = \frac{1}{N}\sum_{i=1}^{N} p_i(1 - p_i)$$

and its variance is:

$$VAR(MSE_{p_i - d_i}) = \frac{1}{N^2}\sum_{i=1}^{N} p_i(1 - p_i)(1 - 2p_i)^2.$$

The Spigelhalter test assesses the null hypothesis H_0: $p_i{=}d_i$ by considering the statistic:

$$Z_s = \frac{MSE - E(MSE_{p_i - d_i})}{\sqrt{VAR(MSE_{p_i - d_i})}}$$

which follows a standard normal distribution.

Normal test

The Normal test allows for cross-sectional dependencies between defaults within a given rating grade and can be applied to multiple periods under the assumption that default events in different years are independent. For a given rating grade at time t, the annual default rate d_t is such that

$$\frac{\sum_{t=1}^{T}(d_t - \frac{1}{T}\sum_{t=1}^{T} d_t)}{\sigma\sqrt{T}}$$

converges to the standard normal distribution as T tends to ∞. The unbiased estimator of the variance of default rates is:

$$\hat{\partial}^2 = \frac{1}{T-1}\sum_{t=1}^{T}\left(d_t - \frac{1}{T}\sum_{t=1}^{T} d_t\right)^2$$

Therefore, the Null Hypothesis H0: "The observed default rates over the years 1 to T are all lower than the forecasted PDs" should be rejected when:

$$\frac{\sum_{t=1}^{T}\left(d_t - \frac{1}{T}\sum_{t=1}^{T} d_t\right)}{\sigma\sqrt{T}} > p + \frac{\hat{\partial}}{\sqrt{T}}\Phi^{-1}(1-\alpha)$$

where the last term on the right-hand side is the α quantile of the standard normal distribution.

Traffic Light test

The Traffic Light test is an extension of the concept introduced by the Basel Committee to assess the performance of market risk models via a binomial test with green, yellow and red intervals (BCBS, 1996). As proposed by Tasche (2003), the approach can be adapted to credit risk models by introducing critical values for the number of defaults that correspond to given probability levels. For example, if the same levels used by the Basel Committee in 1996 for market risk are used, α_l=0.95 and α_h=0.999, then the critical values k_l and k_h will be such that the number of defaults will exceed k_l only with a probability of 1- α_l and k_h only with a probability of 1- α_h. In formulas:

$$k_l = min\{k : P[d \geq k] \leq 1-\alpha_l\} = q(\alpha_l, d) + 1, \quad \text{and}$$

$$k_h = min\{k : P[d \geq k] \leq 1 - \alpha_h\} = q(\alpha_h, d) + 1$$

where d is the observed number of defaults and *q(α,d)* is the *α*-quantile of the distribution of *d*.

Based on the same Vasicek model discussed in the introduction to Part 2, and by following Gordy (2002), it can be proven that each *α*-quantile can be approximated by:

$$q(\alpha, d) = n \cdot \Phi\left(\frac{\sqrt{\rho}N^{-1}(\alpha) + \Phi^{-1}(p)}{\sqrt{1-\rho}}\right)$$

where p is the forecast probability of default and ρ is the correlation parameter.

The outcome of the Traffic Light test will then be green when the realized number of defaults is lower than k_l, yellow when it is between k_l and k_h, and red when it is higher than k_h. It should be noted that the choice of the correlation parameter ρ strongly influences the results and should, therefore, be made conservatively. Tasche (ibid.) suggests not exceeding 0.24, one of the highest values allowed under the Basel Accord (for Corporate, Sovereigns and Banks).

Blochwitz et al. (2011) suggest a version of the Traffic Light test based on an assumption of independence of defaults within each rating grade and on the adoption of the normal approximation for the distribution of defaults. The test yields results for each rating grade according to four coloured zones, namely:

Green for $d < p$
Yellow for $p \leq d \leq p + K^y \sigma(p,N)$
Orange for $p + K^y \sigma(p,N) \leq d \leq p + K^0 \sigma(p,N)$
Red for $p + K^0 \sigma(p,N) \leq d$.

Where p is the forecast probability of default, d is the observed default rate and $\sigma(p,N) = \sqrt{\frac{p \cdot (1-p)}{N}}$, with N the number of borrowers with a given rating grade.

This approach does not need an explicit statement of the correlation coefficient, but requires specifying the two parameters K^y and K^0. Blochwitz et al. (ibid.) observe that, although the probability for the colours to go from green to red should decline, it is in the tail that correlation effects are greater, hence the need to set a large enough value for K^0. They suggest $K^y = 0.84$ and $K^0 = 1.64$, which reflect probabilities of observing green, yellow, orange and red of 0.5, 0.3, 0.15 and 0.05, respectively.

4 On back-testing and benchmarking

One can, at least in theory, compare overnight trading Value at Risk for a particular portfolio with the "clean" P/L distribution over, say, a one-year period, on the basis of slightly more than two hundred daily observations, but the same cannot really be done with default probabilities or operational failure probabilities. First, one cannot observe probabilities of default, but only the events of default and actual losses. Probabilities, therefore, have to be inferred from observed default rates by applying the law of large numbers. However, for each exposure, such observations will typically happen once in a given year. Moreover, the law of large numbers requires that events are independent and identically distributed; two conditions that are in general not met, the former because defaults are always correlated to some extent, and especially so in times of crisis, the latter because defaults will always, at least in part, depend on idiosyncratic causes and hence be generated by different probability distributions. Furthermore, there is no universally agreed-upon definition of default, and which definition is actually adopted will of course impact the results of any exercise. Finally, the chosen model philosophy may make back-testing especially challenging. For instance, in order to back-test a TTC model, one would in fact require default data on the scale of the economic cycle, ideally of multiples thereof, given that the PD is supposed to reflect a long-term average over the whole cycle. Needless to say, all these challenges are magnified for those portfolios that typically exhibit low numbers of defaults.

In absence of reliable or sufficient internal default data, a bank needs therefore to use an external yardstick to perform its tests. The following are the more common approaches, in decreasing order of reliability.

Use of external ratings: When limited internal default data are available and the counterparts within a portfolio are, at least to a relevant part, externally rated (like large corporates, banks or sovereign governments) a bank can perform a number of the tests described above against the ratings provided by S&P, Moody's or Fitch. In order for such analysis to yield meaningful results, the rated portion of the portfolio needs to be large enough and representative enough of the whole portfolio. It should be noted that, as explained above, the validation exercise should encompass both discriminatory power and calibration, with the latter presupposing an ability to compare internal PD estimates with external ones. However, rating agencies, by their own unanimous admission, do not provide PD estimates, but merely a qualitative indication of relative creditworthiness. This creditworthiness may be interpreted as a probability of default, but no direct estimate is provided and consequently, one can only benchmark against observed default rates for each given rating grade. This problem is analogous to the one mentioned above in discussing back-testing: As default probabilities are unobservable, using actual default rates implies relying on the law of large numbers and on its underlying assumptions[1].

Data pooling: When the number of defaults is small, but not irrelevant or nil, banks may consider pooling data with other institutions holding portfolios with similar characteristics and for which the same risk factors used in the internal model are available[2]. This may be done through external data providers or by joining consortia with other market participants to develop databases large and meaningful enough for the application of back-testing techniques that are not feasible in the original portfolio.

Internal assessments: A final alternative, for low-default, nonstandard portfolios for which a bank has specific expertise that is not widespread in the market and where its assessment can be considered more reliable than those of the rating agencies, is to test against an internally constructed benchmark. For example, a bank can create, for each type of counterpart, a sample of counterparts to be listed from the highest to the lowest quality according to an expert-judgment credit risk assessment. The ranked sample can then be used as a benchmarking input for different statistical tests within a validation exercise. Needless to say, it may be very challenging to demonstrate the independence of such benchmarks, and banks need to be very careful in establishing procedures and controls around this approach.

In some cases, provided it is possible to at least distinguish borrowers in different risk categories, the internal set of defaults can be enhanced by a set of "quasi defaults" composed by borrowers who are close to or likely to default. This increases the size of the database and may allow the performance of enough statistical tests to arrive at a validation of the underlying model.

Finally, Pluto and Tasche (2005) developed a methodology to estimate probabilities of default when both the number of internal defaults and external references are practically nonexistent. The resulting PD estimates are usually very high and used as a kind of theoretical upper bound. Therefore, this approach is mainly used to check whether a given set of PD estimates can be considered conservative or not.

5 Conclusions

In looking at the validation of PD models, we have discussed several statistical techniques covering the analysis of individual risk factors as well as of the model as a whole in terms of the ability of the model to discriminate among borrowers. We have also described a number of statistical tests that a validator can apply to assess the estimates of the probabilities of default against external or internal benchmarks. In applying all these techniques, it is important to remember that proper validation is a comprehensive approach to the assessment of a rating system of which statistical methodologies are only one component and have to be applied with awareness of their limitations. In particular, the assumptions behind each test, for instance on correlations or functional forms of distributions, have to be carefully considered.

Also, a validator should never forget that the reliability of the results yielded by back-testing and benchmarking work depends on the availability and quality of relevant data. For some portfolios and sub-portfolios, for instance, the database size required for the observation of a sufficient number of defaults may be impossibly large. In some cases, using data from a period of unusually large volatility to test PDs that have been estimated as long-term averages may cause even a very good system to fail most of the tests. We have examined some key approaches that can be followed in order to respond to the challenge of finding the appropriate data set for validation purposes when internal default data are insufficient or absent. All have advantages and disadvantages that have to be taken into account when presenting validation conclusions and when balancing a trade-off between feasibility of the approach and accuracy of the results.

Notes

1. This difficulty may be further compounded by the fact that the 90-days-past-due criterion mandated by regulation is not in general adopted by rating agencies. As a consequence, there may be a discrepancy between internal and external observed default rates.
2. This last requirement may be hard to fulfill in practice.

References

Asuero, A.G., Sayago, A. and Gonzalez, A. G., "The Correlation Coefficient: An Overview, Critical Reviews," *Analytical Chemistry*, Vol. 36, 41–59, 2006.

Basel Committee on Banking Supervision, "Supervisory Framework for the Use of 'Backtesting' in Conjunction with the Internal Models Approach to Market Risk Capital Requirements," Basel, 1996.

Basel Committee on Banking Supervision, "Update on the work of the Accord Implementation Group related to validation under the Basel II Framework," Basel, 2005.

Basel Committee on Banking Supervision, "Studies on the Validation of Internal Rating Systems," Working Paper N. 14, Basel, 2005.

Bennett, D.A., "How Can I Deal with Missing Data in My Study?," *Aust. N. Z. J. Public Health*, Vol. 25, No.5, 464–469, 2001.

Blochwitz, S., Liebig, T. and Nyberg, M., "Benchmarking Deutsche Bundesbank's Default Risk Model, the KMV Private Firm Model and Common Financial Ratios for German Corporations," presented in Bank for International Settlements: Research and Supervision: A Workshop on Applied Banking Research, Oslo, 12–13 June 2001.

Blochwitz, S., Martin, M. R. W. and When, C. S., "Statistical Approaches to PD Validation," in Engelmann B. and Rauhmeier R. (editors), *"The Basel II Risk Parameters"*, Second Edition, Springer, 2011.

Brier, G. W., "Verification of Forecasts Expressed in Terms of Probability." *Monthly Weather Review*, Vol. 78, 1–3, 1950.

Cantor, R. and Mann, C., "Measuring The Performance Of Corporate Bond Ratings," Special Comment, Moody's, April 2003.

Capéraà, P. and Genest, C. "Spearman's ρ Is Larger Than Kendall's τ for Positively Dependent Random Variables," *J. Nonparametr. Statist.*, 2, 183–194, 1993.

Davison, A. C. and Hinkley, D. V., "Bootstrap Methods and their Application," *Cambridge Series in Statistical and Probabilistic Mathematics* (No. 1), 1997.

Engelmann, B., "Measures of Rating's Discriminatory Power," in Engelmann, B. and Rauhmeier, R. (editors), *The Basel II Risk Parameters,* Second Edition, Springer, 2011.

Fredricks, G. A. and Nelsen, R. B., "On the relationship between Spearman's rho and Kendall's tau for pairs of continuous random variables," *Journal of Statistical Planning and Inference*, Vol. 137, 2143 - 2150, 2007.

Gordy, M. B., "A Risk-Factor Model Foundation for Ratings-Based Capital Rules," Board of Governors of the Federal Reserve System, 22 October 2002.

Hosmer, D., Lemeshow, S. and Klar, J., "Goodness-of-Fit Testing for Multiple Logistic Regression Analysis When the Estimated probabilities are Small," *Biometrical Journal,* Vol. 30, 911--924, 1988.

Pluto, K. and Tasche, D., *Estimating Probabilities of Default for Low Default Portfolios,* mimeo, Deutsche Bundesbank, 2005.

Rauhmeier, R., "PD Validation: Experience from Banking Practice," in Engelmann B. and Rauhmeier R. (editors), *The Basel II Risk Parameters,* Second Edition, Springer, 2011.

Schafer JL. "Multiple Imputation: A Primer," *Stat. Methods in Med.* 1999, Vol. 8, No. 1, 3–15, doi: 10.1191/096228099671525676.

Sobehart, J. R., Keenan, S. C. and Stein, R. M., "Benchmarking Quantitative Default Risk Models: A Validation Methodology," Moody's Investors Service, 2000.

Tabachnick, B. G. and Fidell, L. S., "*Using Multivariate Statistics,*" 6th Edition, Pearson, 2012.

Tasche, D., "A Traffic Light Approach to PD Validation," Deutsche Bundesbank Working paper, 2003.

Tasche, D., "Validation of Internal Rating Systems and PD Estimates," in Christodoulakis, G. and Satchell, S. (editors), *The Analytics of Risk Model Validation,* Academic Press, 2008.

5 Loss Given Default Models

Loss Given Default (LGD) is the second key parameter in the Basel formula discussed in Chapter 3. In fact, by looking at the formula, we can notice how the computed capital requirement is linear in the LGD estimate and less than linear (actually concave) in the PD estimate (which is embedded in the copula-like formula for the inverse normal distribution at 99.9% confidence).

$$K(Capital)=\left[LGD\cdot N\left[\frac{1}{\sqrt{1-R}}\cdot INV(PD)+\sqrt{\left(\frac{R}{1-R}\right)}\cdot INV(0.999)\right]-PD\cdot LGD\right]$$
$$\cdot\frac{1}{(1-1.5\cdot b(PD))}\cdot(1+(M-2.5)\cdot b(PD))$$

In other words, an increase in LGD, everything else being equal, impacts the capital requirement more directly than an increase in PD, and hence a bank's capacity to accurately estimate it has a direct influence on its capital adequacy.

Default is defined in the Basel Accord (BCBS, 2006, §452) as occurring when either: "The bank considers that the obligor is unlikely to pay its credit obligations to the banking group in full," or "The obligor is past due more than 90 days on any material credit obligation to the banking group."

LGD is defined (BCBS, ibid. §297) as a percentage of the exposure at default (EAD). This implies that the adopted definition of both loss and default makes a difference to the estimation of LGD. The Basel Accord (BCBS, ibid. §460) requires that "all relevant factors should be taken into account. This must include material discount effects and material direct and indirect costs associated with collecting on the exposure. Banks must not simply measure the loss recorded in accounting records, although they must be able to compare accounting and economic losses." Peter (2011) suggests that economic loss can be defined as the change in a facility's value due to a default and that LGD can therefore be computed as:

$$LGD_j(t_{DF})=\frac{EAD_j(t_{DF})-NPV(Rec_j(t),t\geq t_{DF})+NPV(Costs_j,t\geq t_{DF})}{EAD_j(t_{DF})}$$

where NPV is the Net Present Value, $Rec_j(t)$ and $Cost_j(t)$ are recoveries and costs observed at time t. The above formula can of course be computed directly from available data when the latter are complete and include information on all the losses incurred. When the information available is incomplete and in particular if the facility has not yet defaulted or is being worked out, LGD is a random variable and needs to be estimated (Bennet, Catarineu and Moral, 2006).

The validation of LGD models is a topic with a relatively short history in technical literature. Bennet, Catarineu and Moral in BCBS (2005) suggest verifying all the elements used in producing LGD estimates including all assumptions made and the minimum regulatory requirements. They posit the development of a reference dataset based on internal and external data and the subsequent estimation of an empirical distribution of realized LGDs, based either on workout or on market LGD approach. On this basis an LGD estimate by facility can be constructed either from statistics of the empirical distribution or by regression-based modelling of a relationship between realized LGDs and other variables present in the reference dataset, like interest rates, GDP values, loan to value ratios and so on. Validation should then be structured along the three dimensions of stability analysis, benchmarking and back-testing. Model stability should be checked with regard to assumptions and regression parameters (when applicable), but also to the timeframe of the reference data set. Benchmarking and back-testing should be performed against external and internal data respectively, taking into account the various consistency issues that could arise: from the various default definitions and measures of losses that can be encountered in external data to the point-in-time nature of internal losses versus the need to produce long-run averages for capital requirements purposes.

Li, et al. (2009) discuss how to analyse the performance of LGD models by means of graphical tools, like scatter plots, histograms or box and whisker plots as well as through the use of confusion matrixes. The latter are developed to compare predicted and observed LGDs in various ways on the basis of loss count, EAD and observed loss. By computing a loss capture ratio, the authors develop a measure of performance similar to the accuracy ratio used to measure PD models' rank-ordering capability that can be used to compare different LGD models.

Loterman, et al. (2014), describe a back-testing framework for LGD models applying statistical hypotheses tests to different performance metrics in order to detect model deterioration at a given significance level.

1 LGD model design

The validation of model design should also encompass an analysis of all the risk factors in order to ascertain that they capture all the relevant information reasonably and consistently. There are, like for the probability of default, several kinds of modelling approaches to estimate loss given default (Peter, 2011 and Schuermann,

2004). One way to look at them is to distinguish approaches that seek to explicitly determine LGD based on the available data and those where estimates are inferred from data containing information which is somewhat related to LGD. In both types of approaches, models may be based on market data as well as on internal data. Modelling approaches could therefore be classified as follows.

- Explicit approaches. LGD is directly estimated from loss data.
  - Market LGD, based on comparing market prices of defaulted bonds or of tradable loans shortly after default with their par values. A comparative analysis of several regression techniques applied to S&P LossStats database can be found in Yashkir and Yashkir (2013).
  - Workout LGD, where all post-default recoveries, carrying costs and workout expenses are discounted in order to estimate the value of the defaulted deal to be compared with the relevant EAD. The determination of the appropriate, risk-adjusted discount rate is challenging, especially for collaterals and costs for which there is no market price available (Hlawatsch and Reichling, 2009). Main issues are the choice of the discount rate, the treatment of zero or negative LGD observations in the data, the measurement and allocation of workout costs and the definition of workout completion.
- Implicit approaches. LGD are inferred from data that contain relevant information.
  - Implied market LGD, where credit spreads on non-defaulted bonds are used, as they reflect the expected loss as perceived in the market[1].
  - Implied historical LGD, as suggested in the Second Basel Accord (BCBS, ibid. §465) for retail exposures, can be estimated on the basis of realized losses and an internal long-run PD estimate.

Another distinction to be made is between models that rely mainly on statistical analysis of data and models that rely more on expert judgement. Although a measure of expert judgement is of course present in any modelling approach, expert-based methods are applied when data is unavailable and/or unreliable, like when dealing with very low-default portfolios. They may include a combination of interviews, peer reviews, expert panels, scenario analysis, reviews of industry studies as well as of technical literature.

The Basel accord requires that the estimation of LGD be based on observed loss rate estimates and in any case be not less than the long-run default-weighted average loss rate given default. An LGD model can be built by performing a regression analysis of historical default data against a number of potential drivers of LGD based on information on of defaulted borrowers available in external, internal, pooled data sources, or a combination of the three.

Dahlin and Storkitt, (2014) list the following approaches for the estimation of LGDs based on observed workout or market LGD.

- Parametric methods
  - Ordinary least squares regression (Qi and Zhao, 2012);
  - Ridge regression (Loterman, 2012);
  - Fractional response regression (Bastos, 2010);
  - Tobit model (Calabrese, 2012);
  - Decision tree model (Logistic-OLS Regressions model (LR-OLS)) (Calabrese, 2012);
- Transformation regressions
  - Inverse Gaussian regression (Qi and Zhao, 2012);
  - Inverse Gaussian regression with beta transformation (Qi and Zhao, 2012);
  - Box-Cox transformation/OLS (Loterman, 2012) ;
  - Beta transformation/OLS (Loterman, 2012);
  - Fractional logit transformation & Log transform (Bellotti and Crook, 2008);
- Non-parametric
  - Regression tree (RT) (Bastos, 2010);
  - Neural networks (Qi and Zhao, 2012);
  - Multivariate adaptive regression spline (Loterman, 2012);
  - Least squares support vector machine (Loterman, 2012);
- Semi-parametric
  - Joint Beta Additive Model (Calabrese, 2012).

In building a LGD model through regression analysis it is important to identify and select the appropriate risk drivers, although statistical analysis may be constrained by the limited number of loss observations. Drivers may be classified according to the following categories (Peter, 2011): borrower, facility, collateral, guarantee, macroeconomic factors, bank internal factors. Borrower characteristics may include: type of borrower (sovereign, corporate, bank, SME, etc.), creditworthiness, country or region, size, the industry sector classification, industry conditions, legal structure, balance-sheet structure. Drivers can also be specific to the type of the borrower; for instance, LGDs for financial institutions may be modelled through capital adequacy, leverage and debt, profitability, liquidity, cash flow, asset quality, management; for sovereign borrowers one may use development indicators (social and political), economic environment, political stability, national debt; for retail customers, social and demographic indicators, financial characteristics and behavioural indicators may be used; while for corporates leverage, profitability, turnover, growth, liquidity, and other financial indicators are used. Features of the facility may include: absolute and relative seniority, debt/transaction type, size and maturity of exposure. Collateral features may include type, current value, depreciation, age, technical characteristics. Guarantee features may include: guarantor (similar characteristics as the one mentioned for the borrower), warranty clauses, coverage. Macroeconomic factors may include interest and FX rate levels, unemployment rates, price indexes, default rate levels, gross domestic product, economic growth, legal system, etc. Finally, internal factors may include valuation procedures, workout strategies, collateralization strategies, relation between the bank and the borrower.

Several empirical studies show (see for example, Altman et al., 2005) that security of debt and priority of claims are the most relevant determinants of final recovery rates, and hence of LGDs. The same studies also show that, while LGDs decrease with security and seniority, they increase with the probability of default, or, better, that they are higher in periods of higher default rates.

The Basel accords require banks to estimate LGD to reflect economic downturn conditions where necessary to capture the relevant risks and that those estimates be no lower than the long-term average Loss Given Default, which was computed based on the average economic loss of all observed defaults within the data source for that type of facility (BCBS, 2006). It also requires that the data observation period in which to build an LGD model consist of at least five years for retail exposures and at least seven years for corporates, sovereigns and bank exposures, in order to ensure that they cover at least one whole economic cycle. Macro-economic variables may also be included in the model in order to capture cyclical effects and economic downturns, either explicitly or by using scenarios or data form periods of, for instance, negative GDP growth or high unemployment rates. The length and complexity of recovery processes makes the reliability and size of available datasets often insufficient, thus further complicating the estimation of downturn figures. Conservative buffers and stressing of estimates constitute an often followed alternative to obtain LGD figures relevant to worsening economic conditions.

2 Model Output

As mentioned above, validating the output of an LGD model should encompass portfolio stability, back-testing and benchmarking. The verification of stability is important both from the model and the portfolio perspective. On one hand, changes in the model results need to reflect actual modifications in the risk profile rather than a lack of stability in the model design or input. The latter in particular; if data of different origins and from different timeframes are used, it may have a negative impact on the stability of results. On the other hand, validators need to be aware, as was already observed, that changes in the composition and risk characteristics of the portfolio need to be taken into account when analysing the performance.

Back-testing an LGD model means comparing and assessing internal estimates against internal observed losses with the objective of evaluating the predictive power as well as of detecting any deterioration in performance.

When the number of internal defaults is too small, benchmarking analyses should be performed on the basis of available data from external rating agencies, published studies or pool consortia.

2.1 Testing stability

Stability testing compares the portfolio to be used in back-testing and benchmarking with the one used during development, to ensure the continued performance of the model. We will discuss the system stability index (SSI), the Chi-squared test and the Kolmogorov-Smirnov test for continuous data (Maarse, 2012).

System Stability Index

The system stability index (SSI) tests whether two discrete samples have a similar distribution. It is defined as:

$$SSI = \sum_{i=1}^{N} (X_i - Y_i) \ln\left(\frac{X_i}{Y_i}\right)$$

where X_i and Y_i are the percentages of the datasets A (back-testing) and B (reference) that belong to segment *i*. The SSI result will be zero in case of perfect stability ($x=y$) and can be interpreted with the help of a Traffic Light scheme. For instance, one may consider a set of thresholds similar to the one below to decide on the level of stability:

- SSI < 0.10: Stable
- SSI in [0.10, 0.25]: Moderately stable
- SSI > 0.25 Unstable.

These values are given merely as examples. At the same time the performance of the model on the different samples has to be assessed in order to gauge the actual impact of the shift in the portfolio.

Chi-squared test

The Chi-squared test also compares discrete distributions, namely the observed frequencies with predicted frequencies within a segment *i*, where segments are assumed to be independent. The test statistic is chi-squared distributed, and conclusions can be drawn based on this distribution:

$$\chi^2_{N-1} \sim \sum_{i=1}^{N} \frac{(X_i - Y_i)^2}{Y_i}$$

where:
N is the number of observations
N−1 the degrees of freedom

Kolmogorov-Smirnov test

The Kolmogorov-Smirnov test (KS-test) checks whether two samples are drawn from the same continuous distribution. It assumes that there are two independent random samples (Xi and Yi) with continuous cumulative distributions FX and FY.

The hypotheses considered are:

H0: The distributions are the same.
H1: The distributions are not the same.

It has to be possible to rank the observations to determine two comparable cumulative distributions and then compute the maximum distance between them.

Given the two distributions:

$$F_X(x) = \frac{1}{N}\sum_{i=1}^{N} I\{X_i \leq x\}$$

$$F_Y(x) = \frac{1}{M}\sum_{j=1}^{N} I\{Y_j \leq x\}$$

where I is the indicator function,
Xi is the observation from sample X, with i=1,..,N,
Yj is the observation from sample Y, with j=1,...,M,

then the maximum distance is then given by:

$$D_{MN} = \max_x \left| F_X(x) - F_Y(x) \right|$$

And the test statistic is calculated as:

$$T = \sqrt{\frac{NM}{N+M}} D_{NM}$$

When the sample size goes to infinity, T is Kolmogorov-Smirnov (KS) distributed. The sample size is sufficiently large to use this distribution when there are more than 40 observations. If it is not possible to rank the observations, the Kolmogorov-Smirnov test will be strongly influenced by the observations' order. The Chi-squared and the SSI both test discrete distributions.

The SSI test weights the shift with the number of observations while the Chi-squared considers each segment as equally relevant. Therefore the Chi-squared test is a much stricter test for the stability of a portfolio as even a shift in a small bucket could lead to rejecting the whole sample.

2.2 Testing performance

There are several performance metrics that can be applied to the task of validating LGD models. We briefly present below a selection of correlation measures (which aim at quantifying a statistical relationship between predicted and observed values), error measures (aimed at measuring the difference between predicted and observed values), and binary classification metrics (which look at how well a model is able to distinguish between high and low losses.

2.2.1 Correlation measures

Kendall

Given a set of predictions and a corresponding set of observations, a pair of observations $[a,b]$ is concordant if those are different, the corresponding predictions are different and the sign of the two differences is the same. Formally, if $o_a \neq o_b$, $p_a \neq p_b$, and the sign of $o_a - o_b$ is the same as the sign of $p_a - p_b$. They are discordant if $o_a \neq o_b$, $p_a \neq p_b$, and the sign of $o_a - o_b$ is equal to minus the sign of $p_a - p_b$.

Kendall's correlation coefficient is defined as:

$$\tau = \frac{n_c - n_d}{\frac{1}{2}N(N-1)}$$

where N is the number of observations/predictions,
n_c and n_d are the number of concordant and discordant pairs, respectively,

Pearson

Pearson's correlation coefficient is defined as:

$$r = \frac{1}{n-1}\sum_{i=1}^{n}\left(\frac{o_i - \mu}{\sigma}\right)\left(\frac{p_i - m}{s}\right)$$

where n is the number of observations/predictions,
o_i and p_i are observations and predictions, respectively,
μ and σ are the mean and standard deviation of the observations,
m and s are the mean and standard deviation of the predictions.

Spearman

Spearman's rank correlation coefficient is also defined as the Pearson correlation coefficient between the ranked variables. For a sample of size n, the n scores X_i, Y_i are converted to ranks: x_i, y_i, and ρ is computed from:

$$\rho = 1 - \frac{6\sum_{i=1}^{n} d_i^2}{n(n^2-1)}$$

where $d_i = x_i - y_i$ is the difference between ranks.
$\rho = 1$ means that the two rankings are the same;
$\rho = 0$ means that rankings are random;
$\rho = -1$ means that the two rankings are the opposite of each other.

Note that $\rho\sqrt{N-1}$ is approximately normally distributed for more than 40 observations and that therefore the null hypothesis can be rejected with 95 percent significance if $\rho\sqrt{N-1} > Z_{0.95}$, were z is the cumulative normal distribution. We also refer to Chapter 4 for a discussion on how to interpret the results of similar correlation metrics.

Determination coefficient

The determination coefficient is one minus the fraction of the sum of error squares over the total sum of squares. These are usually defined respectively as:

$$SS_r = \sum_{i=1}^{N} (P_i - O_i)^2$$

also called residual sum of squares and as:

$$SS_t = \sum_{i=1}^{N} (O_i - \bar{O})^2$$

The coefficient of determination is given by:

$$R^2 = 1 - \frac{SS_r}{SS_t}$$

All the above correlation measures can take values between -1 and + 1

2.2.2 Error measures

Mean Absolute Error

The Mean Absolute Error is the average absolute difference between predicted and observed values and is defined as:

$$MAE = \frac{1}{N}\sum_{i=1}^{N} |P_i - O_i|$$

where N is the number of observations and P_i and O_i are the predicted and the observed values, respectively.

The Maximum Absolute Deviation measures the same differences, but weighted by the respective EADs.

$$MAD = \frac{\sum_{i=1}^{N} |P_i - O_i| EAD_i}{\sum_{i=1}^{N} EAD_i}$$

Root Mean Squared Error

The Root Mean Squared Error is the square root of the average of the squared differences between predicted and observed values and is defined as:

$$RMSE = \sqrt{\frac{1}{N}\sum_{i=1}^{N}(P_i - O_i)^2}$$

Loss Shortfall

The Loss Shortfall measures how much the observed LGD is lower than the predicted LGD and is defined as:

$$LS = 1 - \frac{\sum_{i=1}^{N}(P_i EAD_i)}{\sum_{i=1}^{N}(O_i EAD_i)}$$

2.2.3 Classification measures

ROC and AUC

As already discussed for the validation of PD models, the Receiver Operating Characteristic curve (ROC) and the area under the ROC curve (AUC) are regularly used in assessing the discriminatory power of rating models[2] and in general of binary classification tools. They may be employed to assess the performance of LGD models by measuring how well a model is able to distinguish between large and small losses. The AUC, which varies between 0.5 (random) and 1 (perfect), measures the discriminatory power of the model.

2.2.4 Statistical hypotheses tests

It should be noted that all the techniques discussed above are strongly dependent on the availability of relevant data. When a sufficient number of observations is not available, and particularly in the case of low default portfolios, many statistical techniques may not be meaningful and even a very small number of outliers in the errors made may yield very poor results.

The general problem with most of the metrics described, however, is the difficulty in estimating the distribution of a test statistic for the null hypothesis. For example, the well-known t-test (Gosset, 1908) is based on the assumptions that observations are independent; that the observed distribution is normal; and that both predicted and observed distributions have the same variance. None of these assumptions can be easily validated in the case of LGD predictions and observations, save perhaps the second, when enough observations are available (i.e., at least more than 30), which rules out the case of typically low default portfolios like sovereigns, banks and large corporates.

Alternatively, the distribution of the test statistic may be estimated using a bootstrapping approach, which consists in estimating the theoretically unknown distribution of the test statistic under the null hypothesis. In parametric bootstrapping, a known distribution is fitted to the data and samples are drawn, and statistics computed, repeatedly in order to define the desired confidence levels. In nonparametric bootstrapping, the data in the available sample are re-sampled with replacement, and the statistics calculated in order to build the (unknown) distribution.

As shown above in the case of stability analysis for the KS-test, a statistical hypothesis test posits a null hypothesis (i.e., no difference between the two distributions) and an alternative one (the distributions are different). The null hypothesis is rejected if there is sufficient evidence against it as measured by the p-value. The p-value represents the probability of finding the observed sample results, or "more extreme" results, assuming that the null hypothesis is true (or, otherwise said, to incorrectly reject the null hypothesis). The resulting p-value is compared to a pre-defined significance level, usually. Lower p-values (i.e., <5%) indicate that there is enough evidence to reject the null hypothesis, while higher p-values (i.e., >5%) indicate that there isn't. P-values can also be analysed through a Traffic Light scheme, as in Castermans et al. (2009), where green, yellow and red can be assigned to different ranges of p-values.

Another way to evaluate the results of a statistical hypothesis test is to look at the probability of correctly rejecting the null hypothesis, that is, of not making a type II error, and comparing it to a pre-defined level, usually 85%. This is called test power and is usually indicated denoted as π.

3 Process and data

Bennet et al., (BCBS, 2005) list the following requirements for the reference data set (RDS) to be used in the development of a LGD model. The RDS must:

- Cover at least a complete business cycle,
- Contain all the defaults produced within the considered time frame,
- Include all the relevant information to estimate the risk parameters, and
- Include data on the relevant drivers of loss.

Additionally, validators will need to test and verify the presence of any selection bias in the dataset, the overall consistency in the definitions of default used, the inclusion of a sufficient number of years of economic downturn in the dataset, also with regard to portfolios with cyclical LGD features.

In order to assess the performance of an LGD model, this has to be evaluated on data different from the ones used to develop the model. The two datasets may differ only because they include different observations and represent therefore different portions of the available historical database (in which case they will be used to evaluate how well a certain model fits the available data) or, more strictly, because the one used for validation is made of more recent observations than the development one (in which case they are used to assess the predictive power of the model).

Note that the LGD distributions may be bi-modal, i.e., they may contain one or two spikes around LGD=0 (full recovery) and/or LGD=1 (no recovery). Also, datasets may contain negative or higher than one LGD values, either because of additional income from penalties and collateral sales, or because of the additional costs of collecting the debt. In some cases, banks prefer to set to zero (truncate or censoring) values outside the interval [0; 1] in order to avoid showing negative realized LGDs (i.e., gains on the defaulted asset). On the other hand, removing zero or negative observations altogether from the dataset is equivalent to adopting a stricter definition of default and should be taken into account when checking consistency of default definitions.

Validation of an LGD model should verify the quality of the data used in model development. In case of internal data, this analysis could be very thorough and include verification of consistency with internal default definition, completeness and integrity of the database and also single case analysis on a sample basis. Furthermore, the relevance and representativeness of the data used should be verified also in perspective terms, i.e., whether or not the data used is relevant in light of the expected future composition and risk profile of the portfolio in light of a bank's business and strategic choices.

These issues are especially relevant when internal data is insufficient or absent and model development is based on external sources of data. Such sources will typically be external rating agencies and consortia of banks created for the pooling of default and loss data. For example, Moody's and Standard and Poors both provide access to databases of default and recovery information of defaulted bonds, loans traded in secondary markets and other available workout information. On the basis of these data several studies and analyses are regularly published with estimates, amongst other things, of average recovery rates. When these data sources are used in development, one needs to assess to what extent they are relevant to the portfolios on which the LGD model is going to be applied as observed –recovery rates may vary significantly across industry segments and geographies. Also the consistency of default definitions has to be checked, as external providers and rating agencies will not necessarily use the same definition as the one internally used in a bank[3]. In addition, if external studies based on such data are used in development, validators have to verify that only results that are widely and consistently agreed upon within the scientific community are used and that developers did not select only the ones that more conveniently fit the assumptions or the business objectives.

Finally, several groups of banks have formed consortia for the collection of default and recovery data with the objective of expanding the available databases and allow more reliable statistical analyses. As these databases are normally anonymized, one needs to be careful in assessing the representativeness of the information contained (especially when the consortium is formed by a diverse set of institutions) and the potential for double counting (as more institutions may be exposed to the same defaulting borrower).

4 Use test and internal requirements

The use test refers to the internal use of the LGD estimate required for the calculation of regulatory capital. Besides the computation of regulatory capital in the Advanced Internal Rating Based (A-IRB) approach, the output of LGD models may be used for pricing, stress testing, fair value accounting as well as for risk management and reporting. Validators must verify that the model is used for the intended purposes, but also that the model output itself is appropriate for the different uses, where different estimates (like downturn versus through-the-cycle), different time horizons (one-year versus maturity of the facility), different regulatory and accounting rules for downturn LGD floors, pricing practices and default definitions may be required.

For example, pricing models are likely to use probability of default and loss given default estimates relevant to the entire life of the asset rather than to the next twelve months and downturn estimates of LGD in particular may be considered too conservative and penalizing when used for pricing purposes.

When using LGD figures for accounting purposes it is important to be aware of the differences between the requirements of the International Financial Reporting Standards (IFRS) and those of Basel-derived capital regulations. These differences include, amongst other things, definition of default, time horizons for estimates, and discount rates. For instance, while Basel defines a default based on 90 days past due and/or unlikeness to pay rule, in IFRS, objective evidence of a default can be recognized before the contract is 90 days past due. As a consequence, different default definitions may influence the way expected losses are calculated. The discount rate is also important when discounting cash flows, and shortfalls thereof, over the remaining lifetime of a financial asset. While under IFRS the discount rate can be between the risk-free rate and the effective interest rate, the discount rate within LGD calculations under Basel is not specified aside from the fact that it should reflect the time value of money and a risk premium appropriate to the undiversifiable risk (BCBS, 2005). Finally, while Basel II requires including all direct and indirect costs in workout calculations, IFRS is somewhat stricter and requires that legal and other indirect costs are not considered.

The general principles behind the adoption of an Advanced IRB approach is that such an approach should be an integral part of its business and risk management processes, insofar as credit risk is relevant, and should influence its decision-making. Therefore, if a bank uses LGD estimates in its internal risk management processes that differ from the downturn LGDs used in the calculation of risk-weighted assets, validators should examine not only the documentation available on the reasons for such difference, but also for a demonstration of the reasonableness of any differences between those models.

5 Conclusions

Establishing an effective validation procedure for LGD estimates is crucial for a financial institution because LGD is a fundamental element in the computation of capital requirements under the advanced internal ratings-based (AIRB) approach. In particular, such requirements will be very sensitive to the LGD estimated internally by a bank.

We have identified several classes of methodological approaches as suggested in technical literature and regulatory papers. In particular, we have distinguished explicit methods (explicit market LGD and workout LGD, based on information from defaulted facilities) and implicit methods (implied historical LGD and implied market LGD, based on information from non-defaulted facilities.

We have highlighted a number of elements to be considered in the development and therefore in the validation of LGD models: consistency in default definitions; treatment of negative data (keeping, truncating, or eliminate negative data); choice of the discount rate; calculation and allocation of recoveries and costs.

We have also presented a number of statistical techniques to test the output of LGD models in terms of both stability and performance. However, the application of such techniques is made challenging by the limited amount of available data. Also, most of the data, and the related studies, focus on American corporate bonds, which makes the results difficult to apply in European or Asian contexts, or to noncorporate portfolios of loans like retail, credit cards, banks and others.

The above challenges are compounded by the fact that different requirements may apply with respect to regulatory applications, when LGD figures are used for other internal uses like pricing or accounting disclosure. The lack of data and the limitations of the studies available equally hinder the work of the modeller and that of the validator. The latter has to rely on expertise and exercise judgment in order to compensate for the limited empirical evidence.

Notes

1. Expected loss is of course made up of both PD and LGD estimates, and therefore it may be difficult to separate the two for the purpose of LGD modelling.
2. Note that the CAP measure discussed in Chapter 5 is a linear transformation of the ROC measure.
3. This point is especially relevant for regulatory purposes as external recovery databases may be based on actual bankruptcies rather than on the "90 days past due" Basel compliant definition.

References

Altman, E., Resti, A. and Sironi, A. (editors) *Recovery Risks: The Next Challenge in Credit Risk Management*, Recovery Books, 2005.

Bastos, J., "Forecasting Bank Loans Loss-Given-Default," *Journal of Banking & Finance*, Vol. 34, No. 10, 2510–2517, 2010.

BCBS, Basel Committee on Banking Supervision, "Guidance on Paragraph 468 of the Framework Document," Basel, July 2005.

BCBS, Basel Committee on Banking Supervision, "International Convergence of Capital Measurement and Capital Standards," Basel, June 2006.

Bellotti, T. and Cook, J., "Modelling and Estimating Loss Given Default for Credit Cards," CRC Working paper 08-1, 2008.

Bennett, R., Catarineu, E. and Moral, G., "Loss Given Default Validation," in *Studies on the Validation of Internal Rating Systems*, Basel Committee on Banking Supervision, WP N. 14, May 2005.

Calabrese, R., "Estimating Bank Loans Loss Given Default by Generalized Additive Models," UCD Geary Institute Discussion Paper Series, WP2012/24, 2012.

Castermans, G., Martens, D., Van Gestel, T., Hamers, B. and Baesens, B. "An Overview and Framework for PD Backtesting and Benchmarking," *Journal of the Operational Research Society*, 1–15, 2009.

Dahlin, F. and Storkitt, S., "Estimation of Loss Given Default for Low Default Portfolios," Working Paper, Royal Institute of Technology, Stockholm, Sweden 2014.

Hlawatsch, S. and Reichling, P., "A Framework for LGD Validation of Retail Portfolios," FEMM Working Paper No. 25, August 2009.

Li, D., Bhariok, R., Keenan, S. and Santilli, S., "Validation Techniques and Performance Metrics for Loss Given Default Models," *The Journal of Risk Model Validation*, Vol. 3, No. 3, 3–26, Fall 2009.

Loterman, G., Debruyne, M., Branden, K. V., Van Gestel, T. and Mues, C., "A Proposed Framework for Backtesting Loss Given Default Models," *Journal of Risk Model Validation*, Vol. 8, No. 1, 69–90, 2014.

Loterman, G., Brown, I., Martens, D., Mues, C. and Baesens, B., "Benchmarking Regression Algorithms for Loss Given Default Modelling," *International Journal of Forecasting*, Vol. 28, No. 2012, 161–170, 2012.

Maarse, B., *Backtesting Framework for PD, EAD and LGD*, Master Thesis, Rabobank International Quantitative Risk Analytics, July 2012.

Peter, C., "Estimating Loss Given Default: Experience from Banking Practice," in Engelmann, B. and Rauhmeier, R. (editors), *The Basel II Risk Parameters, Second Edition*, Springer, 2011.

Qi, M. and Zhao, X., "Comparison of Modelling Methods for Loss Given Default," *Journal of Banking & Finance*, Vol. 35, 2842–2855, 2011.

Schuermann, P., "What do We Know about Loss Given Default?," Working Paper, Federal Reserve Bank of New York, 2004.

"Student" (Gosset, W., S.), "The Probable Error of a Mean," *Biometrika*, Vol. 6, No. 1, 1–25, March 1908.

6 Exposure at Default Models

In the Basel Accord A-IRB framework (BCBS, 2006), the exposure at default (EAD) is defined as the size of the credit risk exposure that the bank *expects* to face on a facility assuming that economic downturn conditions occur within a one-year time horizon *and* the associated borrower defaults on its obligations within that horizon.

EAD models cover a wide range of approaches depending on the type of product considered. The Basel Accord classifies both on-balance sheet and off-balance sheet exposures for the purpose of computing EAD for credit risk and counterparty risk under the different approaches. In this chapter we will focus on EAD estimation for credit risk under the A-IRB approach. We will examine EAD models for derivative exposures in Part 3.

Many types of facilities that are carrying credit risk exist; of these, some will produce a fixed and some others a variable credit exposure. A fixed credit exposure is one where the bank has not made any commitment to provide credit in the future, while a variable credit exposure is one where the bank has made such commitment in addition to the current credit. Examples of variable exposures are demand loans, term loans, revolving credit, overdraft protection, and so on. Intuitively the EAD for a fixed exposure is the EAD on the drawn amount. In turn, the EAD on drawn amounts should not be less than the sum of (i), the amount by which a bank's regulatory capital would be reduced if the exposure were written-off fully, and (ii) any specific provisions and partial write-offs (BCBS, 2006).

A variable exposure, however, may default at a (subsequent) time when additional money has been drawn and thus cause a loss higher than the current on-balance sheet value.

An EAD estimates on a variable exposure consists of two components: (1) The exposure on the drawn (disbursed) amount on the facility at the time of estimation; (2) the potential exposure that may materialize in the future due to further withdrawals, subject to any relevant contractual covenant, on the facility by the borrower until it defaults, if it ever does, within a one-year time horizon. The first component (on-balance sheet exposure) is equal to the book value of the drawn amount on the facility and is known with certainty. The book value of the drawn amount on the facility should reflect all the capital repayments (amortization), which means that all capital repayments should be deducted from the total disbursed amount at the time of calculation. As for the interests accrued on the disbursed amount, Basel regulation does not put forward any strict rules; in practice some banks include such interest in this component in order to bring a more economic perspective to the EAD estimates. It is assumed that this current exposure will stay on the bank's balance sheet until the borrower defaults, if it ever does. The on-balance sheet EAD on a facility is considered equivalent to the total of:

- The current drawn (disbursed) amount on the facility;
- The interest and the fees that are expected to be collected from the borrower within the one-year time horizon.

The second component (off-balance sheet exposure), on the other hand, is conditional on the default event and economic downturn conditions. It is not known a priori for the facilities associated with a non-defaulted borrower and has to be estimated.

The off-balance sheet EAD for a facility is the product of two factors:

- Committed but as-yet undisbursed amount on the facility;
- A Credit Conversion Factor (CCF), an estimate of the ratio of the undisbursed amount that will have been converted into an effective drawn amount by the time of the borrower's default, if it ever happens within a one-year time horizon.

To compute the EAD for variable exposures, we need to convert the committed but undisbursed (undrawn) amount of the facility into an effective exposure amount. This is done by estimating a credit conversion factor (CCF) which represents an estimated ratio of the undisbursed amount that will be converted into an effective drawn amount by the time the borrower defaults, if it ever happens, under economic downturn conditions within a one-year time horizon.

For A-IRB banks, the CCF is the key input for computing EAD, and it must be expressed as a percentage of the undrawn (off-balance) amount of the commitment. Other ways of computing CCF, for instance as a percentage of the whole exposure (the on- and off-balance sheet or the entire facility limit), albeit conceptually equivalent, would not be fully in line with regulatory requirements. The CCF, as defined above, shall be zero or positive or, alternatively, that the EAD of an exposure cannot be less than the current outstanding amount. CCF estimates have to take into account drawdowns following a default when these are not reflected in the LGD estimation.

1 EAD model design

There is currently no regulatory prescription as to the design of the model to be used for estimating CCF, but there are a number of regulatory requirements focussing on how to define CCF, how to assign CCF to facilities and how to build the reference dataset to be used for estimation. Banks are also expected to show, and validators consequently to verify, that the approach chosen is properly documented, that reasons for all modelling choices are clearly explained, along with identified strengths and weaknesses, and that the effect of the modelling choices on final CCF values are analysed, including their relationship with time to default and credit quality.

In particular, the European Banking Authority devotes two articles of its Draft Regulatory Technical Standards (EBA, 2014) to the estimation of exposure at default. The guidance contained therein could be summarized as follows.

- EADs have to be estimated by using average CCFs by facility grade or pool (i.e., one CCF for all exposures in the same grade or pool) for all commitment the bank has currently taken on. Realized conversion factors by facility grade or pool have to be computed as an average, weighted with the number of defaults using all observed defaults within the reference dataset; alternatively, banks can directly estimate a grade or pool average CCF without estimating individual CCFs for defaulted exposures.
- CCF estimation should reflect the bank's policies and strategies on account monitoring, including limit monitoring, and payment processing.
- The functional and structural form of the estimation method, assumptions regarding this method, where applicable its downturn effect, length of data series, margin of conservatism, and the human judgement and, where applicable, the choice of risk drivers, should be adequate to the type of exposures to which they are applied.
- A bank might use average CCF for Basel II purposes, provided they are not too volatile around their long-run average. However, if variability during the economic cycle is material, CCF estimates should be adjusted to become appropriate for economic downturn conditions and more conservative than their long-run average. Both estimates should be provided in order to justify the choices made.
- The bank should specify the nature, severity and duration of an economic downturn and incorporate in the conversion factor estimates of any adverse dependencies that have been identified between selected credit and economic factors versus drawing of credit limits.
- A well-documented process should be in place for assessing any effects of economic downturn conditions on drawing of credit limits and for producing conversion factor estimates consistent with downturn conditions.

From the above requirements, we can describe a high-level EAD estimation process as made up of the following key steps.

1. Tracking and recording of all defaults, in order to be able to identify exposure at the appropriate reference point prior to default;

2. Compute the realized CCF for every defaulted exposure within each exposure pool. Compute the average CCF for each pool as the weighted average of the CCF which were estimated for the defaulted individual exposures;
3. Identify EAD risk drivers;
4. Using information on EAD risk drivers and CCFs of defaulted exposures, estimate CCFs for non-defaulted exposures;
5. Determine whether the CCF obtained is appropriate for economic downturn conditions. If the volatility of CCFs is low and lies around the average, average CCF may be used; otherwise, economic downturn conditions should be appropriately incorporated;
6. Apply CCF estimates to every non-defaulted exposure to obtain EADs.

Figure 6.1 summarizes the estimation process.

Most banks estimate CCFs empirically on the basis of a dataset of observed EAD of defaulted facilities at dates preceding the default. Statistics are computed on the increase of the facilities' usage as the default date approaches. One way to compute a realized CCF on the basis of such a dataset is to use the relationship:

$$EAD(t_d) = Exp(t_r) + CCF(t_r) \cdot (ExpMax(t_r) - Exp(t_r))$$

where:
$EAD(t_d)$ is the observed exposure at time of default t_d;
$Exp(t_r)$ if the drawn amount at the reference time t_r;
$CCF(t_r)$ is the realized conversion factor at the reference time t_r;
$ExpMax(t_r)$ is the limit of the facility at the reference time t_r;

Then the realized CCF at time t_r is given by:

$$CCF(t_r) = \frac{EAD(t_d) - Exp(t_r)}{ExpMax(t_r) - Exp(t_r)}.$$

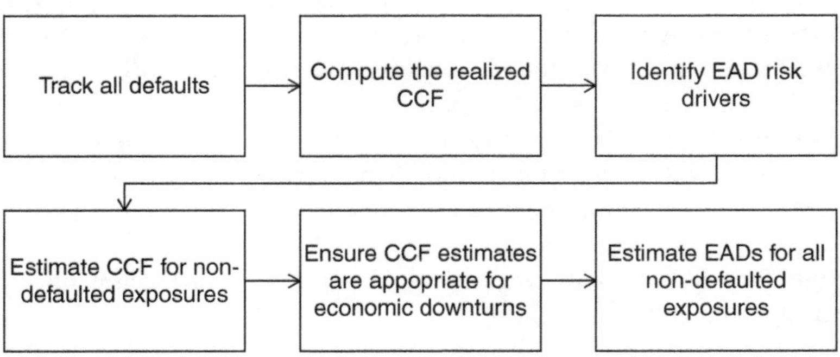

Figure 6.1 EAD estimation process

It should be noted, however, that the above CCF is undefined when the utilization of the facility is maximum and may be inaccurate is the limit of the facility varies over time. A possible alternative is thus to compute the conversion factor simply as:

$$CCF(t_r) = \frac{EAD(t_d)}{ExpMax(t_r)}.$$

Moral (2011) describes three ways to determine realised CCFs: fixed-time horizon, variable-time horizon and cohort approach.

In the first approach a fixed time horizon *H*, usually 1 year, is selected and the CCF is computed at $t=t_d - H$

$$CCF(t_d - H) = \frac{EAD(t_d) - Exp(t_d - H)}{ExpMax(t_d - H) - Exp(t_d - H)}.$$

where,

$EAD(t_d)$: Exposure at the time default occurred;

$Exp(t_d\text{-}H)$: Exposure of the bank at the start of the time horizon prior to default;

$ExpMax(t_d\text{-}H)$: Maximum exposure that the bank could have with the counterparty at the start of the time horizon.

This approach assumes that all the nondefaulted exposures will default at the same time over the time horizon chosen for the estimation. The CCF is the ratio of the increase in the exposure until the default day to the maximum possible increase in exposure over the fixed time horizon. Therefore, the numerator indicates how much the exposure of the bank grew from the exposure at the fixed interval prior to default, and the denominator indicates the maximum increase in the exposure that could have happened over the given time horizon.

In the variable time horizon approach, a range of time horizons rather than a single one is chosen. Realised CCFs are then computed for each defaulted facility and for a set of reference dates within the chosen range (for instance, CCFs for each of the 12 months within a range of one year) as in the formula below.

$$CCF(t_d - j) = \frac{EAD(t_d) - Exp(t_d - j)}{ExpMax(t_d - j) - Exp(t_d - j)}, j = 1,2,\ldots,12 \qquad months.$$

where:

$EADt_d$: Exposure at the time default occurred;

$Exp(t_d\text{-}j)$: Exposure of the bank at the j-th date prior to default;

$ExpMax(t_d\text{-}j)$: Maximum exposure that the bank could have with the counterparty at the j-th date prior to default.

Although this method takes into account more possible default dates than the fixed horizon approach, not all the estimated CCFs can be used, as some of them, for instance those closer to default (especially for borrowers who cannot easily draw after a first impairment) will be less meaningful than others.

In the Cohort approach the time horizon of observations is divided into fixed short time windows (cohorts) with default occurring at any time during the interval. Each facility is included in the cohort which includes its default's date. The CCF is the ratio of the increase in the exposure until the default day to the maximum possible exposure computed from the start of the cohort. The numerator indicates how much the exposure of the bank increased from the exposure at the start of the cohort prior to default. The denominator indicates the maximum increase in the exposure that could have happened during the cohort. As the default can occur at any time within the time window, the time interval between the start of window and the default is not fixed.

The CCF is given by the formula:

$$CCF(t_i) = \frac{EAD(t_d) - Exp(t_i)}{ExpMax(t_i) - Exp(t_i)}.$$

where,
$EAD(t_d)$: Exposure at the time default occurred;
$Exp(t_i)$: Exposure of the bank at the start of the time window prior to default;
$ExpMax(t_i)$: Maximum exposure that the bank can have with the counterparty at the start of the time window prior to default.

Advantages and disadvantages of the three above approaches can be summarized as follows.

Like for the estimation of LGD, the estimation of Credit Conversion Factors for nondefaulted exposures requires the identification of the main determinants or risk drivers (RD) of EAD. These are generally identified in the available literature (see

Table 6.1 Pros and cons of approaches to compute realized CCFs

	Advantages	**Disadvantages**
Fixed time horizon	Results are homogeneous, as they are computed on the same time horizon	Ignores defaulted loans with age lower than the horizon and anything happening in between (assumes that the only time a default can occur is the end of the horizon).
Variable time horizon	Better accuracy due to more observations	More data-intensive
Cohort	Considers that facilities can default at any time during the observation period	Results are less homogeneous as the horizons used are very different

for example Moral, 2011) as belonging to two main categories: type of facility and covenant. Also, certain characteristics of the borrower, like profitability, access to alternative financing and history of its relationship with the bank, may influence the EAD (Bos, 2005). Miu and Ozdemir (2005) investigate a sample of Canadian banks and analyse how EAD relates to industry type, risk rating, facility size and time variation of the exposure.

CCFs for nondefaulted exposures can be estimated using information on risk drivers. A bank can construct a look-up table by assigning defaulted exposures to pools on the basis of combination of EAD risk drivers and then compute the average CCFs of defaulted exposure pools to estimate the CCFs for the non-default exposures.

When using the fixed-horizon approach for estimating realized CCFs, the average CCF for a pool of defaulted exposures should be calculated computed from the individual realized CCFs. When using the cohort approach, the long-run average should be obtained by weighing the period-by-period means alongside the proportion of defaults occurring in each period. Nondefaulted exposures are then assigned an average CCF that corresponds to the relevant combination of risk drivers.

This approach may require a substantial amount of data and be therefore more suitable for treating retail exposures than others. If m is the number of risk drivers and k is the number of values that each can assume, the number of CCF pools will be k^m. On average, each pool will be of size $S=N/k^m$, where N is the total number of observations. In order to have S be sufficiently large, say 50, the total number of observed defaults will have to be at least $N=50 \times k^m$. Even with just 5 risk drivers and $k=2$, we have $N=50x32=1{,}600$. This number of defaults over a one-year horizon may be quite difficult to observe in most cases. Also, exposures may be distributed amongst pools in such a way that some pools contain no defaulted exposures at all, preventing the bank from computing the corresponding CCFs average.

In case of severe lack of data and/or highly specialized portfolios, some banks estimate CFF using expert judgement. This approach may sometimes be combined with the direct estimates discussed above, especially if one is striving for compliance with regulatory requirements, and it will be quite difficult to validate from a model design standpoint, as analysing the underlying reasons for assigning CCFs to exposures will not be straightforward to analyse.

CCFs can also be computed on the basis of the expected cash flows of the facility, in the cases where these cash flows can be reliably estimated. This can be done by simply using the cash flows that have been contractually agreed or combine those with an estimate based on historically observed flows.

Alternatively, a bank can use regression analysis to estimate CCFs for the non-defaulted exposures by considering risk drivers as independent variables and the realized CCFs as dependent variables. This model can be calibrated over the totality of the exposure data or over each individual pool of exposures. In a regression model, CCF is modelled as a function of RDs. In its simplest form, one can model CCF as a linear function of risk drivers RDs:

$$CCF = \beta_0 + RD_1\beta_1 + RD_2\beta_2 + \ldots + RD_n\beta_n$$

Of course, the relationship between the CCF and RDs might not be linear and a more advanced, nonlinear regression model could be required.

Finally, another way to deal with insufficient or unreliable internal data would be to use external information on defaults and recoveries in order to apply statistical models at various level of complexity. A key question both for developers and validators is of course to what extent the external benchmark is representative of the internal portfolio and specifically whether the external database contains enough information on the underlying facilities to ensure the estimated CCFs would be meaningful.

The validation of the EAD models design is complicated by the fact that they attempt to model factors that are in large part not only internal to the bank, but also specific to the portfolio and the individual facility. The complexity of EAD or CCF models is largely caused by their dependence on the contractual details of the underlying products and even to the specific relation with the borrower. That is probably why validation tools and techniques for EAD models are both less developed and less standardized than for PD or LGD models. Validation of EAD model design should therefore focus on the link between the specific facilities and the CCF estimates, how appropriate to the portfolio is the set-up of the model, as well as compliance with both regulatory and business requirements.

2 Model Output

The validation of EAD models output could, to a certain extent, rely on techniques similar to the ones used for PD and LGD models. In this sense, some test of portfolio stability should be carried out in order to verify the portfolio structure against the development sample, for instance by comparing the corresponding realized CCF distributions. Similarly, for models where risk drivers are used either just to segment the dataset or to construct a functional relationship via linear or non-linear regression, the predictive power of the risk drivers used can be analysed through both univariate and multivariate analysis.

In order, however, to test the predictive powers of an EAD model as a whole, some kind of back-testing and/or benchmarking procedure is required, in line with the analysis that is carried out for PD models. For example, one may compare predicted and observed CCF for each facility within a pool of defaulted positions. Alternatively, one may compare predicted CCFs with external sources, although, as already observed, this approach would be greatly complicated by the relation-specific nature of EAD behaviour.

Valvonis (2008), comparing the performance of fixed-horizon and cohort estimates for various types of retail portfolios, uses the following indicators of the accuracy of EAD predictions.

Absolute Accuracy

$$AA_t = \sum_{i=1}^{n} (EAD_t^{est,i} - EAD_t^{real,i})$$

where $EAD_t^{est,i}$ and $EAD_t^{real,i}$ are the estimated and observed exposure at default for facility i at time t.

Relative Accuracy

$$AR_t = \frac{\sum_{i=1}^{N} EAD_{i,t}^{est} (t_d - 1y) \le t \le t_d - \sum_{i=1}^{N} EAD_{i,t}^{real} (t_d - 1y) \le t \le t_d}{\sum_{i=1}^{N} EAD_{i,t}^{real} (t_d - 1y) \le t \le t_d} \cdot 100\%$$

where t_d is the time of default and where the sum of EADs (realized and estimated) are computed for all exposures that existed at time t and where no longer than one year prior to default.

CCF estimates can also be back-tested through a student t-test.

The tested hypotheses are:

H0: The prediction, CCFE is equal to the observation, CCFO.
H1: The prediction, CCFE is different from the observation, CCFO.

The confidence interval is constructed around the observed CCF for different confidence levels in the following way:

$$\text{Conf. int.(CCFO)} = \text{(CCFO)} \pm t_{N-1} \frac{S_O}{\sqrt{N}}$$

where:
t_{N-1} is the t distribution with N-1 degrees of freedom;
S_O is the standard deviation of CCF_O;
N is the number of observations.

The test is based on three assumptions: independence between observations, normal distribution of the average CCF and equal variance of the observed and predicted CCF. Maarse (2012) suggests that the t-test should include weights (the off-balance sheet value) because in the EAD calculation, the CCF factor is multiplied by the undrawn facility amount.

3 Data and other requirements

As mentioned above, EAD modelling is highly dependent on both default data and contractual-related information. It follows that minimum data requirements for the estimation of CCFs based on historical data should encompass all default events (both defaults and recovery date) as well as information on contracts and on exposures one year before default, at default and between default and write-off/ recovery (including credit limits, book values and drawn amounts).

A CCF model establishes a relationship between the customer's behaviour and a number of risk factors. Such factors, or risk drivers, need to be identified and collected. They should include both contract features (e.g. type of contract/ product type, time period after contract signature date, contractual conditions and covenants, time period before maximum disbursement request date, seniority, current utilisation, signature amount) and borrower's features (e.g. counterparty type, country, credit rating, sector or industry, financial ratios, balance sheet data).

From a regulatory compliance perspective, validators should focus on prudential regulatory compliance with the requirements explicitly stated in the Basel II framework documents, which by and large refer to potential losses that may be incurred. In BCBS (2006) paragraphs 308, 316 (incl. par. 82-89 as referenced by par. 316) and 474-478 contain the key requirements for EAD estimates. In particular, paragraph 474 states that the EAD estimate on an on-balance sheet exposure must be at least as large as the current drawn amount. No specific requirement is given on the inclusion of the interest and the fees income in the EAD estimates.

> *EAD for an on-balance sheet or off-balance sheet item is defined as the expected gross exposure of the facility upon default of the obligor. ... Banks estimates of EAD should reflect the possibility of additional drawings by the borrower up to and after the time a default event is triggered.* Par. 474
>
> *Advanced approach banks must assign an estimate of EAD for each facility. It must be an estimate of the long-run default-weighted average EAD for similar facilities and borrowers over a sufficiently long period of time.* Par. 475

The regulatory EAD is meant to capture the uncertainty that a potential default event would introduce into the total exposure of a facility. In principle, as a borrower approaches default, it is likely to increase the drawn amount on a facility as long as the facility limit that a bank has committed to permits. In turn, the bank is likely to take actions (i.e., executing covenants) to limit the exposure on the facility as per the terms of the contract. The EAD should capture the dynamics of such relationship between the bank and the borrower as the default event looms closer.

From a business point of view, validators should primarily be concerned with verifying that risk measures are unbiased and can be effectively used for business and risk management decisions. Risk measurements from this point of view would not necessarily be conservative and would reflect the institution's reasonable expectations regarding the economic values of products, portfolios or business decisions. For example, such measures may take into account the expected cash inflows (in addition to the losses) from products, or, pay more attention to estimation power of models to be able to discriminate risky counterparts, products, businesses from others.

Internal and external requirements are not mutually exclusive and overlap in several areas, but it may be quite challenging to fulfil all such requirements in the design of an EAD model. Nevertheless, validators should at least consider some basic business requirements relevant for EAD estimation. For example, the default of a counterpart may affect the bank's financial position by directly impacting the profit and loss account via a deduction in loan loss provisions (reflecting the expected loss or the best estimate of recovery) or indirectly through a reduction in revenues due to lost interest payments; also, following a liquidation, through the write-off of all or part of the assets from the bank's balance sheet. While the direct impacts on P/L and the balance sheet of the bank relate to the book value of the exposure and are contemplated in the Basel definitions, the reduction in revenues is a forward-looking measure which will be useful for pricing, economic capital and stress testing purposes.

Another element to be considered by EAD measures is the inter-dependency between the borrowers' credit quality (as expressed by the probability of default) and exposure (as expressed by the increase/decrease of EAD with deterioration of portfolio credit quality or under severe stress). Ideally, EAD should capture the likely changes in borrowers' drawdown behaviour as well as the bank's potential reaction when the borrower is in distressed conditions. This is important not only for computation of regulatory capital, but also for achieving a more accurate internal measure of economic capital. As borrowers under stressed economic conditions may be inclined to use their committed credit lines more aggressively than under normal conditions (Jacobs, 2008) a discrepancy may arise between the actual exposure under normal economic scenarios and under stressed scenarios. An EAD model incorporating the effects of such discrepancy may also lead to a bigger difference between the "expected" scenario loss and the "stress" scenario (tail) losses in an economic capital model or a stress-testing exercise.

An advanced EAD measure may also incorporate the impact of the macro-economic environment on CCF. For example, quantitative easing, reference rate reductions and other attempts by various central banks to enhance liquidity may influence the drawdown behaviour of borrowers and therefore the amount of undisbursed commitments on banks' loans. Among other factors, an EAD measure which can capture such effects would certainly allow more accurate estimation of economic capital and more reliable stress testing results.

Internal requirements may encompass risk-weighted asset, estimation of economic capital, calculation of general and specific provisions, the decision to extend credit, pricing, credit risk monitoring and so on. Additional requirements that emerge in the EAD context are typically related to the differentiation of best estimate and downturn EADs (the BCBS prescribes EADs to be calculated in a downturn scenario, whereas the impairment process is typically based on best estimate EADs in accordance with relevant accounting standards).

4 Conclusions

Exposure at Default (EAD) is an estimate reflecting the uncertainty (risk) around the size of the exposure that a bank faces. It is defined in the Basel Accords as the size of the credit risk exposure that the bank expects to face on a facility assuming that economic downturn conditions occur within a one-year time horizon and the associated borrower defaults on its obligations within that horizon. As such, EAD is not merely the current exposure that the bank faces today; it is an estimation of the total future exposure that the Bank would face in case of a default event under downturn conditions within the one-year time horizon.

EAD has so far been the least studied of the parameters required for internal rating models under the Basel regulatory framework. Nevertheless, a number of approaches exist that banks can use, depending on the effectiveness and efficiency of their processes, default data management especially. These range from expert-based approaches (which in the best cases rely on a combination of observation of realized CCF and managerial judgment) to look-up tables constructed on the basis of realized CCFs of appropriately categorized exposures; from models using the expected cash flow of the various facilities to regression models of various level of sophistication. In all these cases, validators face first the challenge of examining the modelled relationship between estimated CCFs and the available data and information, which may be hard to ascertain especially when expert judgment plays a key role. Furthermore, the relationship-specific nature of borrowers' behaviour as default approaches makes estimated CCFs highly dependent on the specificities of the individual facilities at the particular bank, thus greatly reducing the usefulness of external benchmarks. Back-testing is therefore the main tool at validators' disposal for quantitative analysis of the model and its outputs, which renders the quality of validation work equally data-dependent. Finding appropriate thresholds for accuracy ratios and hypothesis tests is one of the key further steps in validation research for this kind of model, and one that will benefit from the systematic accumulation of practical experience as supervisors place more rigorous and comprehensive requirements on A-IRB banks.

References

Araten, M. and Jacobs, M. Jr., "Loan Equivalents for Revolving Credits and Advised Lines," *The RMA Journal*, May 2001.

BCBS, Basel Committee on Banking Supervision, "International Convergence of Capital Measurement and Capital Standards," Basel, June 2006.

Bos, J. W. B., "Exposure at Default Validation," in *Studies on the Validation of Internal Rating Systems,* Basel Committee on Banking Supervision, WP N. 14, May 2005.

European Banking Authority (EBA), *Draft Regulatory Technical Standards On the specification of the assessment methodology for competent authorities regarding compliance of an institution with the requirements to use the IRB Approach in accordance with Articles 144(2), 173(3) and 180(3)(b) of Regulation (EU) No 575/2013,* EBA/CP/2014/36, 12 November 2014.

Hahn, R. and Reitz, S., "Possibilities of Estimating Exposures," in Engelmann, B. and Rauhmeier, R. (editors), *The Basel II Risk Parameters, Second Edition*, Springer, 2011.

Jacobs, M. Jr., "An Empirical Study of Exposure at Default," June 2008, available at SSRN: http://ssrn.com/abstract=1149407.

Maarse, B., "Backtesting Framework for PD, EAD and LGD," Master Thesis, Rabobank International Quantitative Risk Analytics, July 2012.

Miu, P. and Ozdemir, B., "Practical and Theoretical Challenges in Validating Basel Parameters: Key Learnings from the Experience of a Canadian Bank," *Journal of Credit Risk*, Vol. 1, No. 4, 2005.

Moral, G., "EAD Estimates for Facilities with Explicit Limits," in Engelmann, B. and Rauhmeier, R. (editors), *The Basel II Risk Parameters, Second Edition*, Springer, 2011.

Valvonis, V., "Estimating EAD for Retail Exposures for Basel II Purposes," *Journal of Credit Risk*, Vol. 4, No. 1, 79–109, Spring 2008.

References

Part III

Market Risk

7 | Value at Risk Models

Models for measuring market risk have a longer history and have been so far subject to more detailed and extensive scrutiny than credit risk models. This is certainly due to the fact that regulatory prescriptions have been in place for longer (BCBS, 1996), but it is also due to the nature of market risk and, as a consequence, of market risk models. Market risk factors are in fact, for the most part, observable, which is not, in general, the case for other types of risk, and historical time series are available that allow extensively for both calibration and testing. Furthermore, although this advantage is off-traded by the complexity of portfolios, market risk assessment can build on the results of pricing and valuation models, which are readily available for a large number of financial instruments.

Market risk can be defined as the risk of an increase or decrease in the market price of a financial instrument or portfolio, due to changes in stock prices, interest rates, credit spreads, foreign exchange rates, commodity prices, implied volatilities. Market risk measurement aims therefore at predicting the distribution of possible changes in value of a financial instrument over a given time horizon. Measures of market risk may range from distribution moments like volatility (standard deviation), skewness, kurtosis, to Value at Risk (VaR) (i.e., the maximum amount that can be lost over a given time horizon with a specified degree of confidence) to CVaR or Expected Shortfall, Tail VaR, Expected loss in the distribution tail, and so on.

Value at Risk (VaR) at confidence level α for a portfolio of financial instruments, can be defined as the inverse cumulative density function of the changes in portfolio values. Formally, let V_t be the portfolio value at time t, $\Delta V_{t+1} = V_{t+1} - V_t$ and $F_t(P) =$ $Probability(\Delta V_{t+1} \leq P)$ be the cumulative density function of ΔV. Then VaR is defined as follows:

$$VaR_\alpha = F_t^{-1}(\alpha) = \inf(P : F_t(P) = \alpha)$$

VaR is therefore the α-quantile of the inverse cumulative density function of ΔV, representing the larges loss that is expected to occur with probability $1-\alpha$.

Although by far the most widely used measure of financial risk, VaR is less than ideal both for theoretical reasons (it is not a coherent risk measure) and practical ones (it is defined in terms of a parameter, which is by and large arbitrary). A risk measure is called coherent (see Artzner *et al.*, 1999) if it satisfies the following five axioms (where $\rho(\cdot)$ is the risk measure; *X*, *Y* are the values of two portfolios; and *G* is the set of all portfolios).

i. Normalization

$$\rho(0)=0$$

The risk of holding no assets is zero.

ii. Translation Invariance

$$\rho(X+\alpha)=\rho(X)-\alpha$$

If the value of a portfolio is increased by a cash amount, the corresponding risk measure is decreased by the same amount.

iii. Subadditivity for all $X, Y \in G$

$$\rho(X+Y)\leq \rho(X)+\rho(Y)$$

The total risk of two portfolios is no larger than the sum of the risks of the individual portfolios (diversification principle).

iv. Positive homogeneity : for all $X \in G$ and $\lambda \in \Re$

$$\rho(\lambda X)=\lambda\rho(X)$$

An increase in the size of a portfolio causes a proportional increase in the corresponding risk measure.

v. Monotonicity : for all $X, Y \in G$ with $X \leq Y$,

$$\rho(X)\leq \rho(Y)$$

If the value of *X* is always lower than the value of *Y*, then the risk of *X* is less or equal than the risk of *Y*.

Alternative measures of risk are for example the Expected Shortfall or ES (see Cotter and Dowd, 2007), which can be defined as the average of the worst α% of the cases and can be specified, for a continuous loss distribution, by:

$$ES_\alpha = \frac{1}{\alpha}\int_0^\alpha VaR_p dp$$

Unlike VaR, the ES is sub-additive and coherent, but is similarly specified in terms of an arbitrary parameter α.

Another risk measure is the Spectral Risk Measure or SRM (see Acerbi, 2002) which can be defined as a weighted average where worse outcomes are included with larger weights or more formally as:

$$M_{\Phi}(X) = \int_0^1 \Phi_p F_X^{-1}(p)dp$$

where F_X is the cumulative distribution function for the portfolio X, and Φ_p is nonnegative ($\Phi_p \geq 0$ for all p), monotonic ($\Phi_{p1} \geq \Phi_{p2}$ if $p_1 < p_2$), normalized $\left(\int_0^1 \Phi_p dp = 1\right)$.

An advantage of spectral measures is the way in which they can be related to risk aversion, and particularly to a utility function, through the weights given to the possible portfolio returns. For instance, Cotter and Dowd (ibid) suggest the use of an exponential weighting function of the following form:

$$\Phi(p) = \frac{ke^{-k(1-p)}}{1-e^{-k}}$$

where the coefficient k represents the user's risk aversion so that the higher k, the steeper the exponential curve and the faster the rise of the weights with the size of the losses.

In the rest of this chapter we will focus on the validation of VaR models because they are by far the most widely used in the financial industry and because most of the approaches and observations discussed apply as well to other risk measures.

1 Model design

In designing a market risk model, the steps that are typically followed comprise the identification of the relevant risk factors, the estimation of a suitable multivariate distribution of the changes in the risk factors and the establishment of a functional relationship between changes in risk factors and changes in portfolio value (Wehn, 2010). The desired outcome is a univariate predictive distribution of the changes in portfolio value conditional on the risk factor changes. Measures are then extracted from the resulting distribution like α-quantiles for VaR, or weighted averages for the expected shortfall.

In the first modelling step, effective selection of risk factors requires knowledge of the portfolio and products in order to maximize not just their explanatory power, but also the operational efficiency of the resulting model. This leads to limiting the number of factors either because it is impossible to consider them all (e.g., we cannot build a model dependent on each individual point of the yield curve), or because the resulting model may be too complex and statistical and numerical analysis too costly. Large trading portfolios may easily consist of thousands of individual exposures and be exposed to thousands of market factors at the same time. Fully modelling their joint distribution on a daily basis (and in some cases even more often) may exceed the computing power of the largest financial institutions. Furthermore, factors should be liquid and proxies are used when relevant historical data are missing.

Historical observation of risk factors show a number of characteristics that have an influence on the reliability of the estimated joint distribution, including clustering of volatility, leptokurtosis (or fat tails), heteroscedasticity, time varying correlations.

The relationship between risk factor and portfolio values is naturally given by the characteristics of the financial instruments of which the portfolio is composed and is ideally performed through full evaluation of the individual positions. However, as mentioned above, the computational burden of fully re-evaluating all the positions often forces practitioners to model the factor/value relationship in an approximate way, usually through a parametric or semi-parametric model. This introduces an estimation risk that needs to be considered by validators when reviewing the model.

One broad way to classify VaR approaches is between those that make specific assumptions about the functional form of the probability distribution of risk factors (parametric approaches) and those who do not (nonparametric) approaches. The most basic of parametric approaches is the variance-covariance approach, which is based on the assumption that changes in risk factors and portfolio values are normally distributed. By leveraging on the properties of the normal distribution, VaR can be easily computed from variances and covariances of the portfolio positions. Of course the assumption of normality runs against the evidence that most assets' returns are fat-tailed and may cause substantial underestimation of the true risk of a portfolio, especially if it contains positions that are nonlinear in the risk factors.

Another family of parametric approaches relies on Taylor series expansions and on the use of sensitivities (also known as "greeks") to approximate the changes in portfolio values. Within this category we can distinguish between first-order or Delta approximations and second-order or Delta-Gamma approximations. The first one uses a first order Taylor expansion where changes in portfolio values are expressed through the first derivatives with respect to risk factors and time. The second one uses a second-order series expansion with respect to risk factors.

Formally, the Delta approximation can be written as follows:

$$\Delta V(\Delta F_{t+1}, X_t) \approx \frac{\partial V(\Delta F_{t+1}, X_t, t)}{\partial \Delta F_{t+1}} \Delta F_{t+1} + \frac{\partial V(\Delta F_{t+1}, X_t, t)}{\partial t} \Delta t$$

and the Delta-Gamma approximation can be written as:

$$\Delta V(\Delta F_{t+1}, X_t) \approx \frac{\partial V(\Delta F_{t+1}, X_t, t)}{\partial \Delta F_{t+1}} \Delta F_{t+1} + 0.5 \frac{\partial^2 V(\Delta F_{t+1}, X_t, t)}{\partial \Delta F_{t+1} \partial \Delta F_{t+1}} \Delta F_{t+1} + \frac{\partial V(\Delta F_{t+1}, X_t, t)}{\partial t} \Delta t$$

While the Delta approximation is attractive because it is simple and easy to compute, the Delta-Gamma approximation trades some simplicity for the ability to (partially) capture non-linearity. Pritsker (2000) analyses the accuracy of several variations of Taylor-based models, namely the Delta-Gamma-Delta method, the Delta-Gamma-Minimization Method and the Delta-Gamma-Monte Carlo method. He observes that the latter, besides making use of all the information conveyed by the Delta-Gamma approximation on the cumulative distribution function, can be applied without the assumption of jointly normally distributed changes in the risk factors that are required in the other methods to be able to compute the moments of the Taylor series.

A second group of approaches is based on the use of simulation techniques, i.e., on drawing instances of ΔF either from a given distribution or from historical instances of ΔF which are believed to have the same statistical properties as future instances of ΔF. The latter approach, called historical simulation, is both simple and flexible to implement. It does not make assumptions about the shape of the distribution and can be implemented either with full valuation of the positions or using first or second-order sensitivities. However, it does make the crucial assumption that history will repeat itself and its performance is therefore dependent on both relevance and availability of historical data. On one side, it is crucial to have a long enough historical data series in order to be able to account for potentially severe movements, but on the other side, a too-long estimation period may cause recent, and presumably more relevant data, to be given insufficient weight in the computation.

The other important no-parametric method is Monte Carlo simulation, where market factors are assumed to follow specific stochastic processes whose parameters are estimated on the basis of historical data. The corresponding distributions are used to generate many (usually thousands) instances of positions' values which are eventually combined in a joint distribution of returns. Therefore, Monte Carlo simulation generates not just one quantile, but the entire distribution of changes in portfolio values without making normality any assumption. It can also account for any non-linearity in the portfolio to the extent that positions are fully re-evaluated for each stochastic draw of risk factors. This, however, is also a source of weakness in the approach as it implies on one hand that implementation is very expensive, especially in terms of computational time, and on the other that the use of complex pricing models[1] and of specific distributional assumptions about the risk factors increases both operational and model risk. A comprehensive review of Value at Risk methods can be found Dowd (2006) and in Damodaran (2007).

2 Model output

Despite the limitations discussed above, VaR is by far the most widely used and accepted (by regulators as well) method for market risk measurement. The output of a VaR model will be therefore affected not only by the intrinsic limitations of VaR as a risk measure, but also by the assumptions and approximations required to make it feasible for practical purposes and by the fact that risk predictions are based on historical data, which do not necessarily reflect the future evolution of the markets. Although the actual distribution of changes in portfolio values cannot be observed, VaR can be seen as a percentile of the clean[2] P&L distribution. Therefore, unlike the case of credit risk discussed in Part 2, value at risk output can be effectively back-tested by systematically comparing the model estimates to the actual profit and losses, and analyse whether, over a given time horizon, losses larger than VaR are consistent with the relevant confidence level.

According to Cristoffersen (1998) the accuracy of VaR estimates can be tested by determining if the probability of exceeding the estimated VaR at a confidence level of α is precisely α and if the exceptions are independently distributed over time as a Bernoulli variable. The first condition is called unconditional coverage property and the second independence property. For example, if the confidence level selected for calculating daily VaR is 99%, we expect the daily VaR to be exceeded once in every 100 days on average. The frequency of such exceptions is called coverage and an unconditional coverage test is a hypothesis test with the null hypothesis that the actual frequency of exceptions is equal to the expected one. On the other hand, exceptions, even when in the expected number, may exhibit clustering, thus indicating that the model does not accurately capture changes in the risk profile of the portfolio over time. If a VaR model produces exceptions that are also independent of each other, the probability, for instance, of observing an exception after already having already observed one, may be higher than what is implied by the estimated VaR, which would therefore be inaccurate and lead to potentially prolonged periods of underestimation of the true level of exposure. Needless to say, when a VaR model satisfies one property and not the other, it should still be considered inaccurate. If only the independence property is satisfied, the model is on average underestimating the actual exposure because overall actual violations are in excess of the estimated level. If only the unconditional coverage property is fulfilled, the model is still inaccurate, as risk is likely underestimated whenever there is a cluster of exceptions. Tests of conditional coverage examine at the same time whether exceptions are in the correct number and independent from each other.

One of the first proposed VaR back-tests is Kupiec's (1995) "proportion of failures" (PF) unconditional coverage test which compares actual VaR exceptions to predicted ones over *N* observations.

$$POF = 2log\left(\left(\frac{1-\alpha*}{1-\alpha}\right)^{N-I(\alpha)}\left(\frac{\alpha*}{\alpha}\right)^{I(\alpha)}\right)$$

where

$$\alpha* = \frac{1}{N}I(\alpha)$$

$$I(\alpha) = \sum_{t=1}^{N} I_t(\alpha)$$

and is distributed as χ^2 with one degree of freedom.

If the number of *exceptions* α^* *is equal to* α then the POF test takes the value zero, indicating no violations with respect to the VaR estimate. As the number of *VaR* violations grows beyond α, the test increases pointing to the inaccuracy of the estimates. The null hypothesis is rejected if $POF > \chi^2_1$ or if the *p*-value = $P(LR > \chi^2_1)$ is less than α.

Kupiec's is a likelihood-ratio test, i.e., a test that looks at the maximum probability of a result under the two alternative hypotheses. The test is based on the value of a ratio where the numerator is the maximum probability of the observed result under the null hypothesis, and the denominator is the maximum probability of the observed result under the alternative hypothesis. The smaller the resulting ratio, the larger the value of the statistic. If the value becomes too large compared to the critical value of χ^2 distribution, the null hypothesis is rejected.

Perignon and Smith (2008) have suggested a multivariate generalization of Kupiec's test. They select a set of coverage probabilities (confidence levels) and associated buckets (for instance 0-1%, 1-5%, 5-10%, 10-100%), then they compare the expected frequency of observations X(t) falling in each bucket (1%, 4%, 5%, 90% in this case) to the observed frequency. The associated test statistic is asymptotically chi-square distributed with K-1 degrees of freedom. This approach is similar to the Hosmer-Lemeshow test discussed in Chapter 4 for the calibration of default probabilities.

A particularly relevant case of unconditional coverage test is the one specified by regulators under the 1996 amendment to the Basel Accord for internal VaR measures. These measures are required to report 10-day VaR at a 99% confidence level, which is usually computed as a one-day VaR at a 99% confidence level and

Table 7.1 Back-testing framework for internal models (BCBS, 1996)

Zone	Number of exceptions	Increase in scaling factor	Cumulative probability3
Green Zone	0	0.00	8.11%
	1	0.00	28.58%
	2	0.00	54.32%
	3	0.00	75.81%
	4	0.00	89.22%
Yellow Zone	5	0.40	95.88%
	6	0.50	98.63%
	7	0.65	99.60%
	8	0.75	99.89%
	9	0.85	99.97%
Red Zone	10	1.00	99.99%

then scaled by the square root of 10. Then the output has to be back-tested quarterly on the most recent 250 days of data. Depending on the number of exceptions observed, the VaR model is then classified according to the following table (BCBS, 1996) where, to increasing number of exceptions correspond an increase in the scaling factor applied by national regulators to calculate market risk capital charges above the base level of 3.

The scaling factor or multiplier is increased to 4 if the VaR measure falls in the red zone and in general is solely determined by the number of times the 1% *VaR* has been violated in the past 250 trading days. This approach is relevant because it is mandatory for all financial institutions using an internal model to determine their capital adequacy for market risk, but from a theoretical point of view suffers from a number of drawbacks.

- The approach ignores any dependence amongst exceptions, and as such is liable to accept a model that underestimates risk over subsets of the observation period.
- It does not formally test a hypothesis, as the three zones are set intuitively on the basis of the corresponding probabilities.
- By the same token, it does not really provide a distinction between bad and good models, but rather assigns them a "grade" to which growing level of capital and scrutiny are attached.
- The mechanism may also potentially deter financial institutions from sailing too close to the wind and thus encourage a conservative VaR measure that, although likely overestimated, would ensure that the traffic light test is safely passed. This is probably due to the fact that higher capital charges are considered preferable to the consequences (in penalties, inspections, time and resources spent in reporting to supervisors) of failing the test.

- On the other hand, it should be noted that the power of back-testing grows with the number of observations (Dowd, 2006) and the one-year time horizon required under the Basel Accord is such that at, say, a 99% confidence level it takes strong evidence to reject a model.
- Finally, a limitation of unconditional coverage tests, as well as of the regulatory-mandated version, is that they ignore the time at which the exceptions occur.

Tests of conditional coverage analyse not just the frequency of VaR exceptions but also their timing, i.e., they look for clustering of exceptions or autocorrelations in loss percentiles in order to check whether exceptions are independent. Christoffersen (1998) proposes an interval forecast (IF) test for unconditional coverage and independence that uses a likelihood ratio test that looks for consecutive exceptions and verifies whether, besides the expected coverage, the probability of an exception depends or not on whether an exception occurred the previous day.

Let us denote with n_{01} and n_{11} the number of days an exception is observed after either no exception or one exception has been observed on the previous day, and with n_{00} and n_{10} the number of days no exception is observed after either no exception or one exception has been observed on the previous day. Then, if p_0 is the probability of an exception conditional on not having observed an exception the previous day and p_1 is the probability of an exception conditional on having observed an exception the previous day, those are given by:

$$p_0 = \frac{n_{01}}{n_{00} + n_{01}}$$

$$p_1 = \frac{n_{11}}{n_{10} + n_{11}}$$

$$p = \frac{n_{01} + n_{11}}{n_{00} + n_{01} + n_{10} + n_{11}}$$

If exceptions are independent, we should have $p_0 = p_1$. The likelihood ratio:

$$IF = -2ln\left(\frac{(1-p)^{n_{00}+n_{10}}\, p^{n_{01}+n_{11}}}{(1-p_0)^{n_{00}}\, p_0^{n_{01}}\, (1-p_1)^{n_{10}}\, p_1^{n_{11}}}\right)$$

is also approximately chi-squared distributed with one degree of freedom. Hence the null hypothesis is rejected if $IF > \chi^2_1$ or if the p-value = $P(IF > \chi^2_1)$ is less than α.

For instance, the null hypothesis is rejected at the .05 significance level if $IF \geq 3.841$ (the 0.95th quantile of the χ^2_1 distribution) and at the .01 significance level if $IF \geq 6.635$ (the 0.99th quantile of the χ^2_1 distribution). The main limitation of this test is that it checks not independency as such, but frequency of consecutive exceptions. These may still be completely absent without the exceptions being independent and the test would not detect it. This independence test can be combined with Kupiec's POF-test to obtain a joint test that examines both properties, the correct failure rate and independence of exceptions, i.e. conditional coverage. The statistics *POF+IF* is also approximately χ^2 distributed, with two degrees of freedom, as it contains two LR-statistics. If the value of the resulting statistic at a given confidence level is higher than the corresponding quantile of χ^2 distribution, the model is rejected.

Campbell (2005) recommends against the use of joint tests on the grounds that the advantage of being able to detect whether a model violates either the coverage or the independence property is offset by the lower power the joint tests have to detect whether a model violates only one of the properties. For example, an independence test has a greater power to detect a violation of the independence property than a joint test.

Although VaR is usually measured at a given confidence level, there is no reason to limit our analysis to a single VaR level to see if unconditional coverage and independence properties hold. As VaR measures the quantiles of the distribution of changes in portfolio values, it makes sense to ask whether the entire distribution to which it refers is a good predictor of the observed Profit and Loss distribution. A distribution test is a goodness-of-fit tests that tries to assess how well the distribution on which VaR is based approximates the observed one. One basic approach to do this is to examine how well the VaR measure estimates various quantiles, say the 0.99, 0.975, 0.95, 0.90, 0.80, 0.70, 0.50 and 0.25. If the model adequately describes the portfolio distribution then, for instance, the 1% VaR should be violated 1% of the time, the 5% VaR should be violated 5% of the time, the 10% VaR should be violated 10% of the time and so on. Any VaR exception at any level of confidence should also be independent from any other at any other level. Crnkovic and Drachman (1997), Diebold, Gunther and Tay (1998) as well as Berkowitz (2001) have suggested back-tests based on multiple VaR levels.

Let $X(t) = F(Y(t))$ where F is the P&L cumulative distribution function produced by the VaR model and $Y(t)$ is the P&L on day t. Each quantile of the probability distribution corresponding to an observation, Y_{t+1} provides a measure of the magnitude of the realized P&L. If the distribution provided by the model accurately reflects the actual P&L it should exhibit properties of uniformity and independence. Uniformity, because VaR at a confidence level of α should be violated α times (which is equivalent to the unconditional coverage property discussed above) and independence because a violation of the estimated VaR level at a given percentile on one day should give no information on a violation at another percentile the following day (which is equivalent to the independence property discussed above). Therefore, as in the case of the single VaR measure, we can test coverage and independence of the estimated distribution, either separately or jointly.

Pearson's Q test is a goodness-of-fit test that can be used to verify if a given distribution is a good approximation of an empirically observed one. Given a partition of the distribution quantile range in n bins $[l_i, u_i]$, $i=1,2,\ldots n$, and the corresponding frequency of VaR exceptions[4] in each bin of the partition f_i, Pearson's statistics are given by:

$$Q = \sum_{i=1}^{n} \frac{(f_i - D(u_i - l_i))^2}{D(u_i - l_i)}$$

where D is the total number of observations (days). If the model is accurate, the test is approximately chi squared distributed with $n - 1$ degrees of freedom.

One needs to be careful, however, in using distribution tests in validation. A given model may be expressly designed to estimate the risk of extreme losses, by, for instance, making certain assumptions about the functional form of the distribution function, but perform badly when several quantiles over the entire distribution are examined.

Finally Lopez (1999) suggests a test focussing on the magnitude of the exceptions rather than simply on their frequency by using a function of the observed P&L and on the corresponding VaR. Such a loss function may, for instance, be constructed by computing the difference (when positive) between the observed P&L and the estimated VaR, and then comparing such difference to an appropriate benchmark. This approach is attractive because it provides the opportunity to estimate the size of the loss associated with VaR exceptions and hence make a more nuanced assessment of the model, but it requires at the same time that the validator is able to compare each value of the loss function to an "expected" value of the P&L. This in turn requires assumptions on the distribution of the P&L, which will have to be separately tested lest the validator could not distinguish between a test failure due to an inaccurate VaR and one due to an inappropriate modelling of the P&L.

When a model fails a back test it may of course indicate either a design or an implementation flaw, with the latter potentially related to data, coding, parametrization and so on. From a validator point of view, however, the problem is always whether a model is overall fit for purpose and not just whether a certain test has been passed or not. In particular, provided that the model design and conceptual assumptions have been thoroughly analysed and that we are comfortable with their soundness, failure of back-testing may be addressed by systematically multiplying the VaR measures for a fixed amount. Such an amount can be obtained by trial and error by repeatedly back-testing scaled-up VaR measures, or by computing, where possible, confidence intervals for the VaR measures. In the case of Monte Carlo approaches, for example, we can compute confidence intervals to measure the accuracy of VaR measures both in absolute terms and for comparing the performance of different models (Pritsker, 2000) and get an indication of what kind of scaling would be necessary to conservatively correct the results of a model that failed the back test.

A trade-off also exists between the confidence level and the reliability of back-testing as the higher the confidence level the smaller the number of exceptions and the less reliable as a result is the test. It is therefore advisable to supplement a 99% confidence level with, for instance, a 95% one, which gives a lower rate of type 2 error (accepting an incorrect model) for a given rate of type 1 error (rejecting a correct model).

3 Regulatory requirements

The 1996 amendment to the Basel Accord requires financial institutions employing an internal model for estimating their regulatory capital requirement for market risk to compute the maximum loss over 10 trading days at a 99% confidence level, subject to qualitative and quantitative requirements. As the first kind of model to be allowed by the Basel Committee to be developed internally and used to compute regulatory capital, it is no surprise that regulatory requirements are detailed and extensive. We will examine here those that are of more direct concern from a validation point of view.

Besides the general criteria that apply to all kind of internal model, conceptual soundness, integrity, sufficient skilled staff and good accuracy track record, Banks must fulfil a number of requirements that have a specific relevance to the development and maintenance of a Value at Risk model, but may also influence the level of the multiplicative scaling factor discussed in the previous section in relation to the traffic light test. In principle, the minimum amount of three for the factor is reserved for those institutions that meet the criteria in full. Such requirements are broadly classified under the two categories of qualitative and quantitative.

Qualitative standards

A financial institution should have an independent function tasked with the initial and on-going validation of internal models, which should include regular back-testing as well as a regular stress testing program, and whose reports should be read at a sufficiently senior level in the hierarchy to allow for the appropriate actions (including the reduction of positions) to be taken. The internal model should be adequately documented, and its use should not be limited to regulatory capital, but should be integrated in day-to-day risk management and in particular, it should be actively used in limit-setting and monitoring. Finally, the whole risk measurement system should be regularly reviewed by the bank's internal audit function. The most important qualitative requirements pertain to the choice of risk factors, and they aim at ensuring that they capture the risks of all trading positions. In particular, that all factors that are used in pricing are also included as risk factors in the value-at-risk model. Exceptions must be justified to the satisfaction of its supervisor. VaR models should also ensure that they capture nonlinearities for options and that other derivatives products are captured, including correlation risk and basis risk. Moreover, whenever a proxy is employed, for instance an equity index in lieu of a position in an individual stock, they must show a good track record of approximating the actual position held. The following table summarizes the key requirements for the choice of risk factors.

Table 7.2 Qualitative requirements

Risk Factor	Requirements
Interest rates	• Yield curves must be estimated through a generally accepted approach (e.g. through forward rates of zero coupon yields); should be divided into maturity segments in order to capture variation in the volatility of rates along the yield curve; with one risk factor for each maturity segment. • For material exposures, yield curves should be modelled using a minimum of six risk factors. More complex portfolios and trading strategies should warrant a greater number of risk factors. • Separate risk factors to capture spread risk, including separate yield curves for nongovernment fixed-income instruments (for instance, swaps or municipal securities) or estimating the spread over government rates at various points along the yield curve.
Foreign exchange rates	• Risk factors corresponding to the exchange rate between the domestic currency and each foreign currency in which the bank has a significant exposure.
Equity prices	• Risk factors corresponding to each of the equity markets or to each sector of the overall equity market, or to the volatility of individual equity issues in which the bank holds significant positions. • Positions in individual securities or in sector indices could be expressed in "beta-equivalents" relative to the above indexes.
Commodity prices	• Risk factors corresponding to each of the commodity markets in which the bank holds significant positions. • One risk factor for each commodity price to which the bank is exposed. • When aggregate positions are small, one might use a single risk factor for a relatively broad sub-category of commodities (for instance, a single risk factor for all types of oil). • For more active trading, the model must also take account of variation in the "convenience yield" between derivatives positions such as forwards and swaps and cash positions in the commodity.

No particular type of model is prescribed, and the banks enjoy considerable flexibility in developing their internal VaR models, and insofar as the models used capture all the material risks run by banks, they can choose to compute VaR based on, for example, variance-covariance matrices, historical simulations, or Monte Carlo simulations. Nevertheless, certain minimum standards need to be followed for the purpose of calculating the capital charge. Such standards could be made more stringent by local supervisors, but in their standard form they essentially require banks to compute VaR on their trading portfolios with a 99% confidence using an instantaneous price shock equivalent to a 10-day movement in prices, meaning that the minimum "holding period" is assumed to be ten trading days. Shorter holding periods may be used and then scaled up to ten days by the square root of time. On the other hand, sample periods of historical data over which VaR is computed have to be at least one year long and need to be updated at least quarterly, unless supervisors require the use of shorter periods, for instance in periods of higher volatility. In addition, internal VaR models must capture *non-linearity in* options positions and ultimately apply a full 10-day price shock to options positions or positions that display option-like characteristics.

A stressed VaR measure should be computed also based on the 10-day, 99th percentile, one-tailed confidence level, but calibrated to historical data from a continuous 12-month period of significant financial stress, as approved by regulators. Again, different techniques might be used to translate the model used for value-at-risk into one that delivers a stressed value-at-risk. The BCBS (2011) suggests for instance the use of antithetic data, or applying absolute rather than relative volatilities.

The capital requirement is expressed as the sum of the higher of its previous day's VaR and an average of the daily value-at-risk measures on each of the preceding sixty business days, multiplied by a multiplication factor, plus the higher of its latest available stressed value-at-risk number and an average of the stressed value-at-risk numbers calculated over the preceding sixty business days multiplied by a multiplication factor. The following table summarizes the key quantitative requirements.

The multiplication factors m_c and m_s used for the calculations of capital requirements are set at a minimum level of 3 for each of them, subject to the decision of local supervisory authorities who can raise them up to 4 on the basis of their assessment of the quality of the bank's risk management system. In particular, the assessment will take into account only back-testing of VaR and not of stressed VaR.

Table 7.3 Quantitative requirements

Frequency of calculation	**Daily**
Confidence level	99% one-tailed
Time horizon / holding period	Min. 10 days, VaR can be scaled up from shorter periods.
Sample period	Min. 1 year. For weighting schemes, weighted average time lag of individual observations of minimum 6 months.
Frequency of datasets update	Min. every three months
Empirical correlations	Allowed for broad risk categories (e.g. interest rates, exchange rates, equity prices and commodity prices, including related options volatilities in each risk factor category). Subject to supervisory approval across broad risk factor categories.
Options	• Must capture nonlinear price characteristics. • Expected to ultimately move towards a full 10-day price shock to options positions or positions that display option-like characteristics. • Must have a set of risk factors that captures the ***volatilities of the rates and prices*** underlying option positions, i.e. vega risk. • Detailed specifications of the relevant volatilities required for large and/or complex options portfolios should measure the volatilities of options positions broken down by different maturities.
Stressed VaR	Based on the 10-day, 99th percentile, one-tailed confidence interval value-at-risk measure of the current portfolio, with model inputs calibrated to historical data from a continuous 12-month period of significant financial stress relevant to the bank's portfolio (e.g. a 12-month period relating to significant losses in 2007/2008).
Capital requirement	$K = \{VaR_{t-1}; m_c VaR_{avg}\} + \{sVaR_{t-1}; m_s sVaR_{avg}\}$ where: VaR_{t-1} is the previous day *VaR*; VaR_{avg} is the average of the daily VaR over the preceding 60 business days; *SVaR* is the previous day stressed *VaR*; VaR_{avg} is the average of the daily sVaR over the preceding 60 business days; m_c and m_s are supervisory-set multiplicative factors.

4 Conclusions

We have examined some of the issues surrounding the validation of Value at Risk models by looking at some key modelling approaches and their advantages and disadvantages, as well as to the main statistical tools used to test the outputs of VaR models. We focussed our attention on VaR because it is by far the most popular risk measurement approach and because its usage is a key regulatory requirement, but we surveyed some of the characteristics that make it a less than ideal choice for risk measurement and also reviewed some of the most widely used alternatives. Following the 2008-09 financial crisis, it is widely acknowledged amongst academics, practitioners and supervisors alike that a best-practice risk assessment system should rely on a full range of risk measures including, but not limited to Value at Risk. Besides these well-known theoretical shortcomings, Value at Risk models rely on historical data on one side and on a combination of approximations and assumptions on the other, thereby making the systematic assessment of their accuracy a fundamental component of modern risk management practice.

Validators should remember that every test has its limitations and in particular that the regulatory-mandated traffic-light test is not, strictly speaking, a hypothesis test, but merely a common sense mapping between levels of unconditional coverage and potentially conservative scalar adjustments. Therefore, they should also employ a combination of tests in order to verify the relevant properties of the results, possibly not just on the single quantile required by regulation, but on the rest of the distribution as well. Model performance should be validated based on usage, hence, for instance, if the model is used for stress testing then its performance in stress scenarios should be assessed too. Also, model performance may not be the same at every level of usage, and hence it should be tested at multiple levels (product, desk, trading area, the entire firm) including, if possible, testing both the "clean" and the "dirty" P&L.

The current regulatory framework uses a traffic light approach derived from Kupiec's (1995) proportion of failures test, but also on a combination of qualitative and quantitative requirements that are intended to foster the robustness and integrity of the risk measurement system. While the traffic light approach is far from being able to comprehensively test the reliability and accuracy of a VaR estimate, the structure and content of the additional qualitative and quantitative regulatory requirements highlight the importance of ensuring that the models fulfil not just a simple statistical property on their results, but also that, from design to development and from implementation to use the modelling process is appropriately governed and controlled.

Notes

1. Pricing models used for market risk purposes should be validated to similar standards as models used for marking to market, and the validation should encompass a theoretical review of the model, a review of the key assumptions, a comparison to alternative models (including models used for valuation if different and a review of their implementation.
2. The term "clean" P&L in this context refers to the fact that, although VaR is computed as if the portfolio were constant over the holding period, in practice, trading portfolio

positions change during the day. The resulting P&L will therefore generally include fees and commissions, as well as the results of trades that were not considered in the VaR calculation. Depending on how relevant such trades are with respect to the total (or how actively traded the portfolio is on a daily basis), one might want to eliminate (clean) them from the P&L before back-testing. Alternatively, one might perform back-tests on both the "clean" and "dirty" P&L and, in case of significantly different results, investigate further the risk of these intraday trades.

3. Probability of achieving up to the corresponding number of exceptions.
4. For instance, the number of exceptions occurring in the [0.05,1.00] bin is the number of times a loss occurs that exceeds the 5% VaR.

References

Acerbi, C., "Spectral Measures of Risk: A Coherent Representation of Subjective Risk Aversion," *Journal of Banking and Finance*, Vol. 26, No. 7, 1505–1518, 2002.

Artzner, P., Delbaen, F., Eber, J.-M. and Heath, D., "Coherent Measures of Risk," *Mathematical Finance*, Vol. 9, 203–228, 1999.

Basel Committee on Banking Supervision, "Amendment to the Capital Accord to Incorporate Market Risks," Basel, January 1996.

Basel Committee on Banking Supervision, "Supervisory Framework for the Use of 'Backtesting' in Conjunction with the Internal Models Approach to Market Risk Capital Requirements," Basel, January 1996.

Basel Committee on Banking Supervision, "Revision to the Basel II Market Risk Framework," Basel, February 2011.

Berkowitz, J., "Testing Density Forecasts With Applications to Risk Management," *Journal of Business and Economic Statistics*, Vol. 19, 465–474, 2001.

Campbell, S. D., "A Review of Backtesting and Backtesting Procedures," *Finance and Economics Discussion Series*, Divisions of Research & Statistics and Monetary Affairs, Federal Reserve Board, Washington, D.C., 2005, 21.

Christoffersen, P., "Evaluating Interval Forecasts," *International Economic Review*, Vol. 39, 841–862, 1998.

Cotter, J. and Dowd, K., *Evaluating the Precision of Estimators of Quantile-Based Risk Measures*, MPRA Paper 3504, University Library of Munich, Germany, 2007.

Crnkovic, C. and Drachman, J., "Quality Control," in *VaR: Understanding and Applying Value-at-Risk*, Risk Publications, London, 1997.

Damodaran, A., *Strategic Risk Taking: A Framework for Risk Management*, Pearson Education, 2007.

Diebold, F. X., Gunther, T. and Tay, A., "Evaluating Density Forecasts with Applications to Financial Risk Management," *International Economic Review*, Vol. 39, 863–883, 1998.

Dowd, K., "Retrospective Assessment of Value-at-Risk", in Ong, M. (editor), *Risk Management: A Modern Perspective*, Elsevier, 2006, 183–202.

Dowd, K., "A Moments-based Procedure for Evaluating Risk Forecasting Models", in Christodoulakis, G. and Satchell, S. (editors), *The Analytics of Risk Model Validation*, Academic Press, 2008.

Holton, G. A., *Value at Risk: Theory and Practice*, Academic Press, 2003.

Kupiec, P., "Techniques for Verifying the Accuracy of Risk Management Models," *Journal of Derivatives*, Vol. 3, 73–84, 1995.

Lopez, J. A., "Regulatory Evaluation of Value-at-Risk Models," *Journal of Risk*, Vol. 1, 37–64, 1999.

Morini, M., *Understanding and Managing Model Risk*, Wiley, 2011.

Perignon, C. and Smith, D.R., "A New Approach to Comparing VaR Estimation Methods," *The Journal of Derivatives*, Vol. 16, No. 2, 54–66, Winter 2008.

Pritsker, M., "Evaluating Value-at-Risk Methodologies: Accuracy versus Computational Time," in Gibson, R. (editor), *Model Risk: Concepts, Calibration and Pricing*, Risk Books, 2000.

Satchell, S., "The Validation of Equity Portfolio Risk Models," in Christodoulakis, G. and Satchell, S. (editors), *The Analytics of Risk Model Validation*, Academic Press, 2008.

Wehn, C., "Market Risk Modelling: Approaches to Assessing Model Adequacy," in Rösch, D. and Scheule, H. (editors), *Model Risk: Identification, Measurement and Management*, Risk Books, 2010.

8 Interest Rate Risk on the Banking Book

Exposure to changes in interest rates is a fundamental feature of most banking activities, and it is inherently linked to their maturity transformation role. Interest rate risk on the banking book (IRRBB) is defined as *"the current or perspective risk to the bank's capital and earnings arising from adverse movements in the interest rates that affect the institution's banking book positions"* (BCBS, 2015). A financial institution's banking book is composed of all assets that are not actively traded and that are meant to be held until they mature, while those in the trading book are traded on the market and valued accordingly. The different regulatory and accounting treatment of the banking and trading book is considered one of the compounding factors of the 2008-09 financial crisis as banks shifted substantial assets (in particular the infamous collateralized debt obligations) from the banking to the trading book to take advantage of lower capital requirements. Consequently, national and international regulatory authorities have reviewed and modified the treatment of the trading and the banking book, with the latter, at the time of writing, still the subject of consultation, in particular on the issue of capital requirement under Pillar 1 of the Basel framework (BCBS, 2015 ibid.).

Interest rate risk on the banking book arises from a gap in the maturity and repricing dates of both assets and liabilities (repricing risk); from imperfect hedging, for example difference in repricing of otherwise mirroring instruments (basis risk); from embedded optionality, such as prepayment options on mortgages, withdrawing options on deposits, caps and floors on variable rate loans; from asymmetric movements in interest rates at different maturities (yield curve risk). Many features of the banking book positions may influence the interest rate exposure, from the different amortization structures (bullet, installments, annuities), to unscheduled disbursements and drawdowns, redemptions, prolongations, or embedded options, which may be part of many different types of credit facilities. For retail banks, savings and current accounts and short-term deposits are a key source of funding whose contractual maturity will not in general reflect the actual expected cash flow pattern. Bond issues may contain options which might be sensitive to changes in interest rates, and loan commitments may also exhibit option-like features, sometimes with previously agreed interest rates conditions.

Since assets on the banking book are held to maturity, modelling their exposure to interest rates requires the estimation of uncertain cash flows over a long horizon for very different items on both the liabilities and assets sides. This uncertainty is compounded by the fact that many banking products incorporate various types of optionality and do not have specific maturity or repricing dates, which in turn requires assumptions on the customers' behaviour and on the repricing speed and pattern of several classes of assets and liabilities. Such assumptions may turn out to be incorrect or may hold only in part; for instance, depositors may behave as assumed, but interest rates may change unexpectedly. The consequent model risk will be larger the longer the time horizon over which the assumptions are applied. For instance, Préfontaine and Desrochers (2006) analyse interest rate risk disclosures based on the most common IRRBB measures, from a sample of North America's largest commercial banks and conclude that, by and large, the risk measures reported did not explain the subsequent variability of their net interest income over time.

1 Model design

Measures of interest rate risk can be broadly classified (EBA, 2015) in earnings measures and economic value measures, depending on whether they focus on the short-term impact of interest rate changes on profitability and solvency, or on the full long-term impact of such changes on the net present value of the current balance sheet.

The simplest earnings measure of interest rate risk is gap analysis, which looks at the absolute difference between the nominal amounts of assets and liabilities which are sensitive to interest rate changes. A positive gap indicates a positive relationship between income and assets value, while a negative gap reflects the opposite relationship. The product of a change in interest rate and the gap (usually more than one, computed on different time intervals corresponding to maturity or repricing dates) gives an idea of the resulting change in interest income. Static Gap Analysis only looks at the existing portfolio and assumes that all contracts are live for the time their interest rates are fixed and are terminated afterwards. A more sophisticated analysis requires assumptions on prolongations, prepayments and new business as well as a forecast of market conditions.

A more sophisticated earnings measure is the Earnings at Risk (EaR), which measures the loss of net interest income (NII) over a given time horizon and is computed as the difference between NII in a base scenario and in an alternative one. The same measure can be computed over multiple alternative scenarios and, with a sufficient number of them, also produce a statistical measure of maximum losses at a given confidence interval akin to a Value at Risk.

The key economic value measure of IRRBB is called Economic Value of Equity (EVE) and is defined as the present value of the expected cash flow of assets minus the present value of the expected cash flows on liabilities, plus or minus the present value of the expected cash flows on off-balance sheet instruments, discounted to reflect market rates.

EVE = Economic Value of Assets – Economic Value of Liabilities

This measure can be obtained statically, i. e., assuming that cash flows do not change under the different scenarios, or dynamically, re-computing cash flows on the basis of changes in customers' behaviour induced by the various scenarios. The assumptions made for estimating the future cash flows and the choice of discount rates may have of course a major impact on the accuracy of this measure.

Modified duration and PV01 (or basis point value) measures the change in market value of a financial instrument due to a one basis point parallel shift of the yield curve. If we classify all instruments on the balance sheet according to their repricing date and we compute the modified duration for each class, then the modified duration of equity is given by the weighted average (by exposure in each class) of all the modified durations. The PV01 of equity can be computed by multiplying the modified duration by the value of equity and dividing by 10,000.

We can see the present value as a function of the discount factors $d(t_1) \dots d(t_n)$ and therefore define interest cash flows as a function of rates:

$$CF_i(d(t_1),\dots,d(t_n)) = \frac{\partial}{\partial d(t_i)} PV(d(t_1),\dots,d(t_n))$$

The present value of a set of interest rate sensitive cash flow can then be expressed as:

$$PV = \sum_i CF_i d(t_i)$$

The impact of a parallel shift in interest rates of one basis point (1 bp = 0.01%)

To this end one can shift either the market interest rate of standard products (before bootstrapping) or the derived zero rates.

$$BPV = PVBP = PV01 = PV(r_1 + 1bp,\dots,r_n + 1bp) - PV(r_1,\dots,r_n)$$

A shift of one basis point in the zero rates is approximately equal to:

$$BPV \approx \sum_{i=1}^{n} \frac{\partial PV}{\partial r_i} 10^{-4} = -\sum_{i=1}^{n} \frac{\partial PV}{\partial d(t_i)} t_i d(t_i) \cdot 10^{-4} = -\sum_{i=1}^{n} CF_i d(t_i) \cdot 10^{-4}$$

This formula can be rewritten as follows:

$$BPV \approx -\sum_{i=1}^{n} CF_i t_i d(t_i) \cdot 10^{-4} = -D \cdot PV \cdot 10^{-4}$$

$$\text{where } D = \frac{\sum_{i=1}^{n} CF_i t_i d(t_i)}{\sum_{i-1}^{n} CF_i d(t_i)}$$

D is approximately equal to maturity, for a fixed rate instrument, and approximately equal to the time until the next rate fixing for a floating rate instrument.

Although duration and PV01 measures are relatively simple to compute, their usefulness is limited to the analysis of small, parallel shift in the yield curve. They cannot account for large movements, convexity effects (and may for instance overstate the drop in value due to a rise in interest rates), and optionality, nor can it measure yield curve or basis risk.

Finally, Value at Risk applied to the banking book is the maximum loss in the market value of equity that can be incurred over a given time horizon with a certain confidence level. Time horizon for the banking book should be consistent with the intended holding of positions, and is usually set at one year. Similar techniques and similar issues as those discussed in Chapter 7 apply to the estimation of VaR in the banking book. Most regulatory guidance (see for instance EBA, 2015; BCBS, 2015; DNB, 2005) suggests computing VaR for the banking book using the historical simulation, variance-covariance or Monte Carlo simulation approaches, whose advantages and limitations we discussed in the previous chapter in the context of trading market risk. A Value at Risk measure for IRRBB has the advantage of being capable of taking into account both convexity and optionality effects, as well as diversification effects due to less-than-perfect correlations amongst balance sheet positions. As in the case of the trading book, VaR is a measure of losses incurred in normal condition, and its estimation (especially when done through historical simulation or variance-covariance) is largely driven by historical data on price levels and volatility. It is therefore not best suited to anticipate the consequences of very large variations in rates that may occur during a severe crisis. Most importantly, however, the challenge in reliably estimating VaR over long horizons lies in the difficulty of long-term forecasting of returns and volatilities.

For example, the well-known square-root-of-time rule applies to volatility regardless of the underlying distribution provided returns are independently and identically distributed, but it does not apply to VaR unless we also assume that returns are normally distributed. The calibration of long-term VaR using a similarly long horizon (e.g., one year) requires a very large historical dataset stretching many years in the past, with problems both practical and conceptual (for instance, how representative the older information might be). On the other hand, calibration by means of, say, daily data may mean using distributions with substantially different statistical properties from yearly data. The interested reader may consult, for instance, Christoffersen et al., 1998; Dowd et al., 2004; Kaufmann, 2004; Wang et al., 2011.

Finally, both EVE and VaR require in different ways an estimation of future cash flows, which are in turn dependent not only on market rates and contractual terms, but also on borrowers' and depositors' behaviours. The modelling of such cash flows is challenging because they may be partially or even totally unknown upfront, and even when they are specified in the contract, the customer may behave in a manner unforeseen by the contract itself. How cash flows are modelled (in particular for those products where contractual cash flows differ from behavioural ones) is therefore a fundamental feature of IRRBB measures.

Modelling the cash flow of loans involves many possible variations on the basic agreement, which are relevant in different stages of the loan like disbursement, reimbursement, prepayment, prolongation. For instance, the expected partial utilization of a loan allocation with an option to draw down may be estimated on the basis of historical observations or of expert judgment, while prepayment behaviour may be modelled based on borrowers' segmentation in homogeneous groups.

Cash flows for deposits with undefined maturity can be modelled by estimating the stable part of the volume. This can be estimated in various ways, such as using the minimum volume over a given historical period (three months, one year, several years); an average or a moving average over similarly defined historical periods; as a trend approximation, on the basis of historical observations. The deviations from the stable volume as well as the unstable part are typically invested with short maturity, while their stable volume can be invested into longer maturities in line with the modelled behaviour of the customers.

Finally, cash flows in options can be modelled through scenario analysis (using the estimated value of market factors to decide whether or not an option will be exercised under a given scenario); through weighting future cash flows by the probability of exercise (e.g., using the option's delta as a proxy); through a statistical model of exercise probabilities based on historical experience.

2 Model output

Validating the output of an IRRBB model presents two main challenges. On one side, IRRBB models, not unlike credit risk models, produce estimates over long time horizons (typically one year). Obtaining back-testing results of any statistical significance faces a trade-off between size and relevance of the data samples used. It is therefore difficult to design a back-testing framework which is at the same time meaningful and statistically robust. On the other hand, all IRRBB models predict variations in certain measures like net interest income or economic value of equity. But assessing such variations requires forecasting the components of such measures and therefore making assumptions on, and therefore also predicting, the behaviour of other related variables (new, business, interest rates, prepayments, drawdowns and so on). This implies that IRRBB back-testing is as much an exercise in isolating dependencies on interest rates from dependencies on other variables and assumptions, as it is in ultimately assessing the predictive power of the model. The U.S. Interagency Advisory on Interest Rate Risk Management stresses this aspect in providing examples of effective backtesting practices.

> Many institutions back-test model outcomes by determining the key drivers of differences between actual net-interest margin results and the modelled net-interest margin for a given period. This type of analysis attempts to explain the differences by isolating when key drivers, such as actual interest rates, prepayment speeds, other runoff, and new volumes, varied from the assumptions used in the model run (OCC et al., 2012).

The analysis of these discrepancies, rather than producing a single statistical indication, as in the case of trading market risk discussed previously, gives indications about the reasonableness of key assumptions and the appropriateness of inputs and parameters.

Nevertheless, there is also value in testing the ability of the IRRBB model to correctly predict the key risk measures. Matz (2008) suggests comparing the predicted NII to the actual NII adjusted for nonrecurring items, analyse the variations in rates, volume and business mix to identify variations resulting solely in interest rate changes, and then compare such observed variations with the model outcome. EVE, on the other hand, is always an estimate, and as such it is difficult to back-test it against an "observed" value, unless the equity of the financial institution is publicly and actively traded, in which case, one can use the market values.

Another difficulty arises from the way IRRBB models are used. Following the current regulatory framework (EBA, 2015), most banks compute interest rate risk by using a parallel shift of the yield curve and comparing the results to a base case scenario. Interest rate movements, however, do not in general happen in parallel shifts of the entire yield curve, and it is therefore unlikely that the results from a, say, 200bps parallel shock could be meaningfully compared to the observed income or economic value measures. Planned enhancements emphasize the need for anticipating other types of interest rate movements, such as parallel shocks only on the short end or only on the long end of the curve, as well as different types of inversions like steepener or flattener shocks (BCBS, 2015). However, it remains unlikely that any of these scenarios will exactly occur in practice. On occasion, of course, an interest rate move may happen over a short time period that resembles closely one of the alternative scenarios used. In this case a financial institution should compare the model prediction made at the relevant time in the past and, although the match between the scenario and the actual market evolution may still be imperfect, try to use the results to gain a better understanding of the model reliability.

An alternative approach consists in back-testing the base case earnings projections onto the realized ones, although results are only reliable insofar as the model's assumptions turn out to be realistic (Voit, 2015). This may be checked by comparing on a regular basis both income projections and assumptions and predictions on rates, customers' behaviours on prepayments or deposits and new business with observed changes. This may be done regularly on prepayments data for loans, stable volume of deposits, and on interest rates. The evolution of the financial institution's business should also be considered in back-testing, as comparison between observations that incorporate additional income from business growth, change in business mix or any other strategic change with predictions that did not take those evolutionary factors into account would not be meaningful.

Good practice would be to keep historical model settings and results, and then, for a given period of time, re-run the model with the actual interest rates and compare the results with actual rates to the income realized in that period. Long periods of stable interest rates are likely to produce excessively reassuring results in terms of IRRBB models, but at the same time they are particularly appropriate to test and refine the other forecasting capabilities embedded in the model.

3 Implementation and data

IT requirements (see EBA, 2015) are quite demanding mainly because they do not refer solely to the system used to compute the IRRBB measures, but to the system that handles the bank's transactions. Such a system is likely to be large, complex, and primarily designed for front- and back-office business purposes, and it is therefore critical that the modelling team understands to what extent it fulfils requirements for the estimation of IRRBB. It should be able to store and retrieve all interest rate related features of a product, including: rate types and levels, repricing profile, optionality and related costs (if any). Some products are fairly complex and consist of components with different interest-rate-related features. The IT system should allow the classification of the different components according to IRRBB-relevant dimensions, like maturity, optionality or repricing.

In order to model IRRBB, be it through earnings or economic value, Exposure data should be comprehensive and capture all material exposures across business lines, geographies and transactions; interest rates for all relevant currencies and a process to address immaterial ones and an observation history covering the relevant period for IRRBB simulations, forecasting and scenario analysis. This means that a financial institution needs to have available data about virtually all its transactions, including all information about the interest rate risk sensitivities of such transactions, so as to able to generate and analyse a sufficiently large spectrum of scenarios. Such data needs to be checked along several dimensions and validators should verify and seek evidence that such a quality assurance process is in fact in place. This should include a review of data collection and storage procedures; systematic data cleaning to ensure the integrity of the databases, that input errors are identified and corrected, and that any required data modification is carried out appropriately in line with modelling requirements. Full reconciliation of data amongst the various systems (e.g. trading, lending, risk management, accounting) may be desirable, but could be unrealistic. Inputs from all the other systems of the bank records should be reconciled, allowing for some inevitable discrepancies, to the general ledger values so as to ensure that all material assets and liability information are correctly input in the model and that errors do not accumulate.

Furthermore, extensive market data sourced from external providers is needed to perform calculations and simulations on interest rates. The abovementioned reviews should encompass the quality of the external databases as well as the process for integrating them into the financial institution's systems. A modelling team that regularly carries out such reviews is likely to have also a good grasp of the functioning of their IRRBB model. Finally, all data processing related to the measuring and monitoring of IRRBB should be checked against, the BCBS Principles for Effective Risk Data Aggregation and Risk Reporting (BCBS, 2013).

4 Conclusions

Arguably IRRBB is one of the oldest risks in banking, as it is inherent in some of the fundamental roles of a financial institution. But IRRBB is also a very complex risk because it arises from a wide combination of activities and does not always manifest itself in outright losses. On the contrary, as also shown by the metrics employed to measure it, IRRBB is defined as the risk of a variation in earnings or value measures, which most of the time will rather translate in an opportunity cost to a bank.

Furthermore, the nature of IRRBB is complex, as it materializes along different dimensions. For many transactions (fixed rate loans, bonds, derivatives) the interest rate characteristics are entirely contained within the contractual conditions; for others (prepayable loans or savings deposits) interest rate risk stems primarily from customers' behaviour in light of market-changing conditions; for others still (items without a contractual maturity like non-maturity deposits or buildings and equipment) interest rate characteristics are conventionally assigned for modelling purposes.

Because of the long-term nature of many of the transactions involved, IRRBB measures need to be computed on long time frames. This complicates the requirements for data, the complexity and reliability of projections as well as the interpretation of results. Furthermore, there is no analytical formula (as there is for a bond or a swap) expressing earnings or economic value as a function of the interest rates, but rather a simple arithmetic relationship between those measures and cash flows, where cash flows depend on rates in complex and very nonlinear ways.

Given that IRRBB arises from many different types of transactions and requires hypotheses and forecasts of many variables, in modelling IRRBB, one needs to be careful in separating the actual impact of interest rate changes on the various risk measures from the impacts of other variables and of the various assumptions made. This further complicates the task of back-testing, as one typically would want to test the specific exposure to interest rate changes while all other assumptions and predictions will rarely occur in practice in the way they were formulated in the model.

References

Basel Committee on Banking Supervision, "Interest Rate Risk on the Banking Book," Basel, June 2015.

Basel Committee on Banking Supervision, "Principles for Effective Risk Data Aggregation and Risk Reporting," Basel, January 2013.

Basel Committee on Banking Supervision, "Range of Practices and Issues in Economic Capital Modelling," Basel, March 2009.

Christoffersen, P. F., Diebold, F. X. and Schuermann, T., "Horizon Problems and Extreme Events in Financial Risk Management," *FRBNY Economic Policy Review*, October 1998.

De Nederlandsche Bank N.V., "Guidelines on Interest Rate Risk in the Banking Book," July 2005.

Dowd, K., Blake, D. and Cairns, "Long-Term Value at Risk," *The Journal of Risk Finance*, Vol. 5, No. 2, 52–57, 2004.

European Banking Authority, "Guidelines on the Management of Interest Rate Risk Arising from Non-trading Activities," EBA/GL/2015/08, 22 May 2015.

Harris, M., "Backetesting Your Interest Rate Risk Model," *CFO & Finance Digest*, Issue #1, August 2010. Available at http://www.wib.org/publications__resources/cfo__finance_digest/2010-12/aug10/harris.html.

Kaufmann, R., "Long-Term Risk Management," PhD Thesis, ETH Zurich, 2004.

Matz, L., "Back Testing Interest Rate–Risk Models," *Bank Accounting and Finance*, April–May 2008.

Office of the Comptroller of the Currency, Board of Governors of the Federal Reserve System, Federal Deposit Insurance Corporation, national Credit Union Administration, State Liaison Committee, *"Interagency Advisory on Interest Rate Risk Management, Frequently Asked Questions,"* 12 January 2012.

Préfontaine, J. and Desrochers, J., "How Useful Are Banks' Earnings-At-Risk And Economic Value Of Equity-At-Risk Public Disclosures?," *International Business & Economics Research Journal*, Vol. 5, No. 9, September 2006.

Voit, B., "Moving Forward with IRR Back Testing," *Credit Union Times Magazine*, 15 May 2013.

Wang, J.-N., Yeh, J.-H. and Chen, N.Y.-P., "How Accurate is the Square-Root-of-Time Rule in Scaling Tail Risk: A Global Study," *Journal of Banking and Finance*, Vol. 35, 1158–1169, 2011.

Part IV

Counterparty Credit Risk

9 | Counterparty Credit Risk Models

In Part 2, we have discussed the validation of models for credit risk by looking at the three components of the regulatory formula for risk-weighted assets: probability of default, loss given default and exposure at default. In this chapter we turn to a type of credit risk that has become extremely important in the wake of the 2008 financial crisis and the numerous and unexpected downgrades of counterparties (including the largest investment banks) which generated large migration losses in derivative trading books. Consequently, counterparty credit risk proved to be relevant not only for the trading activities of financial institutions, but also, in light of the many interconnections amongst them, for the stability of the financial system as a whole. Counterparty credit risk is relevant in the context of over-the-counter (OTC) derivatives and securities financing transactions (SFT)[1]. Risk in over-the-counter transactions and the combination of credit and market risk has been discussed in Duffie and Singleton (2003), the modelling of CCR is analysed in Pykhtin and Zhou (2006, 2007) and in Canabarro (2010), while Martin (2010) provides an overview of model risk in CCR systems.

Since a derivative contract can have a positive or a negative market value, the default of a counterpart will cause a loss equivalent to the replacement cost of the contract, i.e., its market value if such value were positive. The counterparty exposure will be the larger between zero and the market value of the portfolio of derivative positions with a counterparty that would be lost in the event of counterparty default. The distribution of the CCR exposure in the future will depend on the various market factors underlying each OTC contract and will usually represent only a fraction of the total notional amount of trades with a counterparty. This market value will depend on the credit quality of the counterpart and will go down in case of a downgrade even in absence of any changes in the market parameters. On the other hand, in a derivative contract, even if credit quality does not change, the exposure at default will depend on the future level of market factors. In other words, rather than the current exposure (i.e., the loss that would be expected if the derivative cash flows were known with certainty or if the counterparty defaulted today) one needs to take into account the potential exposure (the loss that would be expected given a range of potential future market scenarios and if the counterparty defaulted at some time before the contract's maturity). As we have seen when discussing the EAD (Exposure at Default) component of the regulatory formula for credit risk, uncertainty on the actual level of exposure at the time of default also needs to be modelled. Counterparty credit risk (CCR) is usually defined as the risk that the value of a portfolio changes due to unexpected changes in the credit quality of trading counterparts, i.e., outright default or downgrading. Because of the nature of the contracts, however, and unlike the case of credit risk on loans, besides the uncertainty on credit quality, one needs also to consider (and model) the uncertainty on the actual exposure. The latter being driven, sometimes in very complicated ways, by market factors, one needs in practice to model the value of all portfolio transactions over, possibly quite long, time horizons, combine this forecast with an estimate of default probabilities and recovery rates, and aggregate the results on a counterparty basis, without forgetting to take into account collateralization and netting arrangements.

The Second Basel Accord provisions on CCR include a capital charge for default risk to cover losses in case the counterparty defaults on its obligations (assuming the instrument is held to maturity). Following the losses incurred during the financial crisis the so called Third Basel Accord (or Basel III) introduced a capital requirement to cover losses from changes in the market value of counterparty risk, as for other risks, proposing different approaches, with increasing levels of complexity. To compute regulatory capital in respect of counterparty credit risk for both OTC derivatives and SFT, a financial institution needs to determine its EAD by using any of four different methods (the original exposure method, the current exposure method, the standardized method and the Internal Model Method, IMM). Specifically, the Capital Requirements Regulation (CRR), specifies the following approaches:

- The original exposure method estimates the exposure at default based on nominal value and time to maturity (only allowed for banks without a trading book).
- The mark-to-market method estimates the exposure at default based on market value, instrument types and time to maturity.
- The standardized method estimates the exposure at default based on a standardized formula regarding market value, instrument type and time to maturity.
- The IMM allows certain approved banks to develop their own models to calculate their exposures at default.

IMM is the most advanced and risk-sensitive method to determine EAD, and the financial institution needs to take into account the interaction between the three components of credit risk (PD, LGD and EAD) as well as the so-called wrong-way risk. The latter is the risk originating from the fact that exposure may be negatively correlated to the counterparty's creditworthiness. For example, a rise in interest rates may have a negative effect on the counterparty's credit rating while at the same time increasing EAD. In order to compute EAD, we need to define the following risk measures.

The Potential Future Exposure (PFE) is defined as the maximum positive exposure estimated to occur on a future date at a high level of statistical confidence, and it is routinely used in monitoring counterparty eligibility and credit limits with respect to CCR.

The Expected Exposure (EE) is defined as the probability-weighted average exposure estimated to exist on a future date.

The Expected Positive Exposure (EPE) is defined as the time-weighted average of individual expected exposures estimated for given forecasting horizons (e.g., one year)

If the distribution of the future values of the exposures computed at different points in the future and up to maturity of the contract or of a netting set, is simulated on the basis of the relevant market factors, EE is the average or expected value of that distribution. EPE is then computed as the average of EEs across time horizons.

The Effective Expected Exposure (EEE) at a specific date is defined as the maximum expected exposure that occurs on or before that date.

The Effective EPE is the average of the effective EE over one year or until the maturity of the longest-maturity contract in the set of netting contracts[2], whichever is smaller.

The EAD, the exposure at default of the counterparty, can be computed as follows:

$$EAD = \alpha \; Effective \; EPE$$

where α represents the ratio between the total economic capital required for CCR and the capital that would be required if counterparty exposures were deterministic and equal to EPE.

The Basel Accord prescribes a value of 1.4 for α, but allows financial institutions to perform their own estimate subject to a floor of 1.2. For a discussion on modelling CCR and α in the context of the Basel Accord see for example Cespedes et al. (2010).

Finally, the Current Exposure (CE) is defined as the larger of zero, or the market value of a transaction or portfolio of transactions within a netting set with a counterparty that would be lost, assuming no recovery, upon the default of the counterparty. The CE is equivalent to the replacement cost mentioned above and represents the value of the contract if it were to be sold on the market.

One of the objectives of CCR estimation is to take into account the credit risk of a counterpart in determining the price of a bank's derivative exposure. The difference between the credit risk-free price of an exposure and the price that incorporates credit risk is the market value of CCR, is called Credit Valuation Adjustment and is the risk-neutral expectation of the discounted loss.

$$CVA = (1 - R)\int_0^T E^Q\left[\frac{DF_0}{DF_\tau}E(\tau)|\tau = t\right]dPD(0,t)$$

where:
R = Recovery rate;
Q = Risk neutral measure;
DF_t = Discount factor;
τ = Time of default;
PD = Probability of Default.

This risk measure is required for both accounting[3] and regulatory purposes, but is also to be incorporated in risk management practices, for instance, economic capital calculations, stress testing and active portfolio management.

If we assume that the institution itself cannot default and that credit exposure and default probability are independent (i.e. we ignore wrong-way risk and Debt Valuation Adjustment or DVA), we can express CVA approximately as follows.

$$CVA \approx LGD\sum_{i=1}^{n} DF_{ti}EE_{ti}PD_{ti-1,ti}$$

where
LGD = Loss Given Default
DF = Discount Factor
EE = Expected Exposure.

1 Model design

One way to understand the various aspects of CCR estimation is to visualize how its different components interact to determine the final risk profile. The approach is similar to what is required under the Basel II formula for RWA, the risk is a combination of the exposure at default, probability of default and recovery rate (or loss given default). However, for CCR the computation of EAD is especially complex, as we need first to estimate the distribution of the exposure in the future. This calculation is done by re-valuing the instruments in the portfolio and thus requires the use of simulation models to generate combination of market factors at future dates as well as of pricing models to produce the future values. The exposure thus generated is then used to compute the exposure at default for the CCR capital charge and is combined with estimates of PDs and LGDs bootstrapped from CDS spreads in order to compute the CVA (or market price of CCR). Figure one presents a schematic view of the process.

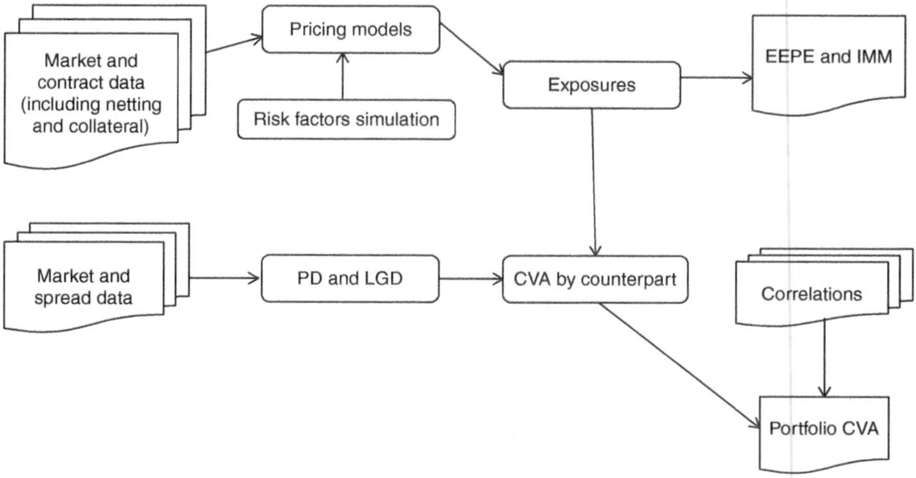

Figure 9.1 CCR calculation

The modelling of the credit exposure requires, therefore, the generation of future scenarios for the market risk factors, the valuation of each instrument for each scenario at each simulation date, and the aggregation of such values across the portfolio taking netting into account. Scenarios for the evolution of the risk factors, which will typically include interest and FX rates, equity and commodity prices as well as credit spreads), can be generated either through path-dependent or direct jump simulations or, otherwise said, could be generated at several times leading up to the maturity date or as a result of a single jump to that same date. Pykhtin and Zhu (2005) show that, if scenarios are specified through a stochastic differential equation (as, for instance, the one for generalized geometric Brownian motion) the price factor distribution at a given simulation date obtained using either method is identical, but note that a path-dependent approach may be preferable for certain path-dependent derivatives like American/Bermudan, barrier options and asset-settled derivatives. Other modelling considerations pertain to the way average and standard deviation of the probability distributions are calibrated depending on whether the factors are modelled using real or risk-neutral measures.

Valuation of contracts also presents challenges, as default can happen at any time in the future and hence exposure needs to be simulated for a potentially large number of future times. As such, valuation also needs to be performed daily, for both accounting and collateral management purposes, the computational requirements grow very quickly with the number of instruments, the number of risk factors, the number of scenarios and the number of points in time. As another example (Pykhtin and Zhu, 2006), path-dependent instruments cannot be valued using techniques that rely on full information about the past as scenarios are generated only for a discrete set of points in the future. These issues render typical front office valuation approaches, like full-scale Monte Carlo based pricing, very difficult to implement and hence suggest the use of closed-form solutions or of acceptable analytical approximations (see for instance Gregory, 2012, Lomibao and Zhu, 2006).

In generating scenarios, the main issues that can affect model performance, and that should be examined by a validator, are the selection of factors, the choice of simulation dates and the choice of the stochastic models for the various factors. The stochastic model may be too simple, as when a model only allows for parallel shift in the term structure of rates, or ignores altogether an important aspect of the factor dynamics, as when volatility is assumed constant or always equal to the implied one from the available options. The financial crisis gave plenty of examples of the dangers of simplifying assumptions in modelling correlations, when relying exclusively on historical experience, and even when using fairly sophisticated modelling choices like multivariate normal and lognormal distributions, or normal copulas (Martin, 2010).

When valuing the instruments present in the portfolio under each scenario, the choice of pricing model has a fundamental impact on the final result and, as already observed, the complexity and size of the computational requirements of a derivative portfolio are such that a trade-off between accuracy and computational efficiency cannot be avoided. However, excessive simplification of the pricing models can lead to substantial inaccuracies.

As an example consider the case where a derivatives portfolio is modelled by exploiting the sensitivities of each derivative product to its risk factors in order to build an approximated linear model for pricing. This approximation assumes constant sensitivities and thus may hold if the derivatives portfolio is one-directional, i.e., hedging underlying exposures that are of a buy-and-hold nature, implying that sensitivities will decrease in time, but it does not necessarily hold in case optionality is involved, and sensitivities can depend on how much the derivative is in or out of the money, possibly causing an upward or downward behaviour of the sensitivities throughout the lifetime of the transactions. It further neglects all possible volatility effects and can thus work acceptably only during a very stable market period or if the derivatives in the portfolio are mostly plain vanilla.

Furthermore, when pricing derivative products, several parameters can have a first-order impact on the price even if they are second-order approximations in mathematical terms. Ignoring such mixed effects can result in an additional loss of accuracy when constant sensitivities are adopted. And finally, since risk measures are concerned mainly with tail events, assuming small movement of the risk factors, which would otherwise justify the assumption of constant sensitivities, is illogical as it is more likely that large variations of the exposure will be caused by large changes in the risk factors.

As a further example, consider the case when the modeller adopts the centering of the distribution on its mean within a historical simulation approach, in order to improve the model performance in back-testing. Since the distributions for the risk parameter are the real distributions and not the risk-free distributions, the drift needs to be kept as part of the pricing process, and no additional adjustment for the average of the exposure distribution is required. Note that the effect of adjusting for the drift can be two-sided. In case the drift is negative, it increases the risk measure, while in case of a positive drift, the risk measure goes down.

Recalibration of the pricing should be performed at each simulation date, but rather than re-perform each calibration, Martin (2010) recommends comparing market value distributions generated under the real measure with those generated under the risk-neutral measure.

Finally, Basel III requires financial institution to compute a stressed EEPE, as counterparty risk tends to be higher in periods of crisis, but its main drivers tend to be low immediately before those periods. Unless stressed measures are used, when spreads, volatilities and correlations are calibrated historically, CCR measure might be too low at the moment when their accuracy is most needed.

2 Model output

We have seen in Chapter 7 how the output of VaR models in the context of trading market risk can be validated through back-testing and the specific regulatory requirements around it. Although in principle, validating the output of a CCR model poses similar challenges, in practice things are more complicated for several reasons. First, while trading market risk models provides daily risk measures that can therefore easily be compared to corresponding daily series of realized P and Ls, time horizons of CCR models are generally longer and of varying length. This creates the need for models that are able to capture long-term exposures, but also for longer time series in order to be able to perform back-testing. Sufficiently long time series are not always available, and this impacts the reliability of the analysis, even in the presence of adapted techniques, like overlapping windows of time horizons. CCR assessment is also more complicated: Exposures profiles are obtained through the combination of the outputs of multiple models of different natures (risk factor models for scenario generation, pricing models, collateral, netting and aggregation models) and have to be computed and aggregated by counterparty portfolios.

Furthermore, the regulatory guidance is a lot less prescriptive than for trading market risk models and does not give clear rules for selecting tests, metrics, horizons and for how to discriminate between acceptable and unacceptable model results. Rather than a set of rigid rules, the Basel Committee on Banking Supervision, in line with an approach followed in the past for other risk areas, provides "sound practices" for back-testing counterparty credit risk models (BCBS, 2010), which contain a set of principles and general guidelines.

BCBS guidance states explicitly the need to backtest the output of EPE models against realized values, separately for each of the risk factors that enter the calculation of EPE and for several distinct time horizons, initialized on a number of historical dates, consistent with the maturity of the trades, incorporating the typical margin period of risk. Although a bank could perform EPE backtesting over a several-year observation window to gain a higher statistical confidence, they should also include back-testing of recent performance, in order to avoid that poor model performance, and in particular low responsiveness to recent market evolution, go undetected.

Frequency of recalibration of parameters should consider that the time series used should not include data posterior to the initialization date and should be the same length as the one originally used for model development. Clear criteria should be established and documented for discriminating between acceptable and unacceptable performance and for how to remedy unacceptable performance. Back-testing of forecast distributions produced by EPE models and risk factor models should not rely on the assessment of a single-risk measure, but should consider multiple percentiles and also an assessment over the whole distribution.

Finally, back-testing should be performed on portfolios that reliably represent the risks in a bank's portfolio. Such portfolios may be made of real trades with actual counterparts or hypothetical ones constructed so as to reproduce the relevant risks. In both cases the dynamics of maturing deals should be taken into account in order to ensure the testing of performance out to the required time horizons.

The BCBS refers to CCR model back-testing as the back-test of the model generating EPE profiles. As we have seen, an EPE model will be composed of several elements: a model for the evolution of risk factors, one or more models for the pricing of the portfolio's instruments, and models for collateral netting and for aggregation across time and trades. Hence, the first issue for a validator in designing a back-testing program is whether to back-test the final EPE measure or the output of the individual models. Some researchers (see for instance Schnitzler et al., 2014) consider that the final result of the model should be subject to ongoing back-testing and that only when the results are unsatisfactory should further analysis be conducted on the different model components in order to identify problems and propose solutions. Needless to say, this also highlights a key disadvantage of this approach, because a failure in back-testing will not give enough information about what exactly is wrong with which model.

Others (see for instance Ruiz, 2014) recommend considering the individual components and focussing on the most critical ones, like the models for the evolution of risk factors, whose inaccuracies may have the greatest impact on the estimated risk profile. This approach undoubtedly simplifies the data requirements, as validators do not need to construct long series of composition and values for counterparty portfolios, a task admittedly both time-consuming and objectively difficult, given that portfolio composition changes as a result of both market evolution and trading activity and that not all banks keep track systematically of such evolutions. The approach is, however, valid, only to the extent that other modelling components, like pricing, collateralization and netting can be relied upon, either because they are straightforward or already established as sufficiently robust for the actual purposes.

When the CCR measure is used for eligibility decisions and to limit monitoring, as in the case of the PFE measure discussed above, back-testing can be performed along the lines examined in Chapter 7. If, however, models are used for EPE (and CVA) computation, the framework needs to consider more than just exceptions to a quantile measure. EPE is a measure on a distribution and exposures, and default, as shown during the financial crisis, cannot be assumed to be independent. Back-testing must therefore look at the entire (positive) mark-to-market distribution predicted by the model rather than a just at a single quantile. In practice this means to compare the predicted distribution with the (observed) empirical one, compute a measure of the distance between the two, and on that basis, establish whether the model's performance is acceptable or not.

Let us define a sequence of non-overlapping time horizons $t_{i,i+\delta}$ $\{i=1,\dots,n\}$ and let us take at each time t_i the distribution function predicted by the model, subject to the value realized at time t_{i-1}. The value F_i $\{i=1,\dots,n\}$ is one if the value realized at time t_i falls in the cumulative distribution function predicted by the model and zero otherwise. F_i $\{i=1,\dots,n\}$ is uniformly distributed if the model perfectly predicts reality and hence the quality of the model can be tested by testing the null hypothesis that F_i $\{i=1,\dots,n\}$ is uniformly distributed. The hypothesis can be tested by measuring the "distance" between the empirical and the predicted distribution in various ways (Schnitzler et al., 2014).

If we indicate with F the theoretical cumulative distribution function given by the model and by F_e the empirical cumulative distribution function obtained from F_i $\{i=1,\dots,n\}$ the Anderson Darling measure is given by:

$$D = n\int_{-\infty}^{\infty} \left(F_e(x) - F(x)\right)^2 w\left(f(x)\right) dF(x)$$

$$w(F) = \frac{1}{F(1-F)}$$

This test gives more weight to the tails of the distribution, and is therefore especially suited for risk management purposes.

However, the Cramér–von Mises test may be more appropriate when we are interested in the entire the distribution function.

$$D = n\int_{-\infty}^{\infty} \left(F_e(x) - F(x)\right)^2 w\left(f(x)\right) dF(x)$$

$$w(F)=1$$

The test A to assess if X_i $\{i=1,\dots,n\}$ (put in increasing order) come from a distribution with cumulative distribution function F_i is:

$$A^2=-n-S$$

where

$$S=\sum_{i=1}^{n}\frac{2i-1}{n}\left[+\ln\left(1-F\left(X_{n+1-i}\right)\right)\right]$$

The test statistic can then be compared against the critical values of the theoretical distribution, which depend on the sample size n and the significance level α.

The two-sided Kolmogorov–Smirnov test compares the largest distance from observed data with a uniform distribution:

$$D=\max_{0\le i\le n}\left\{\left|F_i-\frac{i}{n}\right|\right\}$$

The null hypothesis is rejected if D exceeds a critical value D^n depending on the significance level α and the sample size n. For a sufficiently large n, D^n is approximated by:

$$D_\alpha^n\approx\frac{\log\left(\frac{2}{\alpha}\right)}{2n}$$

Ruiz (ibid. 2014) also introduces an interesting approach to the problem of establishing a threshold for model acceptance. He suggests constructing an artificial time series using the model subject to testing, and then computing a distance D using one of the metrics discussed above. The constructed time series should perfectly match the model, but still the distance D will not be exactly zero as it is the outcome of a numerical simulation. Repeating the computation a large number of times will yield a distribution Φ(D) for the distance D compatible with a "perfect" model that can be approximated numerically if the number of trials is sufficiently large. At this point, if the distance D*, computed by back-testing the model against empirical data, falls with high probability within a given range of Φ(D), then the model can be considered compatible with a perfect one with high probability and vice versa.

As observed in Chapter 7, distribution tests do not completely replace the need for a traffic light approach. Depending on the test statistic, a model may be accepted by distribution tests like the ones above and still fail the traffic light approach. This may happen if the predicted distribution functions are largely accurate except for the tails that contain the outliers.

3 Process and governance

CCR models are complex from both a conceptual and a practical implementation point of view. As a consequence, it is important that a validation exercise includes the way a CCR system is governed and run. This should start with the identification of the key stakeholders in the CVA process, like trading desks, middle office, information technology, but also back office, legal and risk management, and the verification that the appropriate procedures and controls are put in place in order to fulfil all the related financial institution's policy and strategic objectives.

Furthermore, the operational process should be reviewed focussing in particular on the quality of data management, the reliability of reporting, the level of automation and computational efficiency, the existence of a complete documentation of workflow and procedures. The financial institution's internal control framework should be extended to cover the CCR system in its entirety, including all the areas where an operational failure may impact the results of the various models and all the ultimate uses of those results. The latter include daily valuation, collateral management, limit monitoring, pricing, and capital requirements.

CCR systems are elaborate combinations of different models. The practical realization of such models may as well differ in terms of hardware and software as well as implementation and roll-out. Therefore, the way different components are integrated in order to produce the desired results is a critical factor in their performance and an important aspect of a validator's work. This task comprises both the analysis of data flows (market data, trade data, and all relevant contract information) to ensure the system is timely and accurately fed and the verification that it is properly set up in order to fulfil all the relevant requirements.

A validation exercise should therefore ensure that data flows are timely and complete, i.e., that they include all the relevant details (including time series) for factor simulation and pricing. Also, as data will also likely be sourced from other systems, like probability of default and other counterparty risk data, the timing and mapping of such information in the CCR system should be carefully verified. For instance, credit spreads should be consistent with market quotes, and when less liquid quotes or proxies are used, additional verifications should be performed. The possibility of an insufficiently comprehensive testing before implementation should also be verified, for instance, if testing has been performed by comparing model results to those obtained using a more basic and less complex methodology.

Furthermore, validators should check consistency of implementation of accounting standards; regulatory provisions; alignment between relevant agreements, e.g., Credit Support Annexes, and system information; proper allocation of trades to netting sets; existence of any breakage clauses effectively shortening maturity of the contracts; proper consideration of margin period of risk (MPR[4]) and so on. For instance International Financial Reporting Standards mandate a trade-by-trade breakdown of CVA figures and the use of CDS-spreads and other market-sourced parameters for calibration (focussing on market alignment rather than on conservatism) whenever possible; imperfectly collateralized exposures should not be treated as nonexistent; wrong-way risk should be correctly identified in terms of the specific risk related to the nature and structure of the transaction within the specific netting set and second (regulators will also be interested in the contagion and systemic effect stemming from systemically important financial institutions). When wrong-way risk is not taken into account, a test of materiality should at least be conducted. Other approaches (stochastic modelling or expert judgment) should be separately assessed.

4 Conclusions

We have examined the different issues surrounding the validation of credit counterparty risk models. We have, however, not specifically reviewed the validation of derivative pricing models, although the accurate pricing of the individual instruments is essential in estimating the counterparty risk of a derivative portfolio. The literature on the validation of pricing models is already extensive and a comprehensive discussion of the validation of the various pricing approach even for only the main types of derivative contracts available would be outside the scope of a book focussed on risk models.

Validation of the conceptual design of a CCR system and of the models comprising it requires an understanding of the financial institution's business, of the portfolio composition and trade patterns as well as of all the requirements both internal and those imposed by accounting and regulatory frameworks. It also requires an identification of the key model risks embedded in the various CCR components: risk factor simulation, pricing, netting, collateralization and aggregation. Certain quantitative validation approaches may favour an analysis of the final results while others may focus first on the results of the individual models with a CCR system, but in both cases, verification of such a model's output faces challenges different and more arduous than the validation of a trading VaR model. Models used in CCR assessment try to estimate not just a single percentile of a given distribution of values over a single time horizon, but a distribution of credit exposures dependent on multiple market factors simulated over many time horizons. The back-testing of CCR models' results is challenging in terms of the amount of data, the computational time and the complexity of the statistical measures involved, requiring verification of the system's calculation outputs involving a detailed assessment of valuation results, the derivation of various exposure calculation and value adjustment along with sensitivities and scenarios, which can be also integrated with benchmarking by both comparison against analytic results, where available, and by consistency checks and against reference libraries.

System integration is a key aspect of CCR models implementation; assessment of the data flows and processes that integrate the simulation of risk factors, the pricing and the counterparty aggregation into the general IT framework of the bank is needed to verify that the correct data is sent to the system at the correct time in a consistent way, including a complete and correct feed of market data and trades with all required information for pricing,

Validators should verify that the system is set up and parameterized correctly in order to fulfil all requirements for pricing, risk assessment, valuation adjustments for accounting and regulatory requirements, including general reference data, market data setup, product setup, legal data (like netting agreements and CSAs), counterparty information and all the other parameters needed.

Validators should in general be wary of and try to understand the consequences of all the simplifying assumptions contained in the methodological approach adopted. The complexity of the problem does indeed justify a compromise between mathematical precision and practical tractability, but when simplifications are present at every step, from the choice of factors to the generation of scenarios, from the choice of time horizons to the pricing of the individual transactions, from the estimation of correlation to (sometimes) the assumptions that credit and market risk are independent, the rationale, the conceptual implications and the impact of such assumptions need to be both thoroughly comprehended and, to the extent possible, quantitatively assessed.

Notes

1. OTC derivatives are “tailor-made” derivatives created through bilateral negotiations. SFTs are repurchase agreement transactions and securities lending transactions. Counterparty credit risk for exchange traded derivatives is guaranteed by the exchange institution.
2. If counterparties have multiple offsetting obligations to one another, they can agree to net those obligations. In the event of a default or some other termination event, the outstanding contracts are all terminated, marked to market and settled with a single net payment.
3. International Accounting Standards (IAS 39) require banks to account for the fair value of OTC derivatives trades, which includes the recognition of fair-value adjustments due to counterparty risk.
4. MPR is the time period from the last exchange of collateral covering a netting *set* of transactions with a defaulting counterpart until that counterpart is closed out and the resulting market risk is re-hedged. The proper application of the margin period of risk for EAD valuation models handling netting sets (5, 10 or 20 business days) adds a further risk dimension to an already complex modelling approach.

References

Basel Committee on Banking Supervision, "Sound Practices for Backtesting Counterparty Credit Risk Models," Basel, December 2010.

Cespedes, J. C. G., de Juan Herrero, J. A. and Rosen, Saunders, D., "Effective Modelling of Wrong-Way Risk, Counterparty Credit Risk Capital, and Alpha in Basel II," *The Journal of Risk Model Validation*, Vol. 4, No. 1, 71–98, Spring 2010.

Canabarro, E., *Counterparty Credit Risk,* Risk Books, 2010.

Duffie, D. and Singleton, K.J., *Credit Risk: Pricing, Measurement and Management,* Princeton University Press, 2003.

Gregory, J., *Counterparty Credit Risk and Credit Value Adjustment: A Continuing Challenge for Global Financial Markets,* Wiley, 2012.

Lomibao, D. and Zhu, S., *A Conditional Valuation Approach for Path-Dependent Instruments,* Wilmott Magazine, July/August 2006.

Martin, M. R. W., Identification and Classification of Model Risks in Counterparty Credit Risk Measurement Systems, in Rösch, D. and Scheule, H. (Eds), *Model Risk: Identification, measurement and Management*, Risk Books, 2010.

Prisco, B. and Rosen, D., "Modeling Stochastic Counterparty Credit Exposures for Derivatives Portfolios," in Pykhtin, M. (Ed.), *Counterparty Credit Risk Modelling: Risk Management, Pricing and Regulation,* Risk Books, 2005.

Pykhtin, M. and Zhu, S., "Measuring Counterparty Credit Risk for Trading Products under Basel II," in *The Basel Handbook* (2nd edition), edited by M. K. Ong, Risk Books, London, 2006.

Pykhtin, M. and Zhu, S., "A Guide to Modelling Counterparty Credit Risk," *GARP Risk Review*, July/August 2007, 16–22.

Ruiz, I., "Backtesting Counterparty Credit Risk: How Good is your Model?" *The Journal of Credit Risk*, Vol. 10, No. 1, 2014.

Schnitzler, S., Rother, N., Plank, H. and Glößner, P., "Backtesting for Counterparty Credit Risk," *Journal of Risk Model Validation,* Vol. 8, No. 4, 3–17, 2014.

Part V

Operational Risk

10 The Validation of AMA Models

In this chapter and in the following one, we will discuss the validation of models for operational risk. Such models have been developed by financial institutions under the so-called AMA (Advanced Measurement Approaches) to calculate capital requirements in respect of their operational risk profile and the technical standards for their assessment are addressed by the European Banking Authority (EBA, 2014).

In the words of the Basel Committee, "in the AMA, banks may use their own method for assessing their exposure to operational risk, so long as it is sufficiently comprehensive and systematic." Use of AMA is subject to supervisory approval, and banks need to classify transaction incidents according to their impact on business. Recognizing the rapid evolution in operational risk management practices, however, the Basel Committee has stated that it "is prepared to provide banks with an unprecedented amount of flexibility to develop an approach to calculate operational risk capital that they believe is consistent with their mix of activities and underlying risks."

For AMA, however, the Basel Accord, unlike for credit risk, does not specify what the approach should be, neither in terms of methodology nor in terms of a specific quantitative model. It is left to each bank to develop one and submit it to the regulators for approval. Therefore, a bank should develop a risk-sensitive approach to the measurement of operational risk. This will be tailored to the specific features of that bank's risk and control environment and its resulting operational risk profile, while making the most of the information, quantitative and qualitative, available and adhering to the qualifying criteria set by the Basel Committee.

The Basel Accord specifies that a number of criteria be fulfilled in order to qualify as AMA. These criteria are very important from a compliance perspective because their fulfilment will ensure that regulators will agree to review (and possibly approve) the approach and the way it has been implemented. However, and in the absence of any other specific prescription on how the advanced approach should be implemented, they are also important because they provide information on the basic elements and the key features that should be present in the approach and on what should thus be covered. The qualifying criteria also specify requirements related to governance and the organizational structure. We briefly summarize all of them for completeness, but with a singular focus on those that give specific instructions on the design of the advanced approach.

General standards

The general standards refer to the very basic best practices such as:

- the involvement of board members and senior management in overseeing the operational risk management framework;
- soundness and integrity of the operational risk management system; and
- the availability of sufficient resources, both in business lines and in control functions, to implement the approach.

Qualitative standards

The qualitative standards cover the same ground as the general criteria, but with more details and examples relating to the working of the measurement process. Specifically, they cover:

- the independence and definition of responsibilities of the operational risk function;
- the close integration of the measurement process in the day-to-day risk management process;
- the regular reporting of operational risk exposures and losses;
- the documentation of the operational risk management system; and
- review and validation by internal and external auditors of the operational risk management process and measurement systems.

Quantitative standards

The quantitative standards are the most specific and give a number of directions for the development of a measurement process in compliance with AMA. They can be summarized as follows:

1. *Soundness*: Same as for the internal ratings-based approach for credit risk (compatible with a one-year holding period and a 99.9th percentile confidence interval).
2. *Detailed criteria*:
   (a) consistency with the Basel Accord's definition and categorization;

(b) regulatory capital to include expected and unexpected losses;
(c) sufficient granularity to capture major drivers of operational risk;
(d) regulatory capital to be the sum of the various risk estimates (full correlation assumption);
(e) key features to include four fundamental elements: internal data, external data, scenario analysis and factors reflecting business environment and internal control systems; and
(f) a sound approach for the weighting of the above four fundamental elements.

3. *Internal data*: A minimum of five years' observation period (three years for the first move to AMA) covering all material activities and exposures; classification according to Basel categories and mapping to Basel-defined business lines and centralized functions; and inclusion of operational losses related to market and credit risk.
4. *External data*: Systematic process for assessing their relevance – in particular, for covering infrequent, yet potentially severe, losses.
5. *Scenario analysis*: Based on experienced business manager and risk management experts to evaluate the impact of simultaneous operational risk loss events.
6. *Business environment and internal control factors*: Actual and future changes should be captured in order to assess their impact on the overall operational risk profile.

Although the above set of criteria still do not specify which methodology banks should use in order to implement an acceptable AMA, they do provide some guidance both in terms of the capabilities the regulators are expecting and the key components any solution should have in order to qualify.

Whatever specific approach a bank chooses to implement, it must provide quantitative estimates at a 99.9% confidence level, classified and mapped according to the Basel Accord loss and business categories. Such an approach should derive the quantitative measure of operational risk on the basis of a reasoned combination of internal data, external data, scenario analysis and factors, reflecting the business environment and internal control systems.

1 Model design

1.1 Model development

The CEBS (predecessor to the EBA) in an early version of a consultative paper (CEBS, 2006) outlined the fundamental steps in the implementation of an AMA model based on the loss distribution approach (LDA). This part of the paper was subsequently dropped following industry feedback, as it was deemed too prescriptive, but they provide nevertheless a useful frame of reference for model development analysis (see Scandizzo, 2007 and 2010).

a. Preliminary analysis

The preliminary identification of a set of probability distributions to be fitted to the data could be helpful in selecting the most meaningful distributions for the data under investigation. A preliminary exploratory analysis of the data can be carried out either by calculating the first four empirical moments of the severity of data (in particular the empirical skewness and kurtosis to examine the levels of asymmetry and tail heaviness of the data), or by representing the frequency and severity distribution functions by means of histogram and/or kernel plots (these plots may suggest the most meaningful frequency and severity distributions to be fitted to the data).

b. Techniques for parameters estimation

Several statistical techniques are available for obtaining estimates of the parameters of the frequency and severity distributions. Appropriate techniques include Maximum Likelihood Estimation, Bootstrapping, Bayesian methods, etc. Maximum Likelihood Estimation techniques should be used with caution when the volume of data available for parameter estimation is not sufficiently large and when the data show a high levels of kurtosis.

c. Tools for evaluating the quality of the fit of the distributions to the data

The techniques usually adopted to evaluate the quality of the fit of the distributions to the data include graphical methods, which visualize the difference between the empirical and theoretical functions, and quantitative methods, which are based on goodness-of-fit tests.

Where the objective of the analysis is to evaluate the fitness of the distributions to the upper tail of data, preference should be given to tests that are more sensitive to the tail than to the body of the data.

d. Methods for selecting the distributions when the results from point c do not lead to a clear choice

While the diagnostic tools provide information on the quality of the fit of each distribution to the data, they do not always lead to a clear choice of the best-fitting distribution. Moreover, the results of the goodness-of-fit tests are usually sensitive to the sample size and the number of parameters.

Where the diagnostic tools do not clearly identify a unique set of frequency and severity distributions, selection methods that allow for scoring of the probability distributions or that provide the relative performances of the distributions at different confidence levels should be used.

Examples of selection methods include the Likelihood Ratio, the Schwarz Bayesian Criterion, and the Violation Ratio. In particular, the Schwarz Bayesian Criterion adjusts each distribution test for sample size and the number of parameters, while the Violation Ratio measures the performance of the distributions at different confidence levels by comparing the estimated and expected number of violations.

When measuring Value at Risk, be it market, credit or operational, we attempt to estimate the quantile of a loss distribution. Before discussing tools and techniques for the selection and validation of models for estimating VaR, it is worth recalling its exact definition and how it relates to the problem of estimating a distribution function and its parameters.

Value at Risk measures the potential loss over a defined period for a given confidence interval. Thus, if the VaR is €100 million at a one-week, 99% confidence level, there is only a 1% chance that a loss will be incurred that exceeds €100 million over any given week. More formally, imagine a process that generates a random loss over a chosen time horizon. If p is a probability and q_p the p-quantile of the loss density function, then VaR at the p confidence level will simply be the q_p quantile of the loss distribution. In formulas:

$$VaR_p = q_p \quad (1)$$

It follows that a Value at Risk model will need to estimate part or all of the loss distribution function, from which then the appropriate quantile will be calculated. The validation of the model will therefore require an analysis of the distribution fitting process, of the techniques used to estimate parameters and of the tools used for evaluating the quality of the fit of the distributions to the data.

The estimation of the loss distribution can be done using essentially three classes of approaches:

- Parametric methods
- Non-parametric methods
- Monte Carlo methods

Parametric methods

Parametric methods are based on the assumption that the relevant loss distribution takes a predetermined parametric form, which means that it belongs to a parametric family of distributions, formally indicated by:

$$\{F(x;\pi) : \pi \in \Pi\}$$

where π indicates either one parameter or a vector of parameters and Π is the set of all possible parameters.

The choice of the distribution is usually guided by some sort of graphical inspection (histograms, q-plots and the like) as well as by more formal criteria such as one or more goodness-of-fit tests (which will be discussed in more detail further below). In all cases, however, two general principles should be kept in mind: parsimony (the simpler model should be preferred, unless there is considerable evidence of the contrary) and restriction of the universe of potential models (if too many models are tried, chances are that one of them will fit the data, but without telling us anything relevant about the population from which the data come).

Once the distribution is selected, and in order to determine the desired quantile(s), we need to estimate the distribution's parameters. This can be done through a variety of methods (maximum-likelihood, least squares, moments, etc.). Then parameters can be inserted into the distribution's quantile formula to obtain our quantile estimates.

These methods are particularly suited to situations where distributions are well-known. This is not the case when only small samples are available, as unfortunately happens quite frequently in operational risk.

Non-parametric methods

Unlike the parametric approach, non-parametric methods try to estimate quantiles without imposing a parametric distribution on the data, but rather by estimating the relevant quantities directly from the empirical distribution of the available data. Although these methods have the obvious advantage of not risking selecting the wrong distribution, they assume that historical data by themselves contain sufficient information to forecast the future. Although this may prove true in many cases, it tends not to hold where the tail of the distribution is concerned and in general when data are not sufficiently numerous. Again, as operational risk is particularly concerned about handling extremes, this may result in unreliable estimates in many practical cases.

Monte Carlo methods

Monte Carlo or stochastic methods simulate the loss distribution on the basis of a "model" of the loss-generating process. Such models, of which variables, parameters and relevant distributions need to be specified, are used to execute a large number of simulations by feeding it with (pseudo-)randomly generated values of the key risk factors. The resulting distribution of losses provides an estimate of the underlying loss distribution and can be then used to calculate the required quantiles in a manner similar to the non-parametric methods discussed above. Implementing such approaches in market risk is relatively straightforward, given that the model is usually already available through the relevant financial product valuation formulas. In market risk we identify a (relatively small) number of factors that affect the value of a portfolio, and analyse those factors' historical behaviour rather than trying to do the same for a specific portfolio. The actual portfolio may in fact not even have a history; it can very well be totally new and unique. Then, by using our knowledge of pricing models, we link the statistical properties of the factors to those of the specific portfolio. The challenge in applying a similar approach to operational risk lies not so much in a lack of historical information on relevant risk factors, but in linking this information to the probability of an operational failure to occur and to the size of the consequent loss. In other words, the chief obstacle to applying this approach in operational risk is in the specification of the model, given that the underlying loss-generating process varies wildly from case to case and may be very hard to formalize with a reasonably limited number of variables. This is also the reason why it is in general more difficult to (stress) test the results of a Value at Risk calculation in operational risk.

Another reason to be careful in estimating VaR for operational risk is the longer horizon usually required for the calculation of the relevant capital charge. While market VaR is usually estimated over a 24-hour time frame and hence updated daily, operational risk capital needs to be estimated over a one-year horizon, thus exacerbating the problem of obtaining reliable fit of distributions and estimate of parameters. This problem also makes it more difficult to accumulate sufficient historical data as well as a long enough track record to be used for validation purposes.

The aggregate loss model, originally developed in actuarial science in order to treat insurance-related problems, has now become, with some minor adaptations, by far the most widespread approach in operational risk. In this approach the aggregate loss is seen as a sum of N individual losses $X_1, \dots, X_N$.

$$S = X_1, \dots, X_N \quad N = 0,1,2,\dots$$

This model therefore requires first determining the probability distributions of the operational events (frequency) and that of the conditional probability distribution of operational losses (severity) given an operational event. The two distributions will then need to be aggregated into an overall probability distribution that will allow us to estimate operational risk with a desired level of confidence.

The distribution of the *aggregate losses*, a term taken from the insurance industry like most of the mathematics involved, may then be derived in a number of ways both analytically and numerically. For example, mean and variance of the resulting distribution can be calculated as follows:

$$\sigma^2\,(AggregateLoss) = E(\#\,Failures)\sigma^2(Loss\,/\,Failure) \\ + \sigma^2(\#\,Failures)E(Loss\,/\,Failure)^2$$

$$E(AggregateLoss) = E(Loss\,/\,Failure)xE(Failure)$$

Alternatives, especially useful with complex combinations of distributions, are the use of convolution integrals or Monte Carlo simulations (Klugman, Panjer and Willmot, 2012). Finally, a closed-form approximation was derived by Böker and Klüpperberg (2005) which is particularly well-suited for heavy-tailed loss data.

Let us now take a closer look at the task of finding appropriate distributions for frequency and severity of losses.

1.2 Distribution fitting

Frequency

One of the reasons why many practitioners use the Poisson distribution to model frequency is its ease of estimation. The estimator of λ is indeed simply the sample mean. Moreover, the Poisson process is additive, meaning that if monthly frequencies are well-fitted by a Poisson distribution with parameter λ_M, then the annual frequency can be estimated by a Poisson distribution with parameter $\lambda = 12 * \lambda_M$.

For a Poisson(λ) distribution, mean = variance = λ. If, for instance, the average loss event frequency per month is 0.91, with standard deviation of 0.83 (hence a variance of 0.69), the observed data could be considered as reasonably well described by a Poisson distribution, as suggested by a visual inspection of Figure 10.1.

A more formal way to test adequacy of a discrete distribution is to compute the χ^2 test. If, for instance, the value of the test is 5.61 while the 90% confidence interval to reject the null hypothesis (i.e., good fit of the data) is 5.58, then the result in this case would indicate that the Poisson is not clearly rejected (the higher the test value, the worse the fit), but that further investigation could help selecting a more adequate distribution (Binomial for instance).

The Poisson distribution has a single parameter; that is, the mean of the distribution. Accordingly, the average of the number of yearly losses is a descriptive statistic that can be used to parameterize the distribution within the convolution methodology. Of course, the mean of this distribution is also its variance; that is, the shape of the distribution depends on its location. Also, as the mean of the Poisson

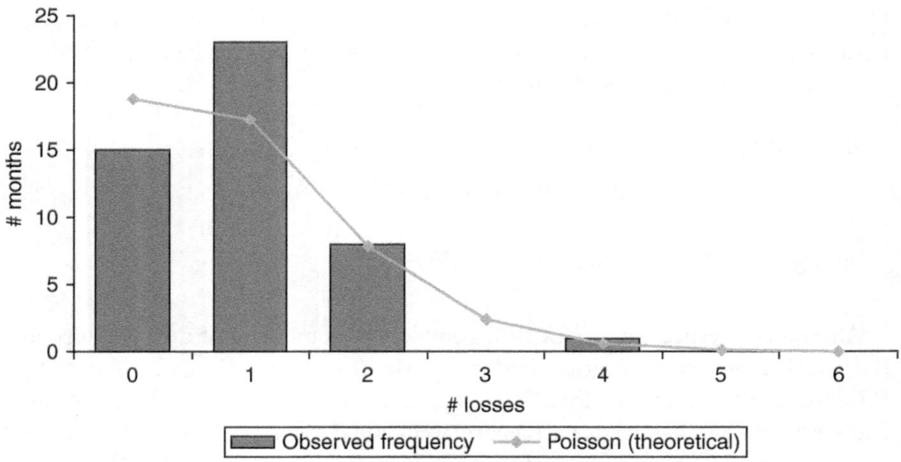

Figure 10.1 Comparison of the observed monthly frequency vs. the theoretical frequency of a Poisson distribution

increases, the distance to the maximum number of losses relative to the mean as measured by an extreme quantile decreases.

The frequency component in the determination of operational VaR is also essential in implementing stress testing. It is not easy to understand why, under stressed conditions, the actual severity of operational losses should increase while the idea that it is the frequency of losses that is related to changing macroeconomic conditions appears more intuitive. Accordingly, for operational risk purposes, it may be more important to stress frequency than severity.

The Poisson distribution is not always adequate to model occurrence of loss events. Three alternatives are the Binomial distribution, the Negative Binomial distribution (see their formal expression below) and the Geometric distribution (which is a special case of the Negative Binomial for $r = 1$).

Binomial (m, q) $$\Pr(N=k)=\binom{m}{k}q^k(1-q)^{m-k}$$

Poisson (λ) $$\Pr(N=k)=\frac{e^{-\lambda}\lambda^x}{x!}$$

Negative Binomial (r, β) $$\Pr(N=k)=\binom{k+r-1}{k}\left(\frac{1}{1+\beta}\right)^r\left(\frac{\beta}{1+\beta}\right)^k$$

The choice between these distributions may be important as the intensity parameter is deterministic in the first case and stochastic in the second.

A way to choose the adequate distribution is to observe the mean and the variance of the frequency series. If the observed mean approximately equals the observed variance, then the Poisson should be used due to its simplicity. If the observed mean is significantly smaller than the observed variance (hence increasing volatility of the frequency), the Negative Binomial is a good candidate. If it is the opposite (i.e., the observed mean is larger than the observed variance), the Binomial distribution might then be adequate.

Severity

Goodness-of-fit tests can be used to formally test the following hypotheses:

H0 (null hypothesis): The observed data is well described by the chosen distribution.
H1: The observed data is not well described by the chosen distribution.

The following are some of the most relevant distributions for modelling severity.

Chi-square(k) $$f(x)=\frac{2^{-0.5k}x^{0.5k-1}\exp\left(-x/2\right)}{\Gamma(0.5k)}$$

Exponential(β)[1] $$f(x)=\frac{1}{\beta}\exp\left(-\frac{x}{\beta}\right)$$

Gamma(α , β) $$f(x)=\frac{\beta^{-\alpha}x^{\alpha-1}\exp\left(-x/\beta\right)}{\Gamma(\alpha)}$$

Lognormal(μ , σ) f(y) = Normal(μ , σ) where y = ln(x).

Normal(μ , σ) $$f(x)=\frac{1}{x\sqrt{2\pi\sigma^2}}\exp\left[\frac{-(\ln x-\mu)^2}{2\sigma^2}\right]$$

LogLogistic(α , β) $$f(x)=\frac{\alpha(x/\beta)^{\alpha-1}}{\beta\left[1+(x/\beta)^{\alpha}\right]^2}$$

Pareto(θ , α)[2] $$f(x)=\alpha\theta^{\alpha}x^{-(\alpha+1)}$$

Raleygh(β)[3] $$f(x)=2\beta^{-2}x\exp\left(-\left(\frac{x}{\beta}\right)^2\right)$$

Weibull(α, β) $$f(x)=\alpha\beta^{-\alpha}x^{\alpha-1}\exp\left(-\left(\frac{x}{\beta}\right)^{\alpha}\right)$$

Several goodness-of-fit tests are used to discriminate the distributions. More specifically, quality of the modelling can be tested with Anderson-Darling, Kolmogorov-Smirnov and Cramér–von Mises tests. When no critical values are available for these tests (for example when using mixture of distributions), the Akaike Information Criteria (AIC) and Bayesian Information Criteria (BIC) can be used.

The following are the main statistical tests.

- The chi-square (χ^2) test. This test can be applied to any univariate distribution (i.e., frequency and severity). The idea is to split the population into k "bins" of equal width, and then to compute the following statistic:

$$Q = \sum_{k=0}^{n} \frac{\left(n_k - E_k\right)^2}{E_k}$$

where n_k is the number of elements observed in bin k and E_k the theoretical expected number of observations in the bin.

- The Kolmogorov-Smirnov (KS) test. It is only valid for continuous (i.e. severity) distributions. It is defined as:

$$D_{KS} = \max_{i=1,\ldots,n}\left[\left|F_n\left(x_i\right) - F\left(x_i;\theta\right)\right|\right]$$

where $F_n(x)$ is the empirical distribution and $F(x_i;\theta)$ is the theoretical distribution. It is thus based on the maximum distance between the observed empirical distribution and the theoretical distribution under investigation.

- The Cramér–von Mises (CVM) statistic (only for severity). This test is similar to the KS test, but introduces a size-based correction. It is computed as:

$$CVM = \frac{1}{12n} + \sum_{i=1}^{n}\left(F_n(x_i) - F(x_i;\theta)\right)^2$$

where $F(x_i;\theta)$ is the cumulative distribution function value at x_i (the i-th ordered value).

- The Anderson-Darling (AD) statistic (only for severity). It is another more sophisticated version of the KS test and is obtained in practices as:

$$AD = -n - \frac{1}{n}\sum_{i=1}^{n}\left\{\left(2i-1\right)\log\left(F(x_i;\theta)\right) + \left(2n+1-2i\right)\log\left(1-F(x_i;\theta)\right)\right\}$$

where F(xi) is the cumulative distribution function value at x(i), the i-th ordered value.

- The Akaike Information Criteria (AIC). This test is similar to the KS test, but introduces a size-based correction. It is computed as:

$$CVM = \frac{1}{12n} + \sum_{i=1}^{n}\left(F_n(x_i) - F(x_i;\theta)\right)^2$$

where $F(x_i;\theta)$ is the cumulative distribution function value at x_i (the i-th ordered value).

- The Bayesian (or Schwartz) Information Criteria (BIC) statistic. It is another more sophisticated version of the KS test and is obtained in practices as:

$$AD = -n - \frac{1}{n}\sum_{i=1}^{n}\left\{(2i-1)\log\left(F(x_i;\theta)\right) + (2n+1-2i)\log\left(1-F(x_i;\theta)\right)\right\}$$

where F(xi) is the cumulative distribution function value at x(i), the i-th ordered value.

However, in the end, a combination of graphical representation, algorithmic tests and the analyst's judgement is always required. Visual inspection may help to concentrate on the key aspects of the problem at hand, like the relevance of the tail or the asymmetry of the distribution. An alternative is to apply a scoring approach, whereby the results of several statistical tests are translated into numerical values so that the model with the best score is selected. But, even in this case, a picture may help better explain and support the choice, and expert judgment will anyway be needed in all cases where the results of the various tests do not agree[4]. For a detailed treatment of these issues, the reader may consult Panjer (2006).

1.3 Parameter estimation

Estimation methods can broadly be classified into two categories: those that establish a system of equation with as many equations as there are parameters to be estimated, and those where the estimate is obtained through the optimization of some relevant criterion.

An example of the first kind is the so-called method of moments, where the population parameters are estimated by equating sample moments with unobservable population moments and then solving those equations for the quantities to be estimated.

An example of the second kind is the so-called Maximum Likelihood (ML) method. The ML method is one of the most popular methods to estimate the parameters of the distributions used to model frequency and severity. The logic of this widespread approach is to determine the parameters that maximize the probability (likelihood) of the sample data. The method of maximum likelihood yields estimators with good statistical properties. In particular, it produces estimates that are asymptotically unbiased[5] and asymptotically efficient[6] as well as functionally invariant[7].

Formally, if x is a continuous random variable with probability density function $f(x; \theta_1; \dots; \theta_k)$ where $\theta_1; \dots; \theta_k$ are k unknown parameters which need to be estimated, then the likelihood function is given by:

$$\ell = \sum_{i=1}^{n} \ln f\left(x_i;\theta_1,\dots,\theta_k\right)$$

The maximum likelihood estimates of the parameters θ_j is then obtained by solving $\frac{\delta \ell}{\delta \theta_j} = 0$.

The ML approach has however a key weakness: it is not robust, i.e. it may produce wrong results when there are errors or outliers in the data or when the distribution is not correctly identified.

An alternative approach consists in evaluating the estimators against the population from which the samples are taken, which, of course, the population being in general not directly observable, needs to be done via simulation. This methodology is called bootstrapping (Efron and Tibshirani, 1993) and can be summarized through the following steps.

1. Generate a random integer number j from the set 1, ... ,n, where n is the sample size.
2. Take the jth member of the original sample.
3. Repeat steps 1 and 2 n times.
4. Compute the estimator (the bootstrap estimate) from the n new values (the bootstrap sample).
5. Repeat steps 1 to 4 a large number of times.

The result is a large number of estimates whose sample mean and variance are good indicators of the expected value and variance respectively of the estimator.

2 Model output

Once the model has produced its output, the two key questions become:

1. Does it make sense?
2. Is it in line with what is required (by the Basel Accord, the CAD, the local regulator and so on)?

The first question calls for a reasonableness check and for a verification that the result is not inexplicably out of line with respect to similar institutions, to previous results, if available, and with what experience and/or theory related to the model applied would suggest. An alternative approach consists in building a different, possibly simpler, model to be used as a benchmark, feeding it with the same data (or with simplified mapping and dataset) and comparing the results.

Along the same line, in order to verify that the model performs according to expectations and exhibits the appropriate stability of relationship between input and output, functional tests should be performed by comparing actual outputs with the outputs that could be expected based on the model's functional specifications. For example, the relationship between extreme losses and Value at Risk can be verified as well as the corresponding increases in low severity/high frequency losses and extreme ones when raising the confidence level[8].

A complete validation methodology cannot ignore that one of the key regulatory requirements (part of the AMA quantitative standards) is to ensure that the model reads at a "soundness standard comparable to 99.9% confidence interval over a one year period."[9] This point, however, thanks also to its not overly precise formulation, leads often to misunderstandings in current practice, the most common of which being that the Value at Risk to be computed simply corresponds to the 99.9 percentile of the distribution of losses.

In fact, in statistical inference, the expression *x% confidence interval* refers to the precision attained, and hence to the error made, while estimating the *x%* quantile (or any other statistic) of a distribution. The 99.9% confidence interval is therefore not the corresponding quantile, but an *interval* within which the *estimate* of the 99.9% quantile is comprised. More formally, a $100(1-\alpha)\%$ confidence interval for a certain statistic θ is a pair of values L and U such that $\Pr(L \leq \theta \leq U) \geq 1-\alpha$ for all θ. It should be noted that, contrary perhaps to what one might think in reading the Basel II quantitative standards, when moving from, say, a 99% to a 99.9% Value at Risk, the reliability of our estimate, everything else being equal, goes *down*.

Technically, the *level of confidence* $(1-\alpha)$ is not a property of the interval, but of the methodology used to obtain the interval itself. Therefore if we use one particular methodology over and over in order to estimate VaR, about $100(1-\alpha)\%$ of the time the true value of VaR will fall within that interval.

Regulatory guidance recognizes that, especially due to lack of sufficient data on high-severity, low-frequency losses, it may be difficult to ensure reliability and stability of result at the 99.9% confidence level. The suggested solution to his problem is twofold: to model the tail of the losses with a different distribution than the one used for the body, derived for instance from external data of some sort, or to use Extreme Value Theory (and the related Peaks-over-Threshold stability property) to compute the highest percentiles of the loss distribution. Although we have already mentioned the use of these approaches in the previous sections, it is worth pointing out that statistical techniques cannot always solve the problem on their own. The first approach of course implies the same issues and assumptions as the ones for the use of external data in general.

The right selection of the loss distribution and its estimation is the most critical part in operational risk modelling. More specifically, the right part of the density (the "tail") has to be carefully modelled, since it is the primary driver of the economic capital charge of the bank.

When the losses are modelled with a two-part distribution, a bank may rely on concepts and methods from Extreme Value Theory (EVT) (more specifically the Peak Over Threshold, or POT, approach). This technique uses information contained in the largest observations of the database to expand the risk profile of the bank beyond the observed (historical) data.

The treatment of extreme values has two steps:

1. Determining the threshold *U*. As no standard method currently exists in the academic literature to select the threshold, a conservative methodology is to use three well-known approaches (Mean Excess Plot, Hill Plot, Maximum Over Sum) and to compare the estimates before making the decision.
2. Estimating the parameters of the extremes distribution (also called Generalized Pareto Distribution, or GPD), using Maximum Likelihood Estimation.

In an dedicated study, Embrechts et al. (2003) examine the applicability of EVT methods to the estimation of regulatory capital for operational risk and discuss specifically the problem of how many exceedances (i.e., extreme observations) are needed in order to obtain acceptable estimates and conclude that "... one should abstain from estimating the VaR at the 99.9% level," as the number of observations required in order to obtain estimates of acceptable accuracy, even under highly idealistic assumptions, is way too large.

Frachot et al. (2003), after having shown the direct relationship between accuracy of Value at Risk estimation and number of observations (and how accuracy declines with the level of confidence), remark on the necessity of systematically estimating the accuracy of capital charges as well as on the fact that a different approach is probably required for high-severity, low-frequency losses and for low-severity, high-frequency ones. They conclude on the likely need for external data when insufficient internal observations do not permit them to reach the required accuracy.

From the above discussion, we can derive two key suggestions. First, and most importantly, industry practitioners should not be waving Value at Risk numbers as accurate and self-contained measures of risk, because their accuracy is wildly variable and should be separately estimated and reported alongside any VaR figure. Sacrificing concision for completeness, risk managers should always say, for instance, that "VaR at the 99% confidence *level* is €10M within a confidence *interval* of €2M" or, perhaps even more clearly, that "the 99% VaR is €10M plus or minus 10%," no matter how feeble such a formulation may look as one of the key outputs of what is often a multi-million dollar investment.

Secondly, banks may consider the possibility of using lower, more realistic confidence levels for capital allocation and other internal purposes, even while continuing to do their best to compute the fabled 99.9% for regulatory computations.

Back-testing

One of the basic tools to verify the accuracy of a model is *back-testing*, a procedure whereby the predictions of the model are compared with the actual results over a certain time horizon and the frequency, size and distribution (clustering) of differences (or violations) is used to decide whether the model is acceptable or not. This technique is currently used in market risk to test the accuracy of daily VaR estimates and the regulators have given specific guidance as to what level of accuracy is expected and how the capital charge should be raised in the presence of excessive violations. This approach, however, may not be very practical to apply in operational risk VaR, as it presupposes a sufficient number of predictions and actual results. Considering that the minimal holding period for operational risk VaR is one year, and that banks are quite unlikely to be able to perform estimates of one-year VaR (at least for most risk categories) with frequency comparable to market risk (where the estimate is done on a daily basis), it is difficult to gather enough data to apply a traditional back-testing approach before quite a long time of application of operational risk VaR models. Furthermore, as it is not possible to directly observe the "actual" 99.9% Value at Risk, aggregated losses should be compared to the estimated Value at Risk, and, if the model computes them, the distributions (actual and observed) of individual losses should be compared.

An alternative approach may rely on the use of actual operational losses incurred not just to test the accuracy of the model, but also to improve its accuracy each time a violation occurs. If operational losses occur that are not in line with the results of the self-assessment, the distribution resulting from the scenario analysis can be adjusted on the basis of the one resulting from those internal data. Internal data are modelled through the Loss Distribution Approach (LDA) whereby two parametric distributions are estimated from the historical frequency and severity for each risk category. The distributions are then combined through Monte Carlo simulation to derive an aggregate loss distribution, which calibrates and validates the results obtained in the scenario analysis.

This is done through Bayesian integration. This method adapts the *a priori* distribution of a given variable with additional information obtained from a second source. The distribution of losses obtained in the scenario analysis (called "prior distribution") is used as starting point. Next, the prior distribution is "updated" with the distribution calculated with the LDA (called "Data Likelihood"). The final distribution is called "posterior distribution,."

Mathematically, imagine that θ represents the relevant variable (Operational risk losses). Bayes' theorem is given by:

$$\pi(\theta|x)=\frac{\pi(\theta)f(x|\theta)}{p_x}$$

In this expression, $\pi(\theta)$ is the prior distribution; it describes what is known about θ without knowledge of the data. It corresponds to distribution obtained as output of the scenario analysis described in section 2.1.2. The sample likelihood $f(x|\theta)$ is the distribution of θ obtained from statistical techniques applied to internal data. Correspondingly, $\pi(\theta|x)$ represents what is known about θ given knowledge of data. It is called the posterior distribution of θ given x. The quantity p_x is merely a "normalizing" constant necessary to ensure that the posterior distribution $\pi(\theta|x)$ integrates or sums to one.

The Bayesian estimator of the parameter θ is the posterior distribution average:

$$\hat{\theta}=\int \theta\pi\left(\theta \mid x\right)d\theta$$

This minimizes the mean square error:

$$MSE\left(\theta\right)=E\left[\left(\theta-\hat{\theta}\right)^2\right]$$

In other words, subjective estimates are updated on the basis of historical data. If historical data reflect experts' opinions, the posterior distribution is very close to the prior distribution. On the contrary, if historical data are very far from experts' opinions, the posterior distribution, and hence the capital charge, records a change in shape and statistics.

3 Data

It is difficult to find a field where the adage: "Garbage in, garbage out" applies more properly than in operational risk. No matter how sophisticated and trusted the statistical methodology, no matter how thorough the testing of the results, without reliable input data, the task of estimating operational risk capital is bound to remain questionable and unconvincing. But an AMA approach is based on more than just one kind of input data and different requirements and different validation techniques will have to be followed depending on the nature of the input considered.

In the following pages we will discuss input data coming from internal and external databases of losses, input data coming from self-assessment/scenario analysis exercises and input data coming from the business and control environment. In each of these cases, we will describe general principles and specific techniques, but in order to give concrete examples, we will have to refer to specific solutions, being aware of course that there are always different ways to implement the various components of AMA. In particular, we will show examples of self-assessment exercises for scenario analysis as well as of the use of Key Risk Indicators for the business and control environment without of course suggesting that other approaches cannot be applied as well.

Internal / external data

Data standards

According to ISO (2002), standards are "documented agreements containing technical specifications or other precise criteria to be used consistently as rules, guidelines, or definitions of characteristics, to ensure that materials, products, processes and services are fit for their purpose." Data standards therefore should ensure that the data collected or produced, entered into a system and stored in a database can be consistently and reliably retrieved, processed and communicated. Data standards cover the structure of the data (the definition and content of each record), the value data can take (terminologies and classifications) as well as the technical framework for exchanging the data with other entities (data communication standards).

The value of data standards is particularly high when, as is the case in operational risk, data is difficult both to collect and to classify and when there is a need to consistently process a combination of hard, objective data (historical financial losses, Key Risk Indicators) and soft, subjective information (results of self-assessment). In the second Basel Accord, the Basel Committee on Banking Supervision (BCBS, 2006) specifies a number of standards that internal data must meet in order for a bank to be allowed to use AMA. They can be summarized as follows:

- Relevance. As any statistician knows, the problem with historical data is that they are, well, historical. They refer to the past and are the result of processes, systems and people which will in general not be exactly the same in the future. Assessing the on-going relevance of historical loss data is a clear Basel II requirement, but how it should be achieved is unfortunately not equally clear.[10]
- Size of the observation period. Historical data should cover a minimum period of three years at the time the bank starts using AMA. As soon as they become available, five years of data should be systematically used. Some of the implication of this standard may contradict the previous one. Using data from five years before does not make sense if substantial changes have occurred, and this holds particularly true for high-severity, low-frequency losses where each instance may have prompted radical management intervention with subsequent changes in people, processes and systems.
- Comprehensiveness. This requirement refers both to the breadth of activities (all the businesses and support functions, all geographic locations and legal entities) and to the losses themselves. Aside from materiality considerations (identifying activities with no material impact, having a de *minimis* threshold), at the core of this requirement is the need to capture *all* material losses in each activity, which is probably the most difficult condition to fulfil, as we will discuss below.
- Classification. Loss data need to be classified according to the loss event type categories and to the business lines established in the Accord. On top of that,

while credit loss due to operational risk should be classified as operational risk losses, but excluded from operational risk capital calculation, market risk losses due to operational risk should be treated as operational risk losses *tout court*.

- Content. The Accord also specifies that the database of operational events and losses should include the following information:
  - Date of occurrence of the event
  - Business Line
  - Loss Event Type
  - Relevant Risk driver
  - Gross loss amount, including any opportunity costs
  - Recovery (if any)

In addition, to facilitate more sophisticated analysis and reinforce the link with management action, the Operational Risk function should collect:
  - Business process in which the operational event occurred
  - Text description of the operational event
  - Date of notification (to assess incident identification timeliness)
  - Date of insurance recovery
  - Accounting information
  - IT system concerned
  - Product concerned
  - Description of the mitigation/corrective action plan to be implemented

Data standards for external data

The problem with data standards is more difficult to treat when it comes to external data, as collection and maintenance of the information are normally not within the bank's direct control. In practice we are faced with two different kind of external databases:

- Those including publicly available losses, that is those losses that are in the public domain and therefore, as banks do not normally divulge this kind of information unless they are forced to do so, those that are too large to be kept confidential. These databases are therefore strongly biased towards high-severity losses or, to put it in another way, are truncated above a very high threshold.
- Those including losses which are privately released by a consortium of institutions. In these cases, collection thresholds are much lower, but losses are drawn only from the banks participating in the consortium and reflect the quality of those banks' data collection procedures.

In both cases, however, using external data to supplement internal data in the calculation of operational risk capital implies the assumptions that external data are drawn from the same underlying distribution as internal ones. Such assumptions, which may be more intuitively reasonable the better correspondence exists with the institutions providing the external data on a number of factors like size, type of business, geographic location, time period considered and so on, need nevertheless to be more rigorously tested.

Frachot et al. (ibid. 2003), argue that, although it is probably not true in most cases that the underlying distributions are the same, nevertheless it seems reasonable, in light of the current status of operational risk knowledge, of the difficulties in developing reliable scaling functions and of available evidence (De Fontnouvelle et al., 2003) on the limited impact that scaling issues may have from an empirical point of view, to stick to that assumption for practical reasons.

Baud et al. (2002) have suggested a methodology for testing the hypothesis that external data are drawn from the same distribution as internal ones (Fair Mixing Assumption), but with the recorded external data truncated above a certain threshold. They distinguish three cases: when the threshold is constant and known, when it is constant but unknown, and when it is stochastic, and they conclude, amongst other things, that ignoring truncation leads to substantial over-estimation of the expected loss and of the subsequent capital charges.

Finally Na et al. (2005), find that a recognizable relationship exists, in the form of the power law,[11] between losses incurred in a specific business unit or a specific institution and gross income. Such a relationship can be used as a scaling mechanism to allow an institution to include external data into their operational risk exposure calculation.

Data from scenario analysis

The key paradigm in Operational Risk measurement consists in assessing the likelihood and impact of individual events. It is therefore in essence a form of systematic and, hopefully, comprehensive scenario analysis, almost regardless of what quantification methodology is chosen. Whether we measure operational risk by applying statistical techniques to historical data, through scoring risk and controls[12] or by relying on managers' self-assessment, we are always analysing scenarios in each of which a specific event takes place.[13]

However, trying to elicit from expert managers the assessment of risks and controls in terms of probability and impact is an interactive exercise where two kinds of problems normally arise. First, and most obviously, business managers are not, as a rule, statisticians, and most have not even a basic background in probability and statistics. It follows that not only do they have trouble following the intricacies of distribution fitting and parameters estimation (this is to be expected and in itself would not be a problem), but they are not used to conceive and describe risks, events and losses in statistical terms. As a consequence, they may have trouble giving coherent assessments, particularly when extrapolations need to be made, like in the case of high-severity, low-frequency losses. It is also very difficult to make quantitative assessment in absence of relevant information like industry benchmarks, historical data, peer comparisons and so on.

The second problem is that managers' expertise is usually highly specialized. They know some specific subset of the bank's activities very well, and they know extremely well the particular way those activities are implemented in their unit. This means that they may have difficulties in making the best use of their expertise if asked to assess events that are too generic or, worse, for which they do not see any concrete link with their specific activities. Asking a manager about the frequency and impact of a software problem is one thing, but asking how often during a month it happens that the automatic download of emerging markets equity prices from Reuters misses more than 5% of the data is altogether another. Similarly, one thing is talking about data entry errors, and another is asking: "How often does it happen that a mis-specified SWIFT code leads to an incorrect payment and hence to a financial loss?"

The validation of the data coming from scenario analysis shall encompass all the assumptions made and the information used to perform the analysis. A typical scenario analysis methodology will consist of:

- A systematic and consistent process for the collection of the experts' estimates. This means that the same approach is applied for each business unit's assessment and that the collected information is the same for each question (for example the expected number of loss events per year for each category and the financial impact of the potential loss events expressed in monetary terms).
- A statistical approach to model frequency and severity of each potential loss event under analysis.

Typically, business units' experts will assess operational risks on the basis of existing information on past losses, events and near misses; on their knowledge of the business; on comparison with similar units within or outside the bank and/or on external data. On this basis, the operational risk function will make assumptions, ideally also based on available statistical and other evidence, about the probability distributions and the parameters to be used in calculating Value at Risk.

The use of statistical and other data as well as the reasons for the ultimate choice of distributions and parameters should be thoroughly documented, and all assumptions used in scenario analysis should be reviewed in order to /confirm their appropriateness. This can be done by submitting them to a regular review by independent business unit experts, i.e., experts from a different (but hopefully still relatively similar) business unit, but also by comparing assumptions as well as results across the bank and with external information.

Another example of validation technique is given by Steinhof and Baule (2006) who suggest an approach to validation where experts are asked to express their opinions in terms of duration, i.e., mean time to the occurrence of one event exceeding a certain severity and are subsequently provided with a comparison between their assessment and an assessment based on available statistical data. The experts are then asked to "validate" their assessment by adjusting, if needed, their own assessment or choosing the one based on statistical evidence.

Data from business and internal control environment factors

The factors constituting the business and internal control environment can be quantitatively captured by means of key indicators (control indicators, risk indicators or performance indicators). Regardless of how such indicators are combined with the other information within the specific AMA implementation, the key element to investigate is how to assess their relevance in operational risk terms and, more specifically, to what extent each of them explains the amount of losses incurred (as well as the number of events that happened). A validation procedure should include wherever possible this kind of assessment of indicators.

One basic approach is the multifactor model suggested by Cruz (2002), where a linear relationship is explored between operational losses and indicators describing control and environmental factors in the form:

$$Y_t = \alpha_t + \beta_{1t} X_{1t} + \ldots + \beta_{nt} X_{nt}$$

where Y_t represents the operational losses or the operational Value at Risk, X_{it} are the business and control environment indicators, α_t and β_{it} are the parameters to be estimated. By performing a linear regression exercise the validity of the various indicators as predictors of operational losses can be analysed and subsequently documented.

It should be noted, however, that such an analysis may not always be possible. Regression models require a minimum amount of observations to be significant, and a bank may not have, especially for certain risk categories, enough of them to test the significance of certain KRIs. In such cases, validation can be performed by reviewing the process of identification and selection of KRIs as the result of a multi-step process involving process mapping, analysis of risk factors and risk drivers, risk identification and loss analysis as described in Scandizzo (2005).

Furthermore, other qualitative criteria could be applied and documented in order to support the validation process. As a first step indicators need to be appropriately and consistently classified in an Indicator Model that should include:

- a definition of types of indicators
- a description of all individual indicators (units, calculation method, assumptions...)
- the sources to collect each indicator (or the information required to compute it)

The main objective of a comprehensive set of key risk indicators is the early detection of any operational risk problem. The most important requirements for the effectiveness of such indicators are the following:

- Relevance - Strongly related to the frequency of operational failure
- Measurability - As much as possible, indicators should be objectively (and independently) quantifiable and verifiable
- Non-redundancy - If two indicators are known to be strongly correlated, only one should be considered
- Completeness – Indicators should cover all the key risk categories
- Auditability – Indicators and theirs sources should be properly documented

The Operational Risk function should, with the help of the business units concerned, identify key risk indicators according to the above criteria and also regularly review and re-validate the indicators by discarding indicators that have become irrelevant or redundant, changing the way key data are collected and processed and developing new ones according to the evolution of the risk and the control environment.

4 Conclusions

We have discussed the validation of Advanced Measurement Approaches to operational risk from the point of view of an institution endeavouring to comply with the requirements of the second Basel Accord as well of the Capital Requirement Directive, but also to follow as closely as possible what regulatory guidance is available on how to implement a proper validation process. The problem of AMA validation is more challenging and vaster than that of the validation of a mathematical model. This is due not just to the composite nature of AMA – the four building blocks; the need to incorporate qualitative information as well as expert judgment; the need to treat non-homogeneous data as if they were related to unique categories of losses – but also to the very nature of operational risk measurement, where we do not have a working model of how the losses are generated.

Validating AMA is thus at the same time trivial and problematic. It is trivial because the model does not purport to represent the way losses are generated, but merely the behaviour of aggregated losses given the occurrence of certain events – not very different from trying to estimate how many claims an insurer will face over a certain time frame if it sells car insurance policies, given the history of car accidents in the area. And it is problematic because, at least in the case of operational risk, the credibility of such estimates is dependent on a number of very strong assumptions which are, as a rule, very difficult to prove.

A credible process of validation for AMA must form an integral part of the measurement model itself. It follows, from the above challenges in validating AMA components, that AMA validation is not an audit exercise. Rather than producing a one-off yes or no result, it should accompany the various components of AMA as they are effected and should form an integral part of the entire process itself, although, to the extent possible, this should happen under the responsibility of an entity independent from the operational risk function.

Notes

1. The Exponential(β) distribution is a special case of both the Gamma and Weibull distributions, for shape parameter $\alpha = 1$ and scale parameter β.
2. The parameter θ is such that both scale and location parameters equal θ.
3. The Raleigh(β) distribution is a special case of both the Weibull distributions, for shape parameter $\alpha = 2$ and scale parameter β.
4. In some cases, for instance, if a model has performed consistently well in the past on a particular type of losses, we may require more evidence (higher scores?) to discard it.
5. Asymptotically unbiased means that the bias in the estimation tends to zero as the sample size increases.
6. Asymptotically efficient means that it has the lowest mean square error.
7. Functionally invariant means that the maximum likelihood estimator does not change under parameter transformation.
8. As shown by Jenkins and others (Jenkins *et al.*, 2005), not only economic capital is mainly driven by extreme losses, but also, for the same increase in the confidence level, the capital requirement for extreme losses increases much faster then that for low-severity/high-frequency ones. In a simulation with a portfolio of two extreme and 10 low-severity/high-frequency exposures, they show how the two extreme risks account for 80% of the overall capital requirement at 99.9% confidence level, whereas an increase in the confidence level from 99% to 99.9% implies a threefold increase in the capital required for the two extreme losses.
9. Directive 2006/48/EC of 14/6/2006, Annex X, Part 3, §1.2.1.8.
10. This problem is especially acute in the case of low-frequency/high-severity losses which, presumably, are promptly followed by substantial changes in the control environment to ensure they do not happen again, thereby immediately reducing the relevance of the related data.
11. The general form of the power law can be described by $L_b = (s_b)^{\lambda} L_{st}$
    Where λ is a constant, L_b is the aggregate loss in a particular unit or institution, s_b is an indicator of size and L_{st} represents the aggregate loss of the standard financial institution.
12. This is called either the Scorecard Approach or the Risk Drivers and Controls Approach.
13. "*Scenario analysis is a systematic process of obtaining expert opinions from business managers and risk management experts to derive reasoned assessments of the likelihood and impact of plausible operational losses consistent with the regulatory soundness standard.*" (Federal Reserve Bank of New York, 2003).

References

Basel Committee on Banking Supervision, "International Convergence of Capital Measurement and Capital Standards," Basel, June 2006, §673.

Baud, N., Frachot, A. and Roncalli, T., "Internal Data, External Data and Consortium Data for Operational Risk Measurement. How to Pool Data Properly," Groupe de Recherche Opérationnelle, Crédit Lyonnais, Working Paper, 1 June 2002.

Böcker, K. and Klüpperberg, C., "Operational VaR: A Closed-Form Approximation," *Risk*, Vol. 18, No. 12, 90–93, 2005.

Committee of European Banking Supervisors, *"Guidelines on the implementation, validation and assessment of Advanced Measurement (AMA) and Internal Ratings Based (IRB) Approaches,"* Brussels, January 2006.

Cruz M., *Modelling, Measuring and Hedging Operational Risk,* J. Wiley & Sons, New York, 2002.

De Fontnouvelle, P., DeJesus-Rueff, Jordan, J. and Rosengren, E., "Using Loss Data to Quantify Operational Risk," Working Paper, Federal Reserve Bank of Boston, Department of Supervision and Regulation, 2003.

European Banking Authority, *"Draft Regulatory Technical Standards on Assessment Methodologies for the Advanced Measurement Approaches for Operational Risk Under Article 312 of Regulation (EU) No 575/2013,"* EBA/CP/2014/08, 12 June 2014.

Federal Reserve Bank of New York, "Supervisory Guidance on Operational Risk, Advanced Measurement Approaches for Regulatory Capital," New York, July 2003.

Frachot, A., Moudoulaud, O. and Roncalli, T., "Loss Distribution Approach in Practice," Groupe de Recherche Opérationnelle, Crédit Lyonnais, Working Paper, May 7 2003.

Information Systems Audit and Control Foundation (ISACF) *"CobiT: Control Objectives for Information and Related Technology,"* 3rd Edition, July 2000.

International Organization for Standardization (5 December 2002). "What are Standards?" Available on line: http://www.iso.ch/iso/en/aboutiso/introduction/index.html.

Jenkins, T., Slade, J. and Street, A., *"A practitioner's guide to the Advanced Measurement Approach to operational risk under Basel II,"* Institute of Actuaries of Australia 2005 Biennial Convention, 8–11 May 2005.

Klugman S. A., Panjer H. H., Willmot G. E., *"Loss Models, From Data to Decisions,"* J. Wiley & Sons, New York, 2012.

Na H. S., Couto Miranda L., van der Berg J, Leipoldt M., *"Data Scaling for Operational Risk Modelling,"* ERIM Report Series Research in Management, December 2005.

Panjer H. H., *"Operational Risk: Modelling Analytics,"* J. Wiley & Sons, Toronto, 2006.

Scandizzo, S., *"Risk Mapping and Key Risk Indicators in Operational Risk Management,"* Economic Notes, vol.34, N. 2-2005, pp.231-256.

Scandizzo, S., *"Validation and Use Test in AMA: A Roadmap to Successful Implementation,"* Risk Books, 2007.

Scandizzo, S., *"The Operational Risk Manager's Guide: Tools and techniques of the Trade,"* (2nd Edition), Risk Books, 2010.

Steinhoff C and Baule R., *"How to validate op risk distributions,"* Oprisk and Compliance, August 2006.

11 Model Implementation and Use Test in Operational Risk

Various regulatory guidelines and requirements demand an independent review and verification process, not just into the AMA model, but into all aspects of the operational risk management process. In addition to focussing on the existence of appropriate policies, procedures, guidelines and standards, it is expected that the independent review function also considers data quality, data completeness and the degree to which risk-related data can be verified and reconciled to day-to-day transactional, accounting and business data. In particular, the two aspects of model implementation and use test should be assessed (Scandizzo, 2007).

1 Model implementation and operations

The first element to look at is the overall input process (i.e., the combination of input data sources and their owners, the process to follow to source and prepare data including the relevant controls).

Operational events and operational losses are normally talked about in the context of database building and quantitative modelling as the cornerstone of statistical analysis in operational risk. Collecting, analysing and storing loss data information is the first step in any solid operational risk measurement framework. And the Basel Committee specifies the minimum requirements for this exercise as follows. The database of operational events and losses should include the following information (see §673 of the second Basel Accord):

- the date of the occurrence of the event
- business line
- loss event type
- relevant risk driver
- gross loss amount, including any opportunity costs
- recovery (if any)

In addition, to facilitate more sophisticated analysis and reinforce the link with management action, the operational risk function should collect data on:

- the business process in which the operational event occurred
- text description of the operational event
- the date of notification (to assess incident identification timeliness)
- the date of insurance recovery
- accounting information
- the IT system concerned
- product concerned
- a description of the mitigation/corrective action plan to be implemented

However, loss events as well as near misses (i.e., those operational failures that only by sheer luck did not result in a financial loss) should not just be buried in a database and disappear into a complex capital calculation. Operational risk management is about analysing causes and implementing corrective actions so that capital numbers are in line with objectives, not merely about measuring. This can only be achieved by ensuring the appropriate level of transparency within the organization and, therefore, it is paramount that key events (those that reveal weaknesses and actually or potentially severe exposures) as well as their causes and consequences are properly disclosed and reported.

As mentioned above, making sure that all material losses are captured is one of the key requirements, because it affects directly the reliability of the results, but also the most difficult one. The reason is twofold. First of all, the identification and collection of operational losses throughout the organization is based on a reporting process. Normally one of the tenets of any operational risk policy is that business managers should report all operational events and losses to the operational risk function. But this is in turn based on the assumption that in each business unit losses are accurately and completely reported to management. As in any process that relies on an uninterrupted chain of human intervention, the potential for errors and omissions (intentional or otherwise) is enormous.

Furthermore, in order to report a loss, one must be aware of it, and this is not always granted. Imagine that a software bug or a manager's mistake causes the bank to misprice one of its products. Not only will the resulting loss not appear anywhere in the bank's systems, but both cause and effect may remain undetected for a long time.

Regulatory guidance[1] on the subject usually points to a process of reconciliation to the general ledger as a means to ensure completeness of the input data. It should be noted, however, that such an approach works only partially and asymmetrically. In fact, only certain losses can be identified in the general ledger. Opportunity losses will of course never appear, and even increases in costs will be in most cases next to impossible to pin down. Whereas hard losses in tightly controlled processes may be clearly posted in accounting (think, for instance, of overdraft interests on Nostro accounts or payment penalties or legal liabilities) others may not be so easy to identify (for instance, an incorrect hedging leading to higher-than-expected market losses). In other words, while items may be find in the general ledger that have escaped detection and/or reporting to the operational risk function, the fact that a reported loss is not identified in the general ledger does not necessarily suggest a problem with the accounting process.

Input validation procedures

Input validation is essentially the checking of data for correctness, or the determination of their compliance with given standards. The objective of input validation is to ensure that the model operates on clean, correct and useful data. This validation, therefore, is not a periodic activity to be performed either ex-ante or ex-post, but rather a systematic process to be embedded in the risk measurement approach through a set of dedicated procedures that in turn will need to be enforced and audited. The regulatory guidance with respect to input validation in AMA implementation is very generic and refers essentially to the existence of appropriate procedures to ensure the required data quality. It is therefore not easy to give specific suggestions as to what kind and level of validation activity would be expected by regulators while examining an AMA approach. However, as this is a subject that has been thoroughly developed in other fields, a good reference could be provided by a framework of recognized quality, albeit more broadly intended for IT management, such as, for instance, the COBIT framework for IT governance (COBIT, 2000), which has been developed to provide an international set of generally accepted information technology control objectives.

The loss data collection process should be designed in such a way to support the operational risk framework by providing input which is consistent and complete. Key elements to be put in place are:

- Risk categories. Although the Basel Accord and the Capital Adequacy Directive provide a structured list of loss event types, any complex-enough organization will need to develop some firm-specific categories to better capture the complexity of its operations. These categories will need to be mutually exclusive, exhaustive and provide enough granularity to allow effective risk management. Needless to say, they will also have to be uniquely mappable to the Basel-provided risk classification scheme.
- Business units as well will need to be mapped to the Basel and CAD classification, but, for data collection purposes, they may also need to be identified so that they align with the underlying risks while at the same time reconciling to the firm's financial and managerial hierarchies.
- Database structure and data fields should be designed to facilitate day-to-day risk management activities like identification of breakdowns and control

improvements. They should also allow for the collection of soft losses (opportunity costs, potential losses, exceptional gains and near misses) as well as for the correct treatment of thresholds. Ideally all losses should be captured, even if Value at Risk calculation only uses data above a certain threshold.

A proper set of procedures to ensure the validity of the input should cover the treatment of source documents including authorization, data collection, error handling and retention. It should foresee checks for the accuracy, completeness and authorization of the data treated and segregation of duties between origination, approval and conversion of source documents into data.

It should ensure that authorized data remains complete, accurate and valid through source document origination and that they are transmitted in a timely manner. It should prescribe the following controls:

- Periodic review of source documents for proper completion and approvals.
- Adequate controls over sensitive information on source documents for protection from compromise.
- Sufficiently long source document retention to allow reconstruction in event of loss, availability for review and audit, litigation inquiries or regulatory requirements.
- Proper separation of duties among submission, approval, authorisation and data entry functions.
- Routine verification or edit checks of inputted data as close to the point of origination as possible.

The procedures should ensure the completeness and accuracy of source documents, the existence of an audit trail to identify source of input, the appropriate handling of erroneously input data and clearly assign responsibility for enforcing proper authorization over data.

2 The use test

The expression *use test* refers to the requirement, contained in the CRD Directive[2], that the internal operational risk measurement system be closely integrated in its day-to-day risk management process. As already observed in the introduction to this work, the fact that the AMA is not just a measurement model, but an approach to measurement, which subsumes a combination of policies, procedures and managerial activities, implies that its validation cannot consist solely of statistical tests. On the other hand, given that "Validation is fundamentally about assessing the predictive ability of an institution's risk estimates" (CEBS, 2006), the use test requirement goes to the heart of the problem: If it is so difficult to establish the accuracy of operational risk estimates, both because of the paucity of statistical data and because of the regulatory obligation to combine those with judgmental and qualitative information, then how to ensure that such estimates are embedded into day-to-day (risk) management?

The attainment of this objective is further complicated by the difficulty of defining what is meant with the expression "day-to-day risk management process." Given that the AMA-generated risk estimates are unlikely to be updated more frequently than quarterly or monthly (at most), it is not immediately clear how a monthly, quarterly or yearly VaR number could be meaningfully embedded in the daily routine of, say, internal controls on settlements or independent verification of traders' P/L.

Furthermore, while the use test requirement for IRB approaches on credit risk naturally refers to the key activity of credit adjudication and is therefore much more specific and easy to prove, the same requirement for AMA suffers from the usual lack of clear boundaries for the scope of operational risk and related management activities. In AMA, on the other hand, it is unfortunately much less clear what day-to-day risk management activity means and, as a consequence, what the use test really requires. In fact, although one might argue that several daily management activities, and possibly all those related to the execution of internal controls constitute day-to-day operational risk management, it is very difficult to identify any of those as either driven by economic capital or impacting the allocation thereof.

In other words, whereas it is very clear in principle that the regulators do not want banks to use two separate systems for operational risk measurement[3], it is far less evident how the chosen system (any system?) translates into daily risk management.

This is of course due more to the very nature of operational risk rather than to any lack of precision on the part of the regulators and demands, as usual, an additional effort in clarifying first what those risk management activities might be and then what role risk measurement should play within them.

Although proving (or disproving) compliance with the concepts of the "use test" can be extremely onerous, there are some broadly valid concepts that a bank needs to take into account in order to meet the requirements of the "use test."

Operational risk management must go significantly beyond calculating Pillar 1 operational risk capital. This means that management has to understand what their operational risk profile is, to include the implications for the operational risk profile in day-to-day decision making and ensure an acceptable level of operational risk awareness across management and staff.

Business units should be able to quantify the impact of operational risk in their decisions, and their performance should be assessed against both the amount of operational risk capital that their decisions explicitly and implicitly use and in ongoing performance against thresholds, budgets and targets.

Finally, most staff should be reasonably operationally risk-aware and should also be aware of applicable policy and procedures and understand when they are required to undertake, initiate or report against some specific operational risk management requirement.

Following are the relevant (and at the time of writing, still in draft form) regulatory technical standards contained in EBA (2014, art. 41-44).

USE TEST

Article 41

Use test (not limited to regulatory purposes)

The competent authority shall verify that an institution ensures that the purpose and use of AMA are not limited to regulatory purposes, rather that:

(a) an institution operational risk measurement system is integrated in its day-to-day business process and used for risk management purposes on an on-going basis;

(b) the operational risk measurement system is used to manage operational risks across different business lines/units or legal entities within the organisation structure;

(c) the operational risk measurement system is embedded within the various entities of the group. In case of use of an AMA at consolidated level, the parent's AMA framework has to be rolled out to the subsidiaries, and the subsidiaries' operational risk and controls have to be incorporated in the group-wide AMA calculations.

(d) the operational risk measurement system is not only used for the calculation of the institution's regulatory own funds requirement in accordance with Articles 92(2)(e) and 312(2) of Regulation (EU) No 575/2013, but also for the purposes of its internal capital adequacy assessment process in accordance with Article 73 of Directive 2013/36/EU.

Article 42

Evolving nature

The competent authority shall verify that an institution ensures that the AMA evolves as the institution gains experience with risk management techniques and solutions, by assessing that:

(a) an institution's operational risk measurement system is robust and responsive to the institution's changing dynamic;

(b) the operational risk measurement system is updated on a regular basis and evolves as more experience and sophistication in management and quantification of operational risk is gained;

(c) the nature and balance of inputs into the operational risk measurement system are relevant and continuously fully reflect the evolving nature of an institution business, strategy and operational risk exposure.

Article 43

Supporting and enhancing operational risk management

The competent authority shall verify that an institution ensures that the AMA supports and enhances the management of operational risk within the organization, by assessing that:

(a) inputs and outputs of an institution's operational risk measurement system contribute to and are used in their management and decision-making processes;

(b) the operational risk measurement system contributes to the regular and prompt reporting of appropriate and consistent information that fully reflects the nature of the business and its risk profile;

(c) remedial action for improving processes is considered upon receipt of information from the operational risk measurement system.

Article 44

Beneficial for operational risk organization and control

The competent authority shall verify that an institution ensures that the use of AMA provides benefits to the institution in the organization and control of operational risk, by assessing that:

(a) the institution's definition of operational risk appetite and tolerance and its associated operational risk management objectives and activities are clearly communicated within the organization;

(b) the relationship between the institution's business strategy and its operational risk management (including with regard to the approval of new products, systems and processes) are clearly communicated within the organization;

(c) there is evidence that the operational risk measurement system increases transparency, risk awareness and operational-risk management expertise and creates incentives to improve the management of operational risk throughout the organization;

(d) inputs and outputs of the operational risk measurement system are used in relevant decisions and plans, such as in the institution's action plans, business continuity plans, internal audit working plans, capital assignment decisions, insurance plans and budgeting decisions.

3 Management versus compliance

That AMA, and the whole Basel Accord for that matter, should not just be a box-ticking compliance effort has been said and written enough times, by both regulators and practitioners, to become a pretty suspicious statement. That such a statement is also a compliance requirement in its own right contained in the Basel Accord itself, the CRD Directive and in every national regulator's guidance, makes the subject slightly self-referential. In fact, there are two issues to consider.

On one hand, as we have mentioned already, there is the fact that AMA (as well as IRB) is not just a measurement model, but an overall approach to risk management. Therefore all the governance, policy and management components which are essential prerequisites for the adoption of AMA should be implemented genuinely for what they are intended to be: steps to permanently improve the management of risk and not just measures to be put in place to achieve regulatory approval and to be forgotten soon afterwards[4] (see Scandizzo, 2007).

On the other hand, the emphasis on incorporating the approach's *measurement* results into the day-to-day risk management process suggests not just a concern on managerial improvement, but also, and more notably, an objective of convergence between internal and regulatory measures of capital at risk. The relationship between regulatory and economic capital has been the subject of numerous studies (see for instance Matten, 2000, and Falkenstein, 1997) discussing, amongst other things, the problems in capital allocation, performance measurement and ultimately market positioning that may result from any substantial and sustained divergence between the two. One of the key ideas behind the New Basel Accord was the objective of rendering regulatory capital requirements more risk-sensitive and hence more in line with economic capital. As already happened for market risk, allowing banks to use an *internal* model for regulatory capital, even if subject to a number of additional requirements, fosters the alignment of the two constraints and the attainment of at least two key benefits.

The first benefit is that the bank faces only one set of constraints: those that, to the best of its knowledge, reflect the distribution of risks in its portfolio. Regulatory capital is no longer a constraint to the profit-maximizing objective of the bank. This simplifies the task of optimizing the allocation of capital and helps reducing underutilized surpluses.

The second is that the bank's books become more transparent, as internally assessed capital at risk is also regulatory capital, and the market can directly respond both to any perceived inaccuracy of such assessment and to any unjustified difference between economic and book capital (Market Discipline).

Therefore, a bank wishing to prove that it is meeting the use test could provide evidence that the risk measurement system is used to manage operational risk exposures across different business lines within the organisation structure. Also, it could show how inputs, estimations and predictions from the risk measurement system are used in the decision making process, for example, as an element in strategic and tactical decision making. Other examples include the computation of specific provisions for certain kind of operational risks (like potential legal or regulatory liabilities), cost benefit analysis to support insurance decisions, as well as improvements in management and internal controls subsequent to a specific operational risk assessment.

AMA risk measures (in particular capital at risk by business lines) can be used to manage the portfolio of operational risk exposures. In theory, given a well-defined risk appetite expressed as a target risk profile for each business line, estimates of operational risk capital can be used in the optimization of available capital and in measuring capital usage and return (Matten, 2000). This task, within the use test framework, is further simplified by the absence of regulatory capital as an external constraint (economic capital *is* regulatory capital). In practice, however, things are more complicated. Providing evidence of such use of operational risk capital means to show how, for instance, a project has been rejected in favour of another on the basis of their marginal capital requirements, or how the decision to enter or exit a certain market has been driven by the estimate of operational risk capital necessary to run a business in that market. Other examples may include documenting the decision to discontinue a particular business line on the basis of its (operational) risk-adjusted performance or to allocate more capital to another one given its attractive (operational) risk-adjusted profitability.

In all these cases, of course, operational risk is unlikely to be the only, or even the main, component of capital at risk, and the challenge in documenting them for the regulatory authorities may lie mainly in showing that considerations like the one listed above are indeed not irrelevant in the decision process vis-à-vis credit and market risk capital requirements.

4 Conclusions

The ability to provide regulators with clear and documented instances of how the Advanced Measurement Approach has been implemented and to what extent it is used in daily operational risk management (use test) is a key prerequisite for AMA approval.

As AMA is not just a computer-implemented set of equations, the relationship between measurement and management and, more specifically the role played by the former in the latter, is going to be relevant. Part of the evidence on the credibility of an AMA model is provided by the fact that the institution itself relies on its results and believes in its value enough to invest considerable resources in maintaining and improving it. Identifying such evidence is what the use test is about, and doing it effectively and convincingly has a lot in common with the process of validating the Advanced Measurement Approach. A model should be extensively tested and thoroughly analysed mathematically, statistically, from a computer implementation perspective as well as in terms of the inputs feeding it. But if a bank is not able to show that it places enough faith into it to base both daily and strategic operational risk management decisions on its results, this may cause doubts both in the credibility of the validation itself and in the commitment of top management to the principles underlying AMA and the Basel Accord. Given all the limitations and challenges in proving the accuracy of operational risk estimates, consistent evidence of an institution's own belief in the soundness of its advanced model is far from being an irrelevant element in judging the model's reliability, and absence thereof will certainly ruin the credibility of the results of the validation performed by the institution itself.

The regulatory requirements for validation and use test are an attempt at bridging the information gap caused by the nature of operational risk. As this is an essentially idiosyncratic form of risk, which depends on the inner workings of each institution, be it in terms of procedures, people, top management culture and so on, its assessment can hardly be based on publicly available market prices fed into well-tested and transparent valuation models. Supervisory authorities requiring banks to perform a regular validation of their AMA are not behaving very dissimilarly from auditors asking business to perform a risk and control self-assessment: It is not conclusive and is no substitute for the actual audit work, but it is aimed at providing a basis for the actual review that will follow by, at least partially, bridging the above mentioned information gap. Validation requirements show an awareness of the potential for inaccuracies and inconsistencies embedded in the regulatory review itself.

One cannot overestimate the importance of the business and control environment surrounding the implementation of AMA. Notwithstanding the regulatory emphasis on the "predictive ability" of Value at Risk estimates, banking crisis after banking crisis have made, and continue these days to make this abundantly clear. If there is a contribution from risk management to the survival of financial institutions, that is unlikely to lie in more or less precise "predictions," but rather in the credible assessment of the potential for catastrophic losses that facilitates the making of risk-mitigating decisions. In order to be credible, such an assessment must rely on a coherent framework, made of policies, control procedures as well as corporate culture, ensuring to the extent possible that the approach is consistent and sound. The validation of the mathematical model and of its software implementation is only one by-product of such framework.

Notes

1. See for example Office of the Comptroller of the Currency; OCC Bulletin 2000-16, page 4; Committee of European Banking Supervisors, Consultative Paper N. 10, 20-1-2006, Annex VI, Part 1; Financial Services Authority, Capital Requirements Directive Implementation, March 2006, section 2.
2. Directive 2006/48/EC of 14 June 2006, Annex X, Part 3, Paragraph 2.
3. This requirement for AMA is also easier to understand in light of the much less prescriptive nature of AMA with respect to IRB.
4. An analogous consideration of course holds for IRB.

References

Committee of European Banking Supervisors, "Guidelines for the Implementation, Validation and Assessment of Advanced Measurement (AMA) and Internal Ratings Based (IRB Approaches," Consultative Paper 10 (Revised), Brussels, January 2006.

European Banking Authority, "Draft Regulatory Technical Standards on Assessment Methodologies for the Advanced Measurement Approaches for Operational Risk Under Article 312 of Regulation (EU) No 575/2013," EBA/CP/2014/08, 12 June 2014.

Falkenstein, E., "Accounting for Economic and Regulatory Capital in RAROC Analysis," *Bank Accounting and Finance*, Vol. 11, No. 11, Fall 1997.

Matten, C., *Managing Bank Capital*, Wiley, 2000.

Scandizzo, S., *Validation and Use Test in AMA: A Roadmap to Successful Implementation*, Risk Books, 2007.

Part VI

Pillar 2 Models

12 | Economic Capital Models

The traditional rationale for measuring risk in banks is that they cannot determine whether an investment decision adds to or detracts from shareholders' value without a reliable estimate of the related risks (Shepheard-Walwyn and Litterman, 1998). In fact a non-financial company would normally go through relatively straightforward steps in its decision process: It would determine how much capital the investment requires, calculate the marginal cost of capital, quantify the expected return on an investment and then assess the corresponding contribution to the company's performance. But for a bank, none of these three steps can be performed without estimating the types and levels of risk involved. The capital required cannot be simply equated to the cost of funding the investment, because taking certain positions, for instance in derivatives, may require little or no funding at all, and yet expose the bank to substantial risks, therefore requiring a corresponding amount of capital. Likewise, the marginal cost of capital for a bank is difficult to estimate on the sole basis of its funding activities, as a bank can fund itself on the interbank market or through deposits at rates that are largely independent of the changes in risk levels on its balance sheet. Finally, even the expected return on a financial investment is hard to determine without knowing the risk profile and hedging strategy of the bank making it.

Bank capital of course is far from being a simple concept and a vast amount of literature is available on its various meanings and uses (a classical reference is Matten, 2002). From the perspective of shareholders, capital represents wealth tied up (measured as market value), requiring an adequate return as risk compensation while at the same time being an instrument for controlling the firm. For a regulator, capital is a buffer to absorb large, unexpected losses, to protect depositors and to ensure the ongoing viability of the financial system. For a risk manager as well, capital is a buffer to absorb losses, but it should also be used to reflect the risk tolerance and risk appetite of the bank, to prevent financial distress and to measure performance on a risk-adjusted basis. The latter task became one of the main motivations for estimating economic capital in the mid-1990s, when several techniques for risk-adjusted measures of performance were developed: RORAA (return on risk-adjusted assets); RAROA (risk-adjusted return on assets); RORAC

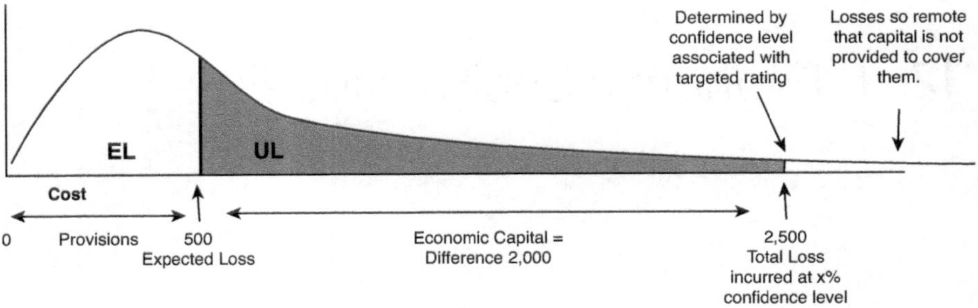

Figure 12.1 Economic capital and unexpected losses

(return on risk-adjusted capital); RAROC (risk-adjusted return on capital). Within this context, the concepts of Expected Loss (EL) and Unexpected Loss (UL) were used to establish a measure of economic capital under the assumption, subsequently allowed for also in the Second Basel Accord, that expected losses (i.e., the mean loss due to a specific event or combination of events over a specified period) would be covered by provisions while unexpected losses (i.e., losses that are not budgeted for) would have to be absorbed by an attributed amount of economic capital). Figure 1 shows a typical illustration of this idea.

Not surprisingly, the potential divergence between regulatory and economic capital and its consequence on banks' performance have been debated since the concepts were introduced (Falkenstein, 1997). The Second Basel Accord (BCBS, 2006) addressed the issue by trying to increase the risk sensitivity of capital requirements (Pillar 1), encourage banks to develop an internal capital assessment process under the supervisors' oversight (Pillar 2) and enforce a level of transparency in the disclosure of risks that would ensure a level of capitalization consistent with market expectations (Pillar 3). Of these three pillars, the second one is the most directly related to the issue of computing economic capital for internal purposes and the one where we find specific indications on the related motivations, approaches and objectives.

The Supervisory Review Process (SRP) is described in the Basel Accord as the interaction and dialogue between supervisors and institutions covering two key areas:

- The Internal Capital Adequacy Assessment Process (ICAAP) on the part of the credit institutions and
- The Supervisory Review and Evaluation Process (SREP) on the part of the supervisory authorities.

The structure and intensity of both of these processes depend heavily on the nature, scale and complexity of the activities of the institution as well as the potential risks posed by its activities. It must consider risks that are not covered under Pillar I (i.e., interest rate risk in the banking book, liquidity risks) and external factors (i.e., the impact of the economic cycle) in light of the fact that methods described under Pillar I cannot fully cover all risks (for instance concentration risk is not integrated into the assessment of credit risk under Pillar I).

The ICAAP prescribes that institutions should have a process for assessing their overall capital adequacy in relation to their risk profile and a strategy for maintaining their capital levels whereby all the relevant risks are identified and measured, and appropriate capital limits and targets are set. It should contain in particular a strategic plan, outlining economic and regulatory capital requirements, anticipated capital expenditures as well as related sources of capital. It should foresee systems and processes for assessing overall capital adequacy against the institution's risk profile including levels, and trend, of risk, verification of key assumptions in all risk models and projected capital requirements as strategy evolves. It should finally incorporate effective (and convincing) means to communicate with the regulator, which are owned by senior management, approved and monitored by the Board, appropriately delineated by business line, customers and product line.

On the other hand, the SREP foresees that supervisors review and evaluate institutions' internal capital adequacy assessments and strategies, as well as their ability to monitor and ensure their compliance with regulatory capital ratios and take supervisory action if they are not satisfied with the result of this process. Supervisors should seek to intervene at an early stage to prevent capital from falling below the minimum levels required to support the risk characteristics of a particular institution and should require rapid remedial action if capital is not maintained or restored. However, within the requirements of implementing a comprehensive risk management system and having a process for assessing their capital adequacy relative to their risk profile, credit institutions are free to choose the methodology. They may employ complex models allowing for correlations between risks as well as simpler models which calculate the necessary capital requirements under Pillar I and account for additional risks to which the respective credit institution is exposed. The emphasis is placed on developing a functioning overall bank control system as well as adequate internal capital management. Supervisors do not precisely determine how ICAAP must be conceived or implemented but would expect that it be integrated in the corporate governance process within a structure of effective internal controls and that it should adequately cover all the potential risks, including those which are not covered under Pillar 1. All in all, credit institutions are expected to *"have in place effective plans and procedures in order to determine on a regular basis the amount, the composition and the distribution of capital available for the quantitative and qualitative coverage of all material risks from banking transactions and banking operations and to hold capital in the amount necessary"* (BCBS, 2006).

1 Model Design

Needless to say, a model providing the kind of comprehensive picture of all of a bank's exposures discussed above is, in current banking practice, more an abstract ideal than anything else. This is the reason why current practice in banks is diverse both in terms of methodological approaches and of sophistication and reliability. The Basel Committee on Banking Supervision (2009) observes that: "*Economic Capital analysis typically involves an identification of the risks from certain activities or exposures, an attempt to measure and quantify those risks, the aggregation of those risks, and an attribution or allocation of capital to those risks.*" This suggests that economic capital modelling faces three key challenges: a comprehensive identification of risks, the selection of suitable (and comparable) risk measures for those risks, the development of an allocation methodology that is capable of correctly accounting for relationships and diversification while at the same time producing a capital charge that can be reliably allocated. Let us look at these challenges one by one.

Providing a comprehensive map of all risks a bank faces has been a regulatory requirement since the inception of the Second Basel Accord. Process mapping is the key preliminary step to risk mapping, as it is obviously hard to identify risks in a vacuum without reference to tasks or activities. It is true that it has been mainly used to identify operational risks (especially those related to transaction processing and IT systems), but analysing all the key processes is a task that should always be performed prior to a risk assessment as it may highlight exposures in many other areas. For instance, an analysis of the risk management process may point out deficiencies in the identification of connected exposures, leading thereby to the underestimation of credit risk, or identify problems in the documentations of credit support mechanisms, leading to higher than expected losses in case of default. Similarly, an analysis of the trading process may help determine whether inappropriate trading or accounting practices are used or if there are hidden liquidity or settlement risks.

The managers and employees who actually run a business are the most important source of intelligence about the risks of that business, first because they know it better than any auditor or risk manager and second because they know what is really happening at the moment, not how the procedure manual says it should be happening. The opinion of the experts is not only a fundamental complement to historical data and statistical indicators, but also a way to recognize that there is always a key difference between the map and the territory and that very few people do actually know every inch of the latter.

Scenario analysis is another important tool in risk identification, as it allows risk managers to go from an abstract description of generic events to concrete examples of what can go wrong and how, thereby providing useful insights for risk management and decision-making. Furthermore, by stretching the analysis to situations far from business-as-usual, it may make certain exposures emerge that might have otherwise remained overlooked. For instance, the formulation of a liquidity crisis scenario may highlight the fact that the replacement cost of certain swaps might be much higher than anticipated, with consequent underestimation of specific risk. Or a carefully constructed rogue trading scenario may help identify a concentration or a volatility exposure in the derivative portfolio.

Once the exposures have been identified, a bank needs to identify a common reliable metric. This issue is well-known to financial practitioners, and the yearning to resolve it has largely been responsible for the almost universal adoption of Value at Risk (Jorion, 2007) based methodologies. Value at Risk, however, similar to other statistically-based risk measures, like the Expected Shortfall (Acerbi and Tasche, 2001), is difficult to apply when the potential losses cannot, either analytically or empirically, be easily modelled through a probability distribution over a given time horizon. That is why there is no such thing as Liquidity Value at Risk or Maturity Transformation Value at Risk. Furthermore, if one really wants to map risks like reputation or strategy, pretending to quantify them in terms of "losses that can only be exceeded 0.01% of the time" is likely to sound preposterous. Risks have also traditionally been assessed on the basis of ad hoc five-point scales, or "mapped" on two dimensional charts according to probability and impact, but neither of these approaches can credibly be applied to the totality of banking exposures and is likely to be used only in the very initial stage of an exposure's assessment, when no analytical models have been developed, historical data are unavailable, and there is no consensus on risk policy or methodology.

Finally, the aggregation methodology depends in the first place on the risk classification structure chosen. This structure may follow the economic nature of the risks or the organizational structure of the firm. The aggregation methodology will then be applied across the different risk types, across business lines or both. A typical classification of risk types may include: market risk; credit risk; counterparty credit risk; interest rate risk on the banking book; operational risk (including legal risk); business risk (risk to future earnings, dividends and equity price); reputation risk; strategic risk. Of course, aggregation requires first that measures are comparable, and, as risk measures are typically expressed through probabilities at a given confidence level over a certain time horizon, comparability means that risk measures need to be consistent in terms of all these features.

The Basel Committee on Banking Supervision distinguishes between several approaches to risk aggregation and discusses benefits and drawbacks thereof. The following table is taken from BCBS (2009).

We should note that all the aggregation methodologies mentioned in the below table, save for the last one (full modelling) consist in taking the outputs of individual (and possibly very different) risk models and aggregating those using correlations

Table 12.1 Pros and cons of risk aggregation approaches

Aggregation methodology	Advantages	Disadvantages
Summation: Adds together individual capital components	Simplicity Typically considered to be conservative	It does not discriminate across risk types; imposes equal weighting assumption Does not capture non-linearities
Constant diversification: Similar to summation but subtracts fixed percentage from overall figure	Simplicity and recognition of diversification effects	The fixed diversification effect is not sensitive to underlying interactions between components. Does not capture non-linearities
Variance-Covariance: Weighted sum of components on basis of bilateral correlation between risks.	Better approximation of analytical method Relatively simple and intuitive	Estimates of inter-risk correlations difficult to obtain Does not capture non-linearities
Copulas: combine marginal distributions through copula functions	More flexible than covariance matrix Allows for nonlinearities and higher order dependencies	Parameterisation very difficult to validate Building a joint distribution very difficult
Full modelling/Simulation: Simulate the impact of common risk drivers on all risk components and construct the joint distribution of losses	Theoretically the most appealing method Potentially the most accurate method Intuitive	Practically the most demanding in terms of inputs Very high demands on IT Time consuming Can provide false sense of accuracy

and dependencies in turn estimated on the basis of a number of assumptions. The full modelling/simulation approach is actually more of a theoretical ideal than an actual modelling approach and is currently of interest in academic contexts rather than in banking practice. Therefore, when we speak of the output of an economic capital model, we refer in practice to a weighted average (of which simple summation is just a special case) of distribution quantiles like Value at Risk measures or the quantile of a multivariate distribution (in case copula functions are used). In the former case, the economic model coincides with the aggregation methodology as the output is nothing else than a weighted average of the outputs of individual models, like market risk, credit risk, operational risk, which have been scaled in terms of time horizon (for instance using the square root of time rule) and confidence interval. Validation should then ensure that the individual risk components have been fully validated and then focus on how the scaling has been performed, on whether the underlying assumptions make sense, and on how the weights (e.g. correlations) for calculating the average have been computed. In the case of copulas, one needs to validate all assumptions and techniques used to derive the full distributions of the various risk components and the parameters of the copula.

2 Model Output

To validate the output of a model means to assess its predictive power in terms of a quantifiable metric. Economic capital "... can be defined as the methods or practices that allow banks to consistently assess risk and attribute capital to cover the economic effects of risk-taking activities" (BCBS, 2009). If the economic effects in the above definition refer to the losses generated by the banks' risk-taking activities, then the model's output consists in an estimate of such losses, against which an appropriate amount of capital is then allocated. Output validation can therefore range from the relatively straightforward (when economic capital is nothing but the simple summation of credit, market and operational risk capital) to the extremely challenging (when economic capital is computed as the output of a model simulating the interactions of all the relevant risk drivers).

Even in the simplest cases, however, there are several problems to solve. One of the most basic examples is when the only risk considered is credit risk and economic capital is computed as the output of a credit risk portfolio model, like CreditMetrics (JP Morgan, 1997) or Creditrisk+ (CSFB, 1997). A discussion on validation of structural portfolio credit risk models providing both default and rating migration predictions can be found in Kalkbrener and Onwunta (2010). The main challenge in this kind of model is the specification of the dependence structure amongst the risk factors used to estimate the probability of defaults or of migration. Correlations can be calibrated using equity prices, credit spreads as well as default and rating data from rating agencies. Equity prices, however, may incorporate information that is not related to credit risk, and they are in any case only available for publicly traded counterparts. Credit spreads are also only available for counterparts issuing debt for which there is a liquid market. Historical default data constitute, of course, an ideal benchmark, but defaults are overall rare, especially for higher-rated borrowers.

An alternative is to use databases of historical defaults as a basis for simulating portfolio behavior. For example, Hu, Levy and Zhang (2013) use data from Moody's Investor Services and Moody's Analytics (including rating-implied probabilities of default, expected default frequencies and correlations) to simulate portfolio value distributions and, assuming 100% loss given default, distributions of realized defaults. They then map numbers of defaults to the corresponding percentiles of the distribution thus obtaining a set of independent and identically distributed percentiles which can then be used for assessing the performance of portfolio VaR models through various statistical tests.

A more complicated instance arises when market Value at Risk for a trading portfolio is combined with credit Value at Risk for a lending portfolio and operational Value at Risk from an Advanced Measurement Approach (AMA) model. Here the challenge is compounded by the difference in time horizons within the risk models (typically 10 days for trading market risk, one year for credit and operational risk) and with the time horizon chosen for economic capital (typically one year, but for some banks, longer, in order to coincide with their strategic planning cycle). However, even if the assumptions behind the chosen scaling methodology are validated as well as the individual market, credit and operational risk models, applying traditional back-testing or benchmarking techniques to the resulting economic capital output remains problematic. As already noted in BCBS (1999), the longer holding period, coupled with the higher target loss quantiles used in credit risk models, makes it difficult to assess the accuracy of such models through back-testing techniques, as this would require an impractical number of years of data, spanning multiple credit cycles.

If the economic capital model produces a convolution of the different risk distributions, then the resulting distribution cannot be compared to a single observed outcome and probability distributions cannot of course be observed. If the economic capital is estimated as a simple sum or as a weighted average of the three different Value at Risk estimates, then the resulting value of economic capital largely depends on the assumptions underpinning the aggregation methodology and it could, at least in theory, be tested against observed aggregate losses. However, it is extremely unlikely that a financial institution would have a sufficiently long and dependable recording of such losses for back-testing to produce reliable results. For these reasons, as noted in BCBS (2009), *"backtesting is not yet a key component of banks' validation practices for economic capital purposes."*

The application of benchmarking, another key approach to output validation, to economic capital estimates may translate into comparing the model's output to the results of another model, from an external consultant, a rating agency, the academic literature, and so on. This would require the use of the same reference portfolio in order to obtain comparable results, and it is of course a lot easier to do in a restricted context – like a credit model applied to a portfolio of publicly traded counterparts against, say, a model from Moody's or S&P – than in the more general case of a model covering market, credit and operational risk. In the latter case finding a benchmark model of comparable breadth may be quite difficult. One might of course try to build such a benchmark model, but the complexity and the data required for calibration may discourage even the most resource-rich validation team.

Another technique consists in trying to replicate the model's results by independently constructing an alternative implementation, in terms of both algorithms and data, of the model itself. This would not, strictly speaking, provide a validation of the output, but could give confidence that the model has been correctly implemented and help highlight any problems with the codes or the databases used.

Sensitivity testing and stress testing should be considered in validation of economic capital models also in light of the close link between regulatory requirements for both economic capital and stress testing. Sensitivity testing and stress testing can be considered as different versions of the same validation approach, with sensitivity looking at the stability of the model's outputs and stress testing attempting to highlight model limitations or capital constraints by stressing both inputs, parameters and assumptions of a model. Jacob (2010) suggests for instance shocking correlations to either regulatory or extreme benchmark values, or drawing a range of outputs from a distribution of correlations, through either bootstrapping or Bayesian techniques. This kind of analysis may also anticipate problems with the reliability of the economic capital model when used in the context of regulatory stress testing under Pillar 2 of the Basel Accord or within specific regulatory mandated exercises.

The challenges described become more and more difficult as the number of risks considered grows larger and the aggregation methodologies attempt at modelling the complex relationships amongst those risks. Furthermore, some risks, like reputation or strategic risk, may not easily lend themselves to the use of quantifiable metrics needed for quantitative validation.

3 Processes, data and the use test

The same reasons why economic capital models are made of different elements, complex and difficult to validate, make them also very demanding in terms of data architecture. The key component of such architecture (source systems, databases, risk applications) as well as the related data flow, should ideally encompass the totality of inputs and parameters required. This means that the input information, the functional logic and the related results of all the models whose outputs are relevant for the computation of economic capital should be integrated.

Furthermore, in order to be able to meaningfully compare estimates of economic capital with the actual book capital, the ECap implementation should be reconciled, to the extent possible, with the relevant accounting rules. For example, impacts on P/L driven by credit migration or other mark-to-market approaches either in loan or in derivative portfolios (through Credit or Debt Valuation Adjustments) should be translated into "book value" estimates of required capital.

Validators should examine evidence that the results of an economic capital model are used for purposes other than only filling the relevant section in an ICAAP reporting. The relevance of an economic capital model from a business perspective can be judged by observing how its results impact a number of important management decisions within the domains of pricing, performance measurement, portfolio management, and strategic planning.

Economic capital estimates can be used for risk-adjusted pricing of deals. While an operation's expected loss can be covered by an expected-loss pricing, the operation's contributions to the total unexpected loss on the portfolio can be reflected by the allocation of economic capital. In order to maintain sufficient economic capital, a bank should hold such capital allocation in the form of equity. The unexpected-loss component of the price can be computed using the appropriate return on equity (as determined by the board or similar governing body). Information about the marginal contribution of a deal to the risk of a portfolio can also be used for portfolio management and relative performance measurement. As observed at the beginning of this chapter, the assessment of financial performance on a risk-adjusted basis is a fundamental need for banks and the original motivation for constructing a risk measurement framework. Such assessment can be used for conducting investment or divestment decisions, for performing a number of different analyses (related to both risk and profitability) as well as for structuring a system of managerial incentives.

In a bank, the economic strategic planning and budgeting process should analyse the key developments in the bank's risk profile and capital management, including measures on how to ensure that the bank can continue to operate in line with its risk tolerance and risk appetite. In this context, capital adequacy is a fundamental consideration in terms of both regulatory, Pillar 1 requirements and economic capital. The planning process should assess the future sustainability of the business plan in terms of internal capital adequacy as measured by the level of capital consumption.

As mentioned above, stress testing constitutes an important technique for the validation of an economic capital model. However, the use of economic capital within a bank-wide stress-testing framework is both a regulatory requirement and a key component of a modern risk management system. This follows from the need, widely recognized after the 2008-09 financial crisis, to supplement the traditional Value at Risk approach with a stress-testing methodology that could anticipate the impact of severe financial and economic downturn. Such a stress-testing framework should comprise not only sensitivity tests, in which the portfolio is stressed to isolated shocks from one or two factors, but also comprehensive downturn scenarios. In scenario-based tests, a narrative is developed to construct a set of plausible, but severe, combinations of shocks that might impact the bank's performance. Economic capital can be included into the strategic and business planning of the bank, and stress-testing such planning means also to stress the economic capital projections for the future, in line with the ones already performed for regulatory capital.

4 Conclusions

The concept of economic capital encompasses the processes and methodologies whereby a bank assesses the risks generated by its activities and estimates the amount of capital it should hold against those risks. More often than not, such processes and methodologies do not materialize into a single, well-identified mathematical or statistical model, but rather consist in a combination of techniques whose outputs are aggregated on the basis of assumptions that can be both complex and strong. Validating these approaches and the resulting estimates requires meeting a number of challenges that are difficult in terms of technique as well as in terms of process and data. Although some classic validation approaches can be used, for example in terms of input validation, sensitivity analysis, model replication or benchmarking to external data, other techniques, like theoretical examination of assumptions, back-testing or comparisons to external models, are more problematic given the scarcity of data combined with the need to validate estimates at high quantiles of distributions on long time horizons.

The real obstacle, however, to define a complete validation process for economic capital is the fact that there is no such thing yet as an established practice for estimating economic capital. This is in turn due to the absence of a comprehensive enterprise-wide model for all the risks faced by a bank. This goal may never be attained, as the diversity of activities and related risks may always defy any such attempt, possibly for good reasons. But this will mean that economic capital will always be, first and foremost, an exercise in integration and thus validation techniques, aside from ensuring the quantitative soundness of the individual components, will have to focus on the quality of data and procedures as well as on the soundness of the theoretical assumptions underpinning the integration process.

References

Acerbi, C. and Tasche, D., "Expected Shortfall: A Natural Coherent Alternative to Value at Risk," Basel Committee on Banking Supervision, May 2001.

BCBS, Basle Committee on Banking Supervision, "Credit Risk Modelling: Current Practices and Applications," Basel, April 1999.

BCBS, Basel Committee on Banking Supervision, "International Convergence of Capital Measurement and Capital Standards," Basel, June 2006.

Basel Committee on Banking Supervision (BCBS), *"Range of Practices and Issues in Economic Capital Frameworks,"* Bank For International Settlements, March 2009.

CSFB, "Creditrisk+, a Credit Risk Management Framework," Credit Suisse First Boston, 1997.

Falkenstein, E., "Accounting for Economic and Regulatory Capital in RAROC Analysis," *Bank Accounting & Finance* Vol. 11, No. 1, 29–34, Fall 1997.

Hu, Z., Levy, A. and Zhang, J., "Economic Capital Model Validation: A Comparative Study," *Journal of Risk Model Validation*, Vol. 7, No. 1, 3–23, Spring 2013.

J.P. Morgan, *"CreditMetrics™—Technical Document,"* J.P. Morgan & Co. Incorporated, 1997.

Jacobs, M. Jr., "Validation of Economic Capital Models: State of the Practice, Supervisory Expectations and Results from a Bank Study," *Journal of Risk Management in Financial Institutions*, Vol. 3, No. 4, 334–365, January 2010.

Jorion, P., *Value at Risk: The New Benchmark for Managing Financial Risk,* McGraw Hill, New York, 2007.

Kalkbrener, M. and Onwunta, A., "Validating Structural Credit Portfolio Models," in Rösch, D. and Scheule, H. (editors), *Model Risk: Identification, Measurement and Management,* Risk Books, 2010.

Matten, C., *Managing Bank Capital: Capital Allocation and Performance Measurement,* 2nd Edition, Wiley, 2000.

Ribarits, T., Clement, A., Seppälä, H., Bai, H. and Poon, S. H.,*Economic Capital Modeling : Closed-form Approximation for Real Time Applications,* FP7 Marie Curie ITN on Risk Management and Reporting, June 2014.
Shepheard-Walwyn, T. and Litterman, T., "Building a Coherent Risk Measurement and Capital Optimisation Model for Financial Firms," *FRBNY Economic Policy Review,* October 1998.

13 | Stress Testing Models

The term "stress testing" refers to several different techniques used to assess the impact of events or combinations of events that, while plausible, are far from business as usual. Approaches to stress testing may vary from basic sensitivity testing (whereby a bank analyses the impact on a portfolio or business unit of a move in a particular risk factor) to scenario analysis[1] (whereby the impact of a simultaneous move in a number of risk factors is assessed).

Within the context of the Basel Capital Accords, the first formal supervisory requirement on stress testing goes back to the 1996 amendment to the First Basel Accord, which made the approval of internal models for market risk conditional on the existence of a firm-wide stress testing programme (BCBS, 1996). In 2000, the Committee on the Global Financial System published a survey on the application of stress testing in banks and found that in most banks, stress testing consisted of individual shocks to prices, rates and volatilities of market factors. It noted that scenarios could be developed by drawing on relevant historical experience (*historical scenarios*) or by analysing the impact of exceptional, but plausible events (*hypothetical scenarios*). Other techniques used to assess exposure to extreme market events included a *maximum loss approach*, in which risk managers estimate the combination of market moves that would be most damaging to a portfolio, and *extreme value theory*, which is the statistical theory concerned with the behaviour of the "tails" of a distribution of market returns (BIS, 2000).

For several years, scenario analysis has not been widely employed except in the form of stress testing for market risk (see "Modern Risk Management: A History," Various Authors, 2003) although the two terms are often used in combination. Most (around 80%) of tests performed were VaR-based and related to market risk in the form of single shocks. Simple models were used for credit and market risk separately, where level and volatility of market factors directly determined the price of assets. There was very little public disclosure, and the results were not necessarily linked to considerations of capital adequacy and did not result in macroprudential measures or capital conservation plans.

According to the Financial Services Authority (May, 2005), *Stress test typically refers to shifting the values of individual parameters that affect the financial position of a firm and determining the effect on the firm's business. Scenario analysis typically refers to a wider range of parameters being varied at the same time.* More recently, the Basel Committee on Banking Supervision (BCBS, 2009) has defined a stress test as *the evaluation of a bank's financial position under a severe but plausible scenario to assist in decision-making within the bank. The term 'stress testing' is also used to refer not only to the mechanics of applying specific individual tests, but also to the wider environment within which the tests are developed, evaluated and used within the decision-making process.*

The role of stress testing has grown in importance after the financial crisis of 2008-09 (Araten, 2013) to become a fundamental component of the risk management of a financial institution, reflecting the wider and more detailed set of regulatory requirements issued thereafter. For instance, in Europe, the European Commission, the Bank for International Settlement (BIS), the Basel Committee on Banking Supervision (BCBS) and the European Banking Authority (EBA) have all contributed to producing guidance on the subject; the main requirements, however, are contained in the Capital Requirements Directive IV (CRD IV, 2013) and in the binding technical standards issued, as mandated in the CRD IV, by the European Banking Authority (EBA, 2014).

Current guidance has therefore become both extensive and detailed, with provisions covering governance as well as methodological aspects. In particular, they underline the importance of stress testing as a key component of both the capital adequacy assessment process (ICAAP) and the risk and capital management process (use test), with clearly established responsibilities and an organic link to the bank's risk appetite and strategy. Methodologies, on the other hand, are discussed in general terms, and no indication is given of specific modelling solutions except to say that they need to be adequate and appropriate to the institution's material risks and that methodologies and data shall be documented in detail. Regulators have, however, indicated what the methodological framework should encompass in terms of key components, namely, sensitivity analyses for specific portfolios or risks (analysis of the model's result when parameters are changed, e.g. the 200 basis point shift in interest rates required under the Basel Accord) and forward-looking scenario analysis incorporating system-wide interactions and simultaneous occurrence of events across the institution. In particular, stress scenarios should be based on historical events or crises (especially if they are likely to recur) as well on hypothetical combinations of exceptional but plausible events (especially considering economic downturns) and be meaningfully translated into risk parameters also considering the impact of concentration risk. Finally, reverse stress tests, whereby scenarios and the related level of losses are identified that would threaten the economic viability of the bank and cause its failure, should also be part of the stress testing framework.

1 Model design

The post-crisis regulatory and industry evolution of risk management practices has spawned a variety of methodological approaches to stress testing where, as for other kinds of risk models, one might broadly distinguish between structural and reduced-form approaches. Structural approaches establish a causal relationship between asset value and probability of default. They posit a particular state of the economy (macroeconomic scenario) and then model the relationship between the economy and the assets' value and hence the relevant risk parameters. On the other hand, reduced-form approaches treat default events as "surprises;" they posit the assets' behaviour directly and give stressed values of risk measures (e.g., default rates) of the portfolio as part of the stress scenario. Reduced form models depend on assumptions about distribution and may have very little connection with macro variables. While they work satisfactorily with random, uncorrelated price movements or volatilities, they are less suitable for modelling systemic events or highly correlated movements. Finally, some market factors may either a structural or a reduced-form role. Interest rates, for instance, may be a factor directly affecting asset value while at the same time also being endogenously determined (for instance as a function of growth, inflation or unemployment).

However, the requirements for the implementation of specific regulatory exercises both in the U.S. and in the EU have given a particular focus to the use of macroeconomic scenarios. Hence, estimating the impact on a financial institution's performance and capital of scenarios where Gross Domestic Product (GDP), unemployment rates, inflation, interest rates, property prices and other macroeconomic indicators reflect severe shocks to the economy is currently at the heart of the industry's modelling efforts. The impact is in turn modelled in terms of risk parameters, and then in risk measures, from individual ones like impairments, provisions and losses to aggregate ones like regulatory capital, economic capital or other metrics of the ICAAP framework (without forgetting to estimate how portfolio exposure is likely to evolve under the considered stress scenario). For each scenario considered, however, the mechanics whereby the macroeconomic shocks translate into risk measures may differ and will be in general modelled in different ways.

In market risk, where stress testing has been performed regularly for many years, models need to take into account certain key features of financial markets, namely, their ability to anticipate economic developments, and the consequent possibility that a recession scenario may not synchronously translate to a corresponding impact on prices. Also, given that traders operate within a complex risk management structure, trading portfolios are usually dynamically hedged in terms of the primary directional risk components, thereby reducing the impact of directional moves in risk factors, especially when these are liquid (Canabarro, 2013). Usually related to large trading portfolios is counterparty risk on derivative transactions, which is measured by the mark to market of Credit Valuation Adjustment (CVA), the value of the credit risk faced by the counterparties of over-the-counter (OTC) derivatives. A model therefore needs to stress the underlying trades and the consequent derivative exposures, the corresponding credit spreads as well as the resulting credit losses.

For credit risk, following the developments of advanced internal rating systems (A-IRB in the Second Basel Accord), stress testing efforts have focussed on translating macroeconomic scenarios into PD, LGD and CCF estimates either for individual counterparties or on the basis of countries and sector portfolios.

Finally, operational risk scenario analysis is a key component of Basel II's Advanced Measurement Approach (AMA). Although the cyclicality of operational risk has been analysed in several studies (Allen and Bali, 2007, Cagan, 2009), establishing a relationship between macroeconomic scenarios and operational losses is especially challenging because of the difficulties in data collection and the complexity in the aggregation of the results.

Since there are no formal requirements as to the specific model to be used for stress testing, validators have to be ready to deal with potentially any kind of model design. In practice one of the most common approaches consists in modelling the relationship between the macroeconomic factors and the bank's internal risk parameters through a multivariate regression model that uses indicators representing those factors as independent variables and the internal risk parameters as dependent ones. A simple version of this approach consists in using an ordinary least squares (OLS) model, where each risk parameter is a function of a set of macroeconomic variables or, more commonly, changes in risk parameters are a function of changes in macroeconomic variables using appropriate time lags. Values of risk parameters may be averaged over portfolios and sub-portfolios based on industry, geographical or other internal segmentation. A simple example of such a model estimating a relationship between changes in Value at Risk (*dVaR*) and changes in a set of macroeconomic variable is given in the equation and table below.

$$dVaR_t = c + a_1 e_{t-2} + a_2 ir_{t-1} + a_3 gdp_t + a_4 dgdp_{t-3} + a_4 \inf_{t-2} + a_5 ind_{t-4}$$

The key assumptions used in model development should be validated together with their economic implications. The choice of indicators should be reviewed as

Table 13.1 Example of OLS model for Value at Risk

Macro variable	Lag	Coefficient
Constant (c)		−2.893
Exchange rate (a1)	−2	+1.025
Interest rate (a2)	−1	+1.981
GDP (gdp)	0	−4.152
Debt-to-GDP ratio (dgdp)	−3	+2.908
Inflation	−2	−5.001
Industrial production	−4	−0.959

well as the documentation explaining the rationale behind the choice. Most stress testing models will use a combination of GDP growth rates, unemployment rates, property prices, interest rates, inflation rates as well as other financial indicators including share price indexes, inventory levels, government debt, and so on. Assessing whether the above factors, or a selection thereof, constitute a sensible choice and whether the economic logic underlying the model is reasonable cannot be done mechanically and will require judgment. Regardless, however, of other considerations, macroeconomic indicators need to be measurable, with enough historical data available at the desired level of granularity to allow extrapolations over the relevant time horizon. It should be possible to reasonably establish an economic link between each macroeconomic indicator and the relevant risk parameters. Relations between rising unemployment and retail defaults, between a fall in the GDP and increased corporate defaults, between property prices and individual defaults, are all typical examples where the resulting impact on default rates may be interpreted in terms of increased PDs for the bank's portfolios.

Model developers may select the final equations by analysing each parameter individually to identify the most relevant economic factors for explaining the risk parameter time series, and they may then use several selection criteria sorting statistical models by their effectiveness for a given focus parameter. Examples are the Akaike information criterion, the Bayesian information criterion, the Deviance information criterion, the Focused information criterion, the Hannan-Quinn information criterion (see Schwarz, 1978; Hannan and Quinn, 1979; White, 1980; Claeskens and Hjort 2003; Ando, 2007).

Assumptions to verify will depend on the choice of model. For many regression models, it is usually assumed that data are stationary, i.e., that their statistical properties remain constant over time. It is also common to assume that residuals of the regression are uncorrelated and normally distributed, and that no heteroscedasticity (i.e., different levels of variability across the dataset) occurs. The reader may consult Durbin and Watson (1950 and 1951), Priestley and Subba Rao (1969) as well as White (1980) for details on how to test for the above properties.

Validators should strive to understand the underlying relationship between input and output, their correlation structure as well as any peculiarity in the data used, like breaks or outliers. Univariate and bivariate analysis, of the type discussed in Chapter 4 for PD models, can be used to estimate the R^2 and test the power of each macroeconomic factor. Furthermore, correlation analysis can help identify factors with a very high correlation and hence similar explanatory power indicating redundancy in the model specification.

Finally, the model used for stress testing should be consistent with the other risk measurement models used within the bank. These will typically be models for estimating PD, LGD, CCF, economic capital, liquidity, counterparty credit risk, market risk and so on. Modelling philosophy (point-in-time or through-the-cycle), model assumptions, and internal and external data should ideally be coherent with risk models used across the bank, so that stressed values obtained for the risk parameters can be meaningfully compared to the corresponding daily estimate and starting values.

2 Model output

The validation of the output of a stress testing model implies the verification of the model's stability as well as of its predictive power. However, the various validation techniques have to contend with both the nature of the models and of the available data.

Stability analysis on a stress testing model can be performed through sub-sampling. The dataset can be split into several samples covering the same time horizon, and outputs are compared. Sub-sampling can be done either randomly, when transaction or counterparty-level data are available, by splitting the dataset into an older and a more recent sample, or across segments (across geographies or sectors). Random or cross-segment sampling allows testing how stable is the accuracy of the model (in the form of goodness-of-fit) on the various samples as well as to verify that the dependencies between macroeconomic factors and risk parameters embodied by the model are structurally robust. A more demanding test is verifying whether running a regression on the different sub-samples would yield the same model, i.e., that the model will exhibit the same dependency of the risk parameters on the macroeconomic indicators. Also, subdividing the dataset according to some reference date validators can test whether the behaviour of older and more recent exposures against the identified macroeconomic indicators is the same or not. Breeden (2008) suggests using the Granger-Newbold and the Diebold-Mariano tests (Granger and Newbold, 1976; Diebold and Mariano, 1995) to test the equivalence of model accuracy over the various kinds of samples.

Sensitivity analysis should be conducted in order to assess the impact on the output of different model parameters as well as to compare the behaviour of different feasible models under various kinds of stressed input. Validators should test for reasonability of results as well as for any breakdown in the economic intuition underlying the model's structure.

The fundamental problem in validating the output of a stress testing model lies in the limited availability of data. Many institutions have around five years' worth of data relevant for risk management purposes, in line with minimal Basel requirements; external data may be available for a longer period in certain sectors, while data series for emerging markets will be in general shorter. But the main problem is that recession data, the most relevant data for stress testing purposes, will be limited to one or two occurrences at most. Therefore, it is very difficult to prove that a model built on data from the most recent economic downturn will be able to predict the next one; there just isn't enough evidence.

Back-testing runs against this problem both in its in-sample and in its out-of-sample version. The objective of back-testing is to assess the predictive power of the model by comparing its forecasts (i.e., the result of the stress test) before the fact with the actual outcome subsequently observed (i.e., with the risk parameters' value observed over the period containing the extreme event used for back-testing). In-sample back-testing uses the same dataset that has been used to develop the model and is therefore less meaningful in terms of validation power. Out-of-sample back-testing is more powerful, because it compares the model output with historical observations other than those used to develop the model. However, it may require internal data from an earlier recession period that may be of lesser quality or plain unavailable. For instance, Chen (2013) suggests running historical scenarios to examine the model output against historically observed events, like the 2008-09 recession, the internet bubble or the 1980s stagflation. Novosylov and Sathcov (2010) use several historical shocks to test a stress testing model: the crisis following the Long Term Capital Management (LTCM) crisis during August 1998; the end of the internet bubble and the impact observed during November 2000; the attack on the twin towers and the consequences recorded over September 2001; the first major impact of the credit crunch over the summer of 2007; the continuation of that crisis over the course of 2008.

Back-testing, of course, does not show whether or not the actual events could have been predicted, but only that the possibility for a worsening of certain economic factors could have plausibly been considered in the stress testing process. Although comparing macroeconomic shocks and changes in risk parameters over several samples and over the available history of actual extreme impacts gives us an understanding of the predictive power of the model, we still need to assume that the stressed scenario was correctly anticipated, if what we are testing is the validity of the stress testing model predictions and not the scenario designing skills of a risk manager. However, even an excellent model will be of no use if the scenario used as input makes no sense or is completely implausible. Unfortunately, there are no foolproof ways for designing scenarios and, although it may be too much to say, as some authors do, that it is more an art than a science, it is a fact that, as a science, it has yet to produce any formalized mechanical technique. Moreover, macroeconomic forecasting is a notoriously inaccurate activity and, even if we believe that a scenario is plausible and internally consistent (i.e., that the various indicators do overall move in manner that does not challenge economic logic), we still do not necessarily know how likely that combination of events is. Finally, the probability of a scenario is in general not in any functional relationship with the probability of losses, as the latter depends on the severity of the scenario and not on how rare (or frequent) that scenario might be.

3 Processes, data and the use test

Analysing the process around a stress testing model requires reviewing the data architecture, the IT infrastructure, as well as the uses and requirements for its outputs. The latter implies considering the business model and risk profile of the institution, including all relevant risk types, portfolios and possible segmentations as well as the risk appetite framework since, after all, stress testing means to specifically probe the boundaries of the organization's risk taking. It also follows from the above discussion that, as aggregation of risk measures lies at the core of stress testing models, aggregation of relevant risk data is what makes stress testing (as well as all effective risk modelling) ultimately possible.

Validators should verify that data can be generated and aggregated by rating grade, by geography, by industry sector and in any other way that facilitates effective stress testing. Data must be available on macroeconomic factors as well as for internal risk parameters, but the nature and structure of such datasets is in general very different, in terms of their relevance to the specific stress testing exercise, the length of the time series, the granularity, and so on. For example, while macroeconomic data may be available over a very long time horizon, and longer than internal data, their relevance may depend on how well they fit the geographical and industry segmentation required internally. Internal data, in turn, may be insufficient in length or inhomogeneous in structure, thereby requiring adjustment and transformation, which are themselves a kind of expert input. Quality of data should be verified in terms of completeness (checking for missing values and structural breaks) as well as availability and representativeness (number of observations, outliers, consistency and relevance).

Aggregation of data requires pre-processing of data to ensure it is homogeneous and adapted to the requirements of the model. This may imply specific interfaces with various internal systems as well as with external data providers whose reliability will need to be verified. Pre-processing will also in general require transformation of data in order to produce the appropriate time series. This part of the process is often manual and therefore both error-prone and difficult to audit. Reviews, at least on a sample basis, should be conducted as part of regular monitoring as well as of validation. Expert judgement, for instance in the form of scenario construction and selection, constitutes another important element of most stress testing models, and its introduction into the model should be controlled, documented and validated.

The IT infrastructure within which the stress testing process is implemented should also be reviewed by validators in order to ensure that data, algorithms, vendor models and internally developed software (including any user interface) are all adequately supporting the process. Ideally, an integrated system should ensure that inputs, algorithms, internal and external interfaces, outputs and reporting are all implemented within a controlled, auditable and secured environment. At a minimum, all the key computing steps should be automated, with appropriate evidence and documentation available around all manually performed steps.

Software implementation and rollout, as well as all the related documentation, should also be subject to validation to ensure that regular stress testing can be performed flexibly and smoothly.

Finally, a key step in the process is the selection of the stress testing model, which may also be based on expert judgment or on a mathematically based set of rules. This part of the process may have a substantial impact on the results, and hence the methodology followed, the rationale behind it, and the documentation of its results should be checked as part of the validation exercise.

4 Conclusions

Validating stress testing models is progressively developing as a standard practice in banking and, although a number of challenges still need to be overcome, we can identify some key elements a validation process should always encompass. All methodological approaches and models should be documented, including assumptions, data, role of expert judgement as well as the results of all tests conducted during and after model development. All assumptions underlying the model estimation process should be checked for reasonability, and their reflection in the model should be verified. If expert judgement has a role in the model, as is always the case to some extent, validators should verify that it is applied reasonably and that its impact on the final result can be identified and assessed. The model selection process should be subject to validation; the techniques used, including the extent to which they are based on expert input, should be reviewed and assessed. The review of the models should encompass IT implementation and software programming. Results in the form of stressed risk measures should be tested through sensitivity analysis and back-testing. Finally, the use of the stress test results, their reporting to the appropriate senior audience and their use for risk management and strategy should be verified and documented.

Although, as already widely adopted in the industry, scenario analysis can be successfully applied in conjunction with management assessment of elementary scenarios corresponding to the piecemeal shocking of individual variables, a key contribution of this technique is in identifying and analysing complex and catastrophic combinations of events. Such extreme scenarios have long been overlooked in risk management reports, on the grounds that they are difficult to conceive, let alone assess, given the lack of specific data, like historical losses, available. Nevertheless, the discipline of constructing complex and entirely new scenarios from simpler historical occurrences and variations thereof is not only technically feasible, but also very worthwhile, as it can afford management a window on the elusive "fat tails" that lie behind so many financial disasters. Furthermore, it provides a means to systematically address what a substantial body of financial literature identifies as the key value added of risk management: the prevention or avoidance of financial distress.

Note

1. Modern scenario analysis, like many other management techniques, can be traced back to World War II, first in the military and later in the civil domain. The RAND Corporation and subsequently the Hudson Institute developed this approach through the seminal work of Herman Kahn (1967). It was then adopted as a key planning tool by most large corporations (see for example van der Heijden, 1996 for a history of its introduction at Shell) as well as for smaller ones (see Linneman and Kennel, 1977 for an application to small enterprises).

References

Akaike, H. (1974), "A New Look At The Statistical Model Identification (PDF)," *IEEE Transactions on Automatic Control*, Vol. 19, No. 6, 716–723.

Allen, I. and Bali, T., "Cyclicality in Catastrophic and Operational Risk Measurements," *Journal of Banking and Finance*, Vol. 31, No. 1, 191–235, 2007.

Ando, T., "Bayesian Predictive Information Criterion for the Evaluation of Hierarchical Bayesian and Empirical Bayes Models," *Biometrika*, Vol. 94, No. 2, 443–458, 2007.

Araten, M., "The Advancement of Stress Testing at Banks," in Zhang, J. (editor), *CCAR and Beyond: Capital Assessment, Stress Testing and Applications*, Risk Books, 2013.

BIS, Committee on the Global Financial System, "Stress Testing By Large Financial Institutions: Current Practice and Aggregation Issues," Bank for International Settlements, April 2000.

Basel Committee on Banking Supervision, "Amendment to the Capital Accord to Incorporate Market Risks," Basel, January 1996.

Basel Committee on Banking Supervision, "Principles for Sound Stress Testing Practices and Supervision," Basel, May 2009.

Breeden, J. L., "Validation of Stress Testing Models," in Christodoulakis, G. and Satchell, S. (editors), *The Analytics of Risk Model Validation*, Elsevier, 2008.

Cagan, P. "Managing Operational Risk through the Credit Crisis," *The Journal of Compliance, Risk and Opportunity*, Vol. 3,No. 2, 19–26, 2009.

Capital Requirements Directive IV (CRD IV), Directive 2013/36/EU of the European Parliament and of the Council of 26 June 2013 on access to the activity of credit institutions and the prudential supervision of credit institutions and investment firms, Official Journal of the European Union, 27 June 2013.

Capital Requirements Regulation (CRR), Regulation (EU) No 575/2013 of the European Parliament and of the Council of 26 June 2013 on prudential requirements for credit institutions and investment firms. Official Journal of the European Union, 27 June 2013.

Canabarro, E., "Market and Counterparty Risk Stress Test," in Zhang, J. (editor), *CCAR and Beyond: Capital Assessment, Stress Testing and Applications*, Risk Books, 2013.

Chen, J., "Stress Testing Credit Losses for Commercial Real Estate Loan Portfolios," in Zhang, J. (editor), *CCAR and Beyond: Capital Assessment, Stress Testing and Applications*, Risk Books, 2013.

Claeskens, G. and Hjort, N. L., "The Focused Information Criterion" (with discussion), *Journal of the American Statistical Association*, Vol. 98, 879–899, 2003.

Committee of European Banking Supervisors (CEBS), GL32 – CEBS Guidelines on Stress Testing, 26 August 2010.

Diebold, F. and Mariano, R., "Comparing Predictive Accuracy," *Journal of Business and Economics Statistics*, Vol. 13, 253–263, 1995.

Durbin, J. and Watson, G. S., "Testing for Serial Correlation in Least Squares Regression, I." *Biometrika*, Vol. 37, No. (3–4), 409–428, 1950.

Durbin, J. and Watson, G. S., "Testing for Serial Correlation in Least Squares Regression, II." *Biometrika*, Vol. 38, No. (1–2), 159–179, 1951.

EBA/CP/2014/36 – Draft Regulatory Technical Standards On the specification of the assessment methodology for competent authorities regarding compliance of an institution with the requirements to use the IRB Approach in accordance with Articles 144(2), 173(3) and 180(3)(b) of Regulation (EU) No 575/2013, 12 November 2014.

Financial Services Authority, *Stress Testing*, Discussion Paper, May 2005.
Granger, C., and Newbold, P., "Forecasting Transformed Series," *Journal of the Royal Statistical Society B*, Vol. 38, 189–203, 1976.
Hannan, E. J. and Quinn, B. G., "The Determination of the Order of an Autoregression," *Journal of the Royal Statistical Society Series B*, Vol. 41, 190–195, 1979.
Hughes, A., "Validating Stress-Testing Models," *Moody's Analytics*, June 2012.
Kahn, H., *The Year 2000: A Framework for Speculation on the Next Thirty-Three Years,"* Macmillan, New York, 1967.
Linneman, R. E. and Kennell, J. D., "Shirt-Sleeve Approach to Long-Range Plans," *Harvard Business Review*, Vol. 55, No. 2, 141, March/April 1977.
Novosyolov, A.and Satchkov, D., "Portfolio Crash Testing: Making Sense of Extreme Event Exposures," *The Journal of Risk Model Validation*, Vol. 4, No. 3, 53–67, Fall 2010.
Priestley, M. B. and Subba Rao, T., "A Test for Non-Stationarity of Time-Series," *Journal of the Royal Statistical Society Series B*, Vol. 31, 140–149, 1969.
Schwarz, G. E., "Estimating the Dimension of a Model," *Annals of Statistics*, Vol. 6, No. 2, 461–464, 1978.
Stein, R., "The Role of Stress Testing in Credit Risk Management," *Journal of Investment Management*, Vol. 10, No. 4, 64–90, 2012.
Van der Heijden, K., *Scenarios: The Art of Strategic Conversation,* John Wiley & Sons, New York, 1996.
Various Authors, *Modern Risk Management: A History,* RISK Books, London, 2003.
White, H., "A Heteroskedasticity-Consistent Covariance Matrix Estimator and a Direct Test for Heteroskedasticity," *Econometrica*, Vol. 48, No. 4, 817–838, 1980.

14 Conclusion: A Model for Measuring Model Risk

A book on model validation is necessarily, if not always explicitly, about model risk, in that all the analyses and measures discussed and suggested are either looking at the many things that can go wrong in managing a model (from original conception to final use) or at how much its outputs are off with respect to some benchmark (historical data, alternative external or internal model). However, the validation practices presented in this book, while covering several dimensions of model risk, fall short of providing a systematic way of formally assessing it and of crisply discriminating between what constitutes a good and a bad model. The latter objective requires specific criteria that are only partially embedded in the practices described. For instance, although we have looked specifically at fitness for purpose, in order to assess model design, it is only by looking at the specificities of a real portfolio that one can establish clear criteria for accepting or rejecting a model. Similarly, the criteria for assessing the adequacy of the implementation and modelling process strongly depend on the size and complexity of the organization (what would be sufficient for a local savings and loans would be unacceptable for a large international bank). The former objective, however (a framework for the formal assessment of model risk) should be achievable within the scope of this work and should go some way to meet the expectations of regulators and supervisors on this subject.

In the immediate aftermath of the financial crisis, in its Revision of the Basel II Market Risk Framework (BCBS, 2009), the Basel Committee on Banking Supervision required that financial institutions quantify model risk. The Committee further stated that two types of risks should be taken into account: *"The model risk associated with using a possibly incorrect valuation methodology, and the risk associated with using unobservable (and possibly incorrect) calibration parameters in the valuation model,"* and that the resulting adjustments impact Tier I regulatory capital and be implemented by the end of 2010. In 2011, the U.S. Office of the Comptroller of the Currency issued specific guidance on model risk management where the nature of model risk is described in a somewhat more comprehensive manner.

Model risk occurs primarily for two reasons:

- *The model may have fundamental errors and may produce inaccurate outputs when viewed against the design objective and intended business uses. The mathematical calculation and quantification exercise underlying any model generally involves application of theory, choice of sample design and numerical routines, selection of inputs and estimation, and implementation in information systems. Errors can occur at any point from design through implementation. In addition, shortcuts, simplifications, or approximations used to manage complicated problems could compromise the integrity and reliability of outputs from those calculations. Finally, the quality of model outputs depends on the quality of input data and assumptions, and errors in inputs or incorrect assumptions will lead to inaccurate outputs.*
- *The model may be used incorrectly or inappropriately. Even a fundamentally sound model producing accurate outputs consistent with the design objective of the model may exhibit high model risk if it is misapplied or misused. Models by their nature are simplifications of reality, and real-world events may prove those simplifications inappropriate. This is even more of a concern if a model is used outside the environment for which it was designed. Banks may do this intentionally as they apply existing models to new products or markets, or inadvertently as market conditions or customer behavior changes. Decision makers need to understand the limitations of a model to avoid using it in ways that are not consistent with the original intent. Limitations come in part from weaknesses in the model due to its various shortcomings, approximations, and uncertainties. Limitations are also a consequence of assumptions underlying a model that may restrict the scope to a limited set of specific circumstances and situations.* (OCC, 2011)

Just a few years later, a full-scale assessment of model risk was the de-facto objective of the ECB (planned to start in 2015) review of internal models of Eurozone banks.

In the introduction to this book, we briefly discussed some contributions to the problem of measuring model risk and argued that they were limited to the problem of pricing specific derivative products and that their practical applications faced considerable challenges in specifying the alternatives and benchmarks of the approaches required. In addition to those, it is worth mentioning the work of Glasserman and Xu (2013), who look at model risk as an entropy-based measure of the worst-case change in the probability law affecting the relevant risk measure, and that of Danìelsson et al. (2014) who examine Value at Risk and Expected Shortfall, computed using a range of models applied to a particular asset at a given point in time and measure model risk using the ratio of the maximum to the minimum result obtained. All these "multiple benchmarks" approaches focus on the output of the model but do not give any consideration to the model design, to the data, to the implementation process or to the use and experience of a model within the organization. However, when examining the output of a model, we are always looking at the result of an imperfect implementation of an inaccurate model. That is why, in the following pages, we will try to develop a methodology to assess model risk comprehensively and in a manner that is, as much as possible, practically achievable.

1 Model design

One common way to distinguish risk models is between structural and reduced-form. Structural models are so called because they aim not just at predicting a certain outcome, but also at explaining the mechanism (the structure) whereby such output is produced as a function of certain factors. In credit risk the Merton model (Merton, 1974) is usually cited as a classical example of a structural model, using an analytical formula (Black, Scholes, 1973) to model the relationship between leverage, volatility, interest rate and probability of default. Structural models are also used in pricing fixed-income and other derivative products.

A reduced-form model, on the other hand, postulates no economic causality or any form of relationship between risk factors and financial impact, but merely models the dynamics in question (be they defaults, other events, losses) as random events whose statistical properties can be analysed insofar as enough data are available. Aggregate loss models as used routinely in insurance and, more recently, in operational risk, are reduced-form and so are some credit risk models like Creditmetrics.

Modelling model risk, however, presents a special set of challenges. First of all, although we can identify a set of factors driving model risk, it is very difficult to postulate a structural relationship between these factors and either the corresponding impact on the model output or a level of model risk. Moreover, the impact itself is elusive, as it depends on what the model output is used for and, normally, on additional external circumstances. For example, an underestimation of a borrower's probability of default may result in an underestimation of exposure against limits, of risk pricing and of regulatory capital. These inaccuracies may in turn translate into losses, but only if default actually happens. Similarly, an underestimated trading Value at Risk will translate into underestimated market exposure against limits and capital as well as in imperfect hedging, but these will in turn generate losses depending on both direction and size of market movements.

The classical reduced-form approach is not easy to apply either. Unlike in an insurance model, where one can observe a sequence of events and measure the related consequences, a model risk "event" is itself quite complicated to pinpoint. In fact, unless we only consider catastrophic events, where a model completely fails to produce a viable output (because of a fundamental design flaw or a coding mistake, for instance), a model may be routinely affected by all sorts of issues (from inappropriate assumptions to IT glitches, from improper use to inadequate data) without these issues being recognized or even observed, before a validation review is carried out.

In line with the validation framework which we discussed in Chapter 2 and have followed throughout this book, we will consider that model risk is driven by how the model is designed, by the data that are used as input, by the way it is implemented and used, and by how wide and relevant is the model use within the organization. The risk driven by these factors will manifest itself in the model output, affecting its predictive power and/or its accuracy. We will therefore define a model event in a very generic manner: as any failure or inadequacy in the design, implementation or use of a model as well as in any of the data used in its development, testing and use.

The interpretation we suggest is that every time a model is used there is a certain probability that the model will experience one or more model events driven by the risk factors above and that the impact of such failure on the accuracy of the output will be in turn a random variable drawn from a certain probability distribution. The problem then becomes how to estimate the unconditional probability distribution of a model event happening and the probability distribution of the impact on the accuracy of the model conditional on the model event. From these two distributions, we can the estimate the aggregate probability of an impact on the output of the model and from this, in turn, any eventual financial loss given the various uses of the model output.

Therefore, we can summarize the general structure of our model as a sequence of steps (see Figure 1) covering: the probability of a model event (rating model), the impact on the model output given the event, the aggregate (unconditional) impact on the model output, the map of model uses, the financial impact (possibly conditional on other factors).

2 The rating model

The first step in developing a reduced-form model is the estimation of the probability distribution that governs the generation of the relevant events. In the case of model risk, we do not have a historical database of model events from which to elicit a probability distribution directly. For the same reason, even if we identify a set of risk factors driving the occurrence of model events, we are unable to apply econometric techniques to develop a functional relationship that allows us to model and predict those events. Therefore, in order to assess the probability of a model event, we will develop a rating model, and we will use the validation framework developed in Chapter 2 in order to identify key risk factors that affect the likelihood of a model event.

A risk rating model ranks certain objects (borrowers, operational processes, deals, portfolios) by identifying a number of risk factors which presumably drive the corresponding risk exposure, scoring them against a fixed scale and then aggregating the scores, possibly using a system of weights, in order to produce an

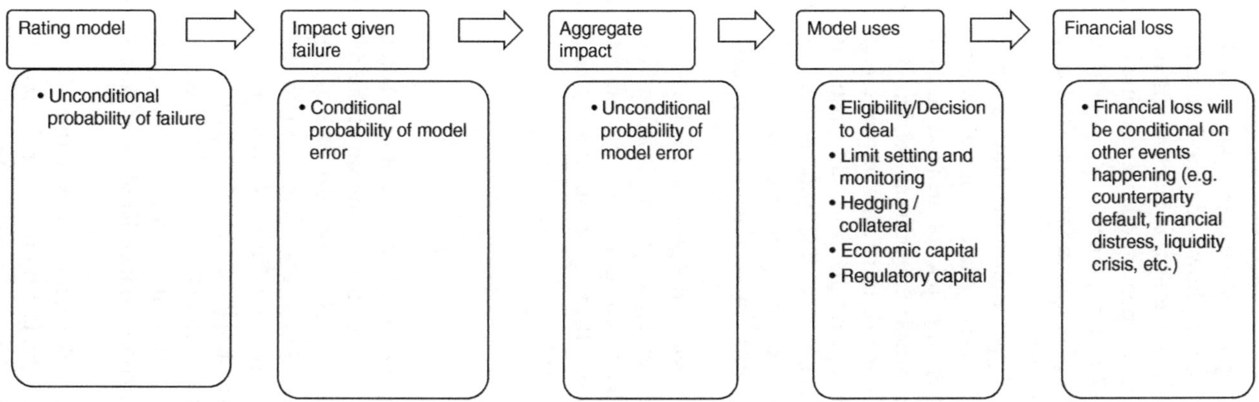

Figure 14.1 General model structure

overall score which can then be mapped to a given rating scale. Scoring models have been developed for credit risk (Thomas et al., 2002) and operational risk (Scandizzo, 2005, Scandizzo and Setola, 2003).

A rating is in general not an absolute assessment of risk, but a relative one. For example, a credit rating from one of the main agencies is not in itself a probability of default, but merely an indication that borrowers with that rating will have the same probability of default and that it will be lower than those of lower-rated borrowers and higher than those of higher-rated ones. A rating is therefore a ranking or a classification based on a comparative assessment of certain given criteria.

We will start from the key areas of focus for validation presented in Chapter 2 (model design, data, model implementation and use test) in order to develop a structured set of model risk factors. For model design we identify the choice of model, the key assumptions and the documentation as the relevant factors. The choice of model needs to reflect both mathematical soundness and fitness to the specific task. It also needs to be such that modellers and users alike can intuitively understand, rather than mechanically apply it. Assumptions, sometimes strong ones about anything from distributions to functional relationships, are unavoidable in most modelling endeavours, and it is important that they are appropriate, clearly articulated and documented, and their impact understood. The importance of completeness and quality in the documentation should not be underestimated as it reflects both the diligence around model development and maintenance, and the level of understanding of the model's complexities.

The best possible model will not perform satisfactorily unless it is first developed and then used with data whose quality and completeness can be ensured, traced and audited on a regular basis. Accordingly, the quality and functionality of the related IT infrastructure will have an impact on the model's performance. Furthermore, given the size and complexity of banks' portfolios, how the model is implemented in practice (how it is coded into a software application, integrated within the financial institution's IT system, fitted with the necessary data and user interfaces) is of fundamental importance, as it is deployed and rolled out within the organization.

Finally, fulfilment of the use test is not just relevant as a regulatory requirement to ensure the model is not just used for compliance purposes, but it gives an idea of the degree of confidence the institution places in it and of how well the model's workings are understood.

Table 14.2 provides a summary of the main criteria just discussed. To make the approach operational, one will need to establish how to weight the individual factors, how to aggregate them, how to produce a ranking from the aggregate score, and how to estimate a probability from the ranking. Although it is in theory conceivable to establish the relative relevance of the various risk factors by, for example, comparing the performance of several models over several years, the problem remains that observing the individual model events is very hard, and that any mathematical or statistical analysis of the relationship between the risk factors we identified and any

Table 14.1 A simple framework for model rating

Risk factor – Level 1	Sub factor – Level 2	Sub factor – Level 3	Questions
Model design	Model selection	• Conceptual soundness • Suitability • Intuitive / understood	Is the model conceptually sound, appropriate for the intended use, sufficiently intuitive and understood by senior and business management?
	Key assumptions	• Clarity/motivations • Appropriateness • Impact / sensitivity	Are key assumptions clearly stated and motivated? Are they appropriate and has sensitivity analysis with respect to assumptions been performed?
	Documentation	• Completeness • Availability • Quality	Are assumptions, parameters, key relationships, inputs and outputs adequately described so that a reasonably competent person can understand them?
Model data	Data quality	• Availability • Traceability • Functionality	Are all parameters and data exhaustively and consistently stored, historicized and maintained on an integrated platform?
	Documentation and reporting	• Completeness • Availability • Quality	Is all the information (including relevant metadata) available that describes nature, quality, coverage and storage of data?
	IT infrastructure	• Systems • Databases • Applications	Is the data architecture, including hardware, databases and other software applications adequate, integrated and functional to the operation of the model?

Risk factor – Level 1	Sub factor – Level 2	Sub factor – Level 3	Questions
Model implementation	Process	• Governance • Procedures • Internal control framework	Are roles and responsibilities clearly established? Are procedures unambiguous, up-to-date and appropriate? Do internal controls address the main operational risks?
	IT	• Interfaces • Coding • Integration	Are all the IT interfaces effective and consistent with the model's intended use? Is coding and integration in line with the model design and specifications?
	Implementation and roll-out	• Planning • Testing • Deployment	Is model implementation properly planned? Is enough time devoted to testing and is the model effectively deployed within the organisation?
Use test	Risk management and decision making	• Strategy and planning • Dealing/pricing • Assessment/reporting	Is there evidence that the model output is used in planning the RM strategy, in individual business decision, and in risk assessment and reporting?
	Capital management	• Capital allocation • Performance measurement • Compensation	Is the model used for economic capital allocation, in risk-adjusted performance measures, including variable compensation?
	Experience test	• Model understanding • Risk management years of use • Independent review	Is the model well understood by modellers, business users, senior management? For how long has it been used and has it been subject to independent review?

observable model failures will require a difficult data collection exercise over several years. It is likely therefore that initially, this approach will require expert judgement not only in assigning score, but also in establishing weights for the individual risk factors. Such weights could be based on loss data, empirical evidence, technical literature available on the subject, management information, auditors' opinion, company experience and best practice.

An aggregated rating requires that individual scores are not only weighted, but also normalized, meaning that each of the scores has to be expressed on a common scale. The following table gives an example of a five-point scale.

	Risk factor assessment
1	Very poor
2	Poor
3	Average
4	Good
5	Very good

The calculation of an overall rating can be based on a weighted average of the individual scores and of the weights discussed above. Such aggregation can provide sub-scores for each sub-factor as well as for each model.

For example, score I_i for risk factor *i* within a specific model (or sub-factor *i* within a specific risk factor) could be calculated as follows:

$$I_r = \sum_{j=1}^{m} w_j i_j$$

wherei_j are scores on risk factor *r* e w_j are the corresponding weights.

A rating for each model line can be calculated by aggregating all the relevant scores. In our example risk rating for a specific model will be calculated as:

$$R = \sum_{r=11}^{n} I_r$$

An alternative methodology, suitable for the aggregation of both quantitative and qualitative information, is discussed for instance in Scandizzo (1999, a, b).

A rating system allows us to rank models and, combined with a system of thresholds (e.g., a traffic light approach), to decide whether to accept, reject or modify a model. In order to obtain an assessment of model risk, and possibly of a model risk capital charge, we need to assign a probability measure to each rating.

Inspired by Pluto and Tasche (2005) who estimate PDs for portfolios with no or a very low number of defaults in the overall portfolio, we will apply the Most Prudent Estimation Principle (MPEP)[1] which, for each rating category, produces an upper bound, or the most conservative estimate of the default probability. Thus, we will try to estimate with a degree of conservatism the maximum probability of failure for a given rating grade such that no more failures occur than the current and lower grades. The approach estimates the probabilities by upper confidence bounds with the probabilities ordered as indicated by the rating grades. It is applied under an assumption of independent events but can be adapted to the case of correlated events.

For example, suppose we have four model rating classes: *A*, *B*, *C* and *D*, and no historical data to estimate the corresponding probabilities defined as:

p_A – probability of failure for grade *A*,
p_B – probability of failure for grade *B*,
p_C – probability of failure for grade *C*,
p_D – probability of failure for grade *D*.

Probabilities reflect the decreasing quality of the grades, in the sense of the following inequality:

$$p_A \le p_B \le p_C \le p_D$$

The confidence region for p_A can be described as the set of all admissible values of p_A with the property that the probability of not observing any default during the observation period is not less than $1-\alpha$ (for instance for α= 90%).

Let n_A, n_B, n_C, n_D be the size of groups *A*, *B*, *C* and *D* respectively. Using the formula for probability of no success in Bernoulli trials, we get confidence intervals for desired probabilities:

$$p_A \le 1-(1-\alpha)^{\frac{1}{n_A+n_B+n_C+n_D}}$$

$$p_B \le 1-(1-\alpha)^{\frac{1}{n_B+n_C+n_D}}$$

$$p_C \le 1-(1-\alpha)^{\frac{1}{n_C+n_D}}$$

$$p_D \le 1-(1-\alpha)^{\frac{1}{n_D}}$$

The above formula will hold assuming ours is a **correct ordinal rating** of the models.

3 Modelling the impact

To model the impact of model failures we need a suitable error measure. The nature of such a measure, however, will have to depend on the nature of the model and on the specifics of the model implementation. In fact, while it is relatively straightforward to measure the mean and the variance of a model error in certain cases, that is definitely not the case in certain others. For example, one may use the mean and variance of the square error (see for instance Joseph, 2005, Loterman et al. 2014) computed comparing predicted and realized defaults and losses from a PD or LGD model for portfolios where default data are abundant, but would find the same technique a lot harder to apply to a sovereign or a financial institution portfolio. The same holds for an operational risk model, at least for loss categories characterized by low-frequency and high-severity losses. When the risk measure is the result of a Monte Carlo simulation, confidence intervals for the error (i.e., the difference between the estimate and the realized measure) can be constructed, using the empirical distribution from a sample of Monte Carlo draws under the assumptions that errors are independently and identically distributed, and employed as an accuracy measure (see Pritsker, 2000). The previous chapters provide some examples of error metrics whose suitability will depend on the specific model and on the circumstances of its implementation.

In order to estimate the aggregate input on model accuracy, we will use again the results from Klugman et al. (2008) already mentioned in Chapter 10, under the assumption that impact sizes are mutually independent random variables from a common distribution that does not depend on the number of events. In particular, let N be the distribution of model events and X the distribution of impacts, and S the distribution of aggregate impacts on the model accuracy. The first two moments of S are:

$$E(S) = E(N)E(X)$$

$$Var(S) = E(N)Var(X) + Var(N)E^2(X).$$

When $E(N)$ is large and N is distributed according to Poisson, binomial or negative binomial, the distribution of S is well approximated by a Normal distribution. In cases when $E(N)$ is small, the distribution of S tends to be skewed and other distributions (e.g. lognormal, beta) might be appropriate. Figure 2 shows the process visually.

This aggregate distribution, of course, merely describes the risk in terms of its impact on the model output. The final financial consequence on the institution, as already observed, will in turn depend on what that output is used for. Identifying the final uses of a model, however, may not be sufficient if one wants to understand

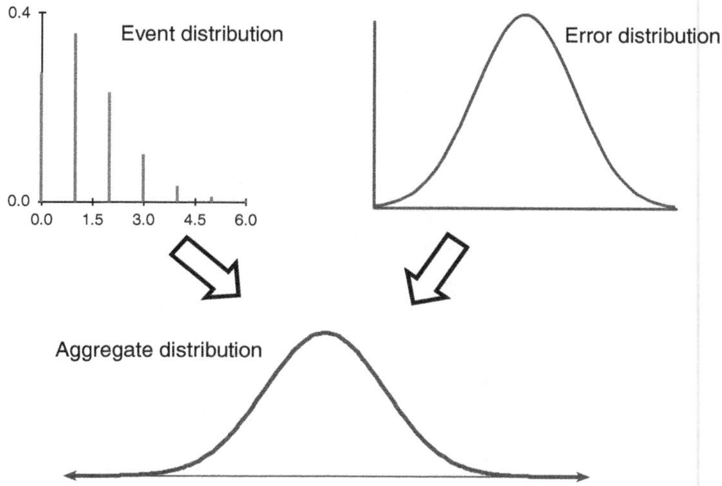

Figure 14.2 Event, error and aggregate distribution

all the possible ways model risk can impact the risk management activities of a financial institutions. In fact, it is not just the sheer number of different models, diverse in their objectives as well as in their conceptual structure, that makes model risk relevant, but also the growing complexity of the many interconnections between data, models, and uses. Developing a framework for mapping these interconnections starting from the above three categories can be extremely complex, especially for a large international bank. Figure 3 below shows a high level example of the various elements to consider for this mapping.

The structure presented above, however, is still too simple, as there is a lot of overlap across both the data and the model categories listed as well as within different type of models. For example, the same counterparty spreads can be used in derivatives and in credit risk models, while the same market risk data can be used in trading models and in macroeconomic stress testing models. The output of one model can serve as input for another; take for instance the case PD, LGD and EAD models' output feeding a portfolio model; or take credit, market and operational risk models feeding an economic capital model. Finally, the same model can serve multiple uses, as in the case of a credit rating model that is used to decide the eligibility of a counterpart both as a borrower and for derivative transactions; or the case of a VaR model used for limit monitoring and reporting as well as for regulatory capital purposes.

Depending on the number of models, the size of the portfolios, and the complexity of a financial institution's activities and organizational set-up, a complete model map of the relationships discussed above can grow very complex, and yet still be very useful to ensure the completeness of a validation exercise as well as to allow an

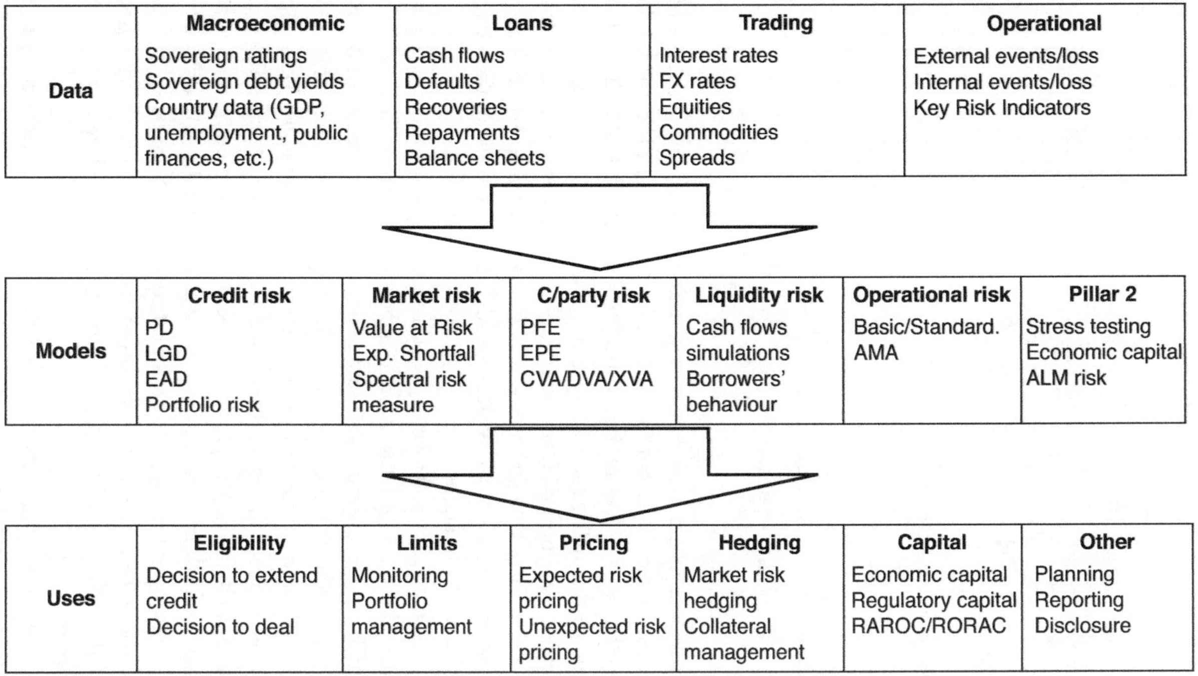

Figure 14.3 Data, models and uses

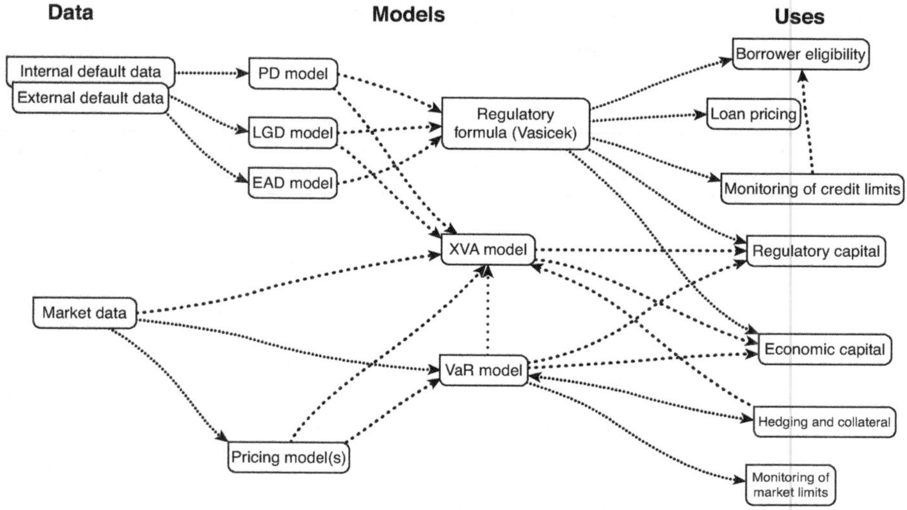

Figure 14.4 A simplified example of a model map

assessment of model risk down to the ultimate financial impact. Figure 4 depicts, only for illustrative purposes, how complicated even a partial map can become when all these interrelationships are taken into account.

4 A simple example

To illustrate how the methodology presented could be used to assess the risk of a model and ultimately compute a capital charge, we will apply it to a model used to estimate regulatory capital requirements within a hypothetical financial institution. We will use our rating methodology to estimate a probability for model failure and assume that a similar assessment has been made for the accuracy of the output using one of the statistical testing techniques discussed in the previous chapters. We will start by making some simplifying assumptions about the use of our rating model, although it is easy to imagine a different and more complex implementation, both in terms of rating scale, weighting of factors and sub-factors, as well as factors aggregation methodology.

Let us assume that all factors and sub-factors are equally weighted, that each of them is scored on a four-point scale and that the resulting overall score is mapped to ratings A, B, C and D using the following simple rule:

Score	Rating grade
4–3.001	A
3– 2.001	B
2–1.001	C
1–0	D

Table 3 shows the results of the scoring of our hypothetical model, which, according to the above rule, will be rated A.

Table 14.2 An example of model scoring

Risk factor – Level 1		Sub factor – Level 2	Level 2 Weight	Level 2 Score	Sub factor – Level 3	Level 3 Weight	Level 3 Score
Model design	Level 1 Weight		0.33	3.67	• Conceptual soundness	0.33	4.00
		Model selection			• Suitability	0.33	4.00
	0.25				• Intuitive / understood	0.33	3.00
			0.33	3.33	• Clarity/motivations	0.33	4.00
	Level 1 Score	Key assumptions			• Appropriateness	0.33	4.00
					• Impact / sensitivity	0.33	2.00
	3.44	Documentation	0.33	3.33	• Completeness	0.33	2.00
					• Availability	0.33	4.00
					• Quality	0.33	4.00
Model data	Level 1 Weight	Data quality	0.33	2.67	• Availability	0.33	3.00
					• Traceability	0.33	3.00
	0.25				• Functionality	0.33	2.00
		Documentation and reporting	0.33	3.33	• Completeness	0.33	4.00
	Level 1 Score				• Availability	0.33	3.00
					• Quality	0.33	3.00
	3.22	IT infrastructure	0.33	3.67	• Systems	0.33	3.00
					• Databases	0.33	4.00
					• Applications	0.33	4.00
Model implementation	Level 1 Weight	Process	0.33	3.67	• Governance	0.33	4.00
					• Procedures	0.33	3.00
	0.25				• Internal control framework	0.33	4.00
		IT	0.33	3.67	• Interfaces	0.33	3.00
	Level 1 Score				• Coding	0.33	4.00
					• Integration	0.33	4.00
	3.33	Implementation and rollout	0.33	2.67	• Planning	0.33	2.00
					• Testing	0.33	3.00
					• Deployment	0.33	3.00
Use test	Level 1 Weight	Risk management and decision making	0.33	2.67	• Strategy and planning	0.33	3.00
					• Dealing / pricing	0.33	3.00
	0.25				• Assessment / reporting	0.33	3.00
		Capital management	0.33	2.33	• Capital allocation	0.33	4.00
	Level 1 Score				• Performance measurement	0.33	2.00
					• Compensation	0.33	1.00
	2.89	Experience test	0.33	3.67	• Model understanding	0.33	3.00
					• Risk management years of	0.33	4.00
					• Independent review	0.33	4.00
Final Score	**3.22**						

Let us now also assume that we have used the same model to rate several other models within the financial institution and that the number of models rated *A*, *B*, *C* and *D* respectively are:

$n_A = 5, n_B = 5, n_C = 5, n_D = 5.$

As explained in section 2 above, in order to establish confidence intervals for probabilities corresponding to the rating grades, we apply the formula for probability of no success in Bernoulli trials and, for a confidence level of 95%, we obtain:

$p_A \leq 0.14;$

$p_B \leq 0.18;$

$p_C \leq 0.26;$

$p_D \leq 0.45.$

Conservatively, we will use *0.14* as our estimate of the average probability of a model event for models rated *A* and will assume that such events are Poisson distributed with parameter $\lambda=0.14$.

Furthermore, suppose back-testing and/or benchmarking on the model output have shown the model percentage error being normally distributed with $\mu=-0.05$ and $\sigma=0.15$. By applying the formulas for the first two moments of the aggregate distribution, we compute the latter mean and standard deviation, and we get $\mu^*=-0.007$ and $\sigma^*=0.0056$. The 99th percentile of the corresponding normal distribution is -0.02.

We can interpret this result by saying that our model will at most be off by 2% at a 99% confidence level every time it is used. When, for instance, the model is used for regulatory capital purposes, 2% indicates the size of a prudent add-on to the capital charge while the expected inaccuracy would be $\lambda \cdot \mu = 0.14 \cdot 0.05 = 0.007$ or 0.2%.

5 Conclusions

The approach presented in this chapter is an attempt at providing a practical way to solve a theoretically difficult problem and thus, inevitably, relies on simplifications and assumptions in equally large measure. The problem of model risk assessment is difficult because the definition of model risk is multifaceted and, to an extent, elusive. The regulators' definition of model risk as the financial loss suffered as a consequence of a model's inaccuracy or inappropriate use points explicitly to a model's intrinsic accuracy on one side and to its various uses on the other. The latter aspect implies not only that no model can be judged out of context, because its performance may be completely different depending on what asset or portfolio it is applied to, but also that the nature of the use – be it capital, pricing, hedging, planning, and so on – will determine the ultimate financial impact of any inaccuracy.

Through our insistence on a methodology that combines systematic statistical testing of outputs with conceptual and evidence-based assessment of design, process, data and implementation process, we have also tried to convey the notion that validation as well is intrinsically two-sided. On one hand, the objective of validation is to give assurance. This appears evident from the regulatory emphasis on independence, process and full documentation. In this sense, a validator, not unlike an auditor, is required to give an opinion, possibly with some qualification, as to whether a model should be used in its current form or not. Not surprisingly, this leads to financial institutions focussing on the final results and to a lot of effort being devoted to managing the action required as a consequence of those results, with relatively less attention been given to understanding the technical aspects and the more quantitative component of the assessment. On the other hand, validation is also intended as a means to manage model risk, which, like any other risk management activity, comprises the well-known steps of identification, assessment, monitoring, control and reporting. This second objective may somehow be at odds with the first, as it may require more closeness (not to say some level of involvement) with the actual modelling process than an independent provider of assurance should be comfortable with. It also calls for a more nuanced approach to articulating results and implies a bigger concern for the specific drivers of model risk and for how they can be managed than with the final yes/no outcome of the process.

Furthermore, the assessment of model risk, like any other form of risk assessment, requires quantification, possibly in financial terms, so that issues can be properly prioritized, resources efficiently allocated, and adequate cushions against losses established. Quantification, however, does in turn require some kind of modelling itself, prompting the inevitable observation that it risks merely replacing one kind of risk with another, possibly even more elusive. This is unavoidable, however, if we interpret the task of validation as more than a verification of compliance with certain given rules (regulatory or otherwise).

At the same time, validators need to think in terms of process analysis and management actions as a fundamental component of their reporting, lest their work be viewed as confined to a mere statistical analysis and only taken into consideration by few "experts." They should cultivate an attitude and a way of working whereby measurement of outcome, far from being unconnected to process and from management, is actually driven by them, and where any quantification should always be accompanied by an elaboration of what mitigating measures could possibly be taken.

Not of secondary importance in this process is the ability to develop working relationships with model owners and developers, as they could not otherwise be credible in their recommendations nor could they hold a lot of confidence in any of their suggestions being actually put in place (a point that further differentiates validation from audit tasks). This quality is fundamental if, as discussed above, we need to develop an approach to model risk management that involves the model owners more deeply than just as providers of model documentation or as the occasional sounding board.

Balancing the dynamics between the main validation objectives of assurance and risk management is the key to the successful implementation of this very complex task. Validators, in light of the sceptical nature of their trade, have hopefully realized early on that mathematical formulas and computer models as well as the panoply of tools and techniques that they routinely employ, do not shield them from inaccuracies, mistakes and risk. Hopefully this shall ensure that they will be the least prone of all financial practitioners to be deluded by mathematical chicanery, but the most willing to explore reasonable solutions to make things work in practice.

Note

1. The MPEP imposes the constraint that default probabilities for a given rating category and those below it are the same. The only requisite for using the MPEP is that the ordinal ranking implied by the ratings is correct.

References

Basel Committee on Banking Supervision, "Revision to the Basel II Market Risk Framework," Basel, 2009.

Board of Governors of the Federal Reserve System, Office of the Comptroller of the Currency, *Supervisory Guidance On Model Risk Management,* OCC, 2011–2012, 4 April 2011.

Cohort, P., dit Vehel, P-E., L. and Patras, F., "Toward Model Value-at-Risk: Bespoke CDO Tranches, a Case Study," *Journal of Risk Model Validation,* Vol. 7, No. 3, 21–34, 2013.

Danìelsson, J., Kevin R. J., Valenzuela, M. and Zer, I., "Model Risk of Risk Models," FEDS Working Paper No. 2014-34, 16 July 2014. Available at SSRN: http://ssrn.com/abstract=2425689 or http://dx.doi.org/10.2139/ssrn.2425689

Glasserman, P. and Xu, X., "Robust Risk Measurement and Model Risk," *Quantitative Finance,* September 2013.

Joseph, M., *A PD Validation Framework for Basel II Internal Ratings-Based Systems,* Edinburgh CS&CC IX Conference, 2005.

Klugman, S. A., Panjer, H. H. and Willmot, G. E., *Loss Models: From Data to Decisions,* Third Edition, Wiley, 2008.

Loterman, G., Debruyne, M., Branden, K. V., Van Gestel, T. and Mues, C., "A Proposed Framework for Backtesting Loss Given Default Models," *Journal of Risk Model Validation,* Vol. 8, No. 1, 69–90, 2014.

Pluto, K. and Tasche, D., "Thinking Positively," *Risk Magazine,* 1 August 2005.

Pritsker, M., "Evaluating Value-at-Risk Methodologies: Accuracy versus Computational

Time," in Gibson, R. (editor), *Model Risk: Concepts, Calibration and Pricing*, Risk Books, 2000.

Scandizzo, S., "Risk Mapping and Key Risk Indicators in Operational Risk Management," *Economic Notes*, Vol. 34, No. 2, 231–256, 2005.

Scandizzo, S. and Setola, R., "Mark up the scorecard," *Operational Risk*, Vol. 4, No. 12, December 2003.

Scandizzo, S., *A Fuzzy Clustering Approach for the Measurement of Operational Risk*, Knowledge-Based Intelligent Information Engineering Systems, 1999. Third International Conference, December 1999a, 324–328.

Scandizzo, S., "Operational Risk Measurement in Financial Institutions: A Fuzzy Logic Approach," in *Uncertainty in Intelligent and Information Systems* (Bouchon-Meunier, B., Yager, R. R. and Zadeh, L. A. editors), World Scientific, Singapore, 1999b.

Thomas, L. C., Edelman, D. B. and Crook, J. N., *Credit Scoring and Its Applications*, SIAM, 2002.

Index

Printed and bound by CPI Group (UK) Ltd, Croydon, CR0 4YY